MORE PRAISE F

WHAT
JEFFERSON READ, IKE WATCHED,
AND OBAMA TWEETED

"Tevi Troy's tour through how presidents consume—and are consumed by—popular culture is very interesting reading. Readers who pick up this book, whether they love history or pop culture, will find the history of our presidents and their free time predilections not just educational but also entertaining."

—**WILLIAM J. BENNETT**, former U.S. secretary of education,
host of *Bill Bennett's Morning in America*

——➤➤➤•●•◄◄◄——

"Tevi Troy has written a fast-paced, surprising, and shall I say it, very entertaining look at how presidents have affected the culture, how the culture has affected them, and the nature of the presidency itself. A fun and illuminating read."

—**KARL ROVE**, former deputy chief of staff and senior advisor
to President George W. Bush and author of *Courage and Consequence*

——➤➤➤•●•◄◄◄——

"As someone who does not know Kardashian from Kissinger, I find a primer on how presidents deal with popular culture not only useful but indispensable. Tevi Troy gives us a good road map here to understand how every White House has kept a finger on the popular pulse without getting overly palpitated."

—**MIKE McCURRY**, former WI

"Tevi Troy's witty and informative book reminds us that, from the beginning, presidents have been consumers—and manipulators—of popular culture. It's comforting, sort of, to learn that our current media- and celebrity-obsessed age isn't really new. Troy makes it all fun and riveting to read."

—**ROB LONG**, Emmy- and Golden Globe–nominated writer, former executive producer of *Cheers*, and contributing editor of *National Review*

"Tevi Troy has written a brilliant, witty, refreshingly novel and insightful book about how the engagement of our American presidents in the popular culture of their era provides insights into their personalities and shaped their presidencies—from the books they read, the theater they saw, later the television and movies they watched, and, with President Obama, the social media he employs. We will look at our presidents in a different light after reading his book."

—**STUART E. EIZENSTAT**, former U.S. ambassador to the European Union and former chief domestic policy advisor to President Jimmy Carter

"This is an excellent account of the impact popular culture increasingly has had on the American presidency from George Washington into the Obama administration. Beginning with Andrew Jackson, although educated people with intellects were not excluded, having a common touch now was essential to winning. Troy presents well the reality of changes in culture and politics, changes which do not enthrall him."

—**JOHN M. PAFFORD, Ph.D.**, author of *The Forgotten Conservative: Rediscovering Grover Cleveland*

WHAT

JEFFERSON READ,

IKE WATCHED,

AND OBAMA

TWEETED

WHAT JEFFERSON READ, IKE WATCHED, AND OBAMA TWEETED

200 YEARS OF POPULAR CULTURE IN THE WHITE HOUSE

TEVI TROY

REGNERY
Publishing, Inc.

An Eagle Publishing Company • Washington, DC

Cataloging-in-Publication data on file with the Library of Congress

ISBN 978-1-62157-039-4

Published in the United States by
Regnery History
An imprint of Regnery Publishing, Inc.
One Massachusetts Avenue NW
Washington, DC 20001
www.RegneryHistory.com

Manufactured in the United States of America

10 9 8 7 6 5 4 3 2

Books are available in quantity for promotional or premium use. Write to Director of Special Sales, Regnery Publishing, Inc., One Massachusetts Avenue NW, Washington, DC 20001, for information on discounts and terms, or call (202) 216-0600.

Distributed to the trade by
Perseus Distribution
250 West 57th Street
New York, NY 10107

To my parents, Dov and Elaine Troy
For their unyielding faith in me and, more importantly, in this great country

CONTENTS

CONTENTS

FROM CICERO TO SNOOKI: HOW CULTURE SHAPES OUR PRESIDENTS

During the Congressional battle over his health-care bill, President Barack Obama joked, "The following individuals shall be excluded from the indoor tanning tax within this bill: Snooki, J-WOWW, the Situation, and House Minority Leader John Boehner." The line was delivered before the White House Correspondents' Dinner, an annual gathering of Washington insiders and glitterati, and the president received the expected laughs from the crowd. A short time later, Obama professed on the daytime talk show *The View* that he didn't know who Snooki was. He reaffirmed his ignorance the next day before the National Urban League, saying, "I was on the *The View* yesterday, and somebody asked me who Snooki was. I said, I don't know who Snooki is. But I know some really good teachers that you guys should be talking about."[1] Three months and three presidential references to the diminutive denizen of the Jersey Shore.

By the end of 2012, Obama was not the only presidential candidate to discuss the social phenomenon that is Nicole Elizabeth "Snooki" Polizzi. On a daytime interview with Kelly Ripa, Mitt Romney acknowledged that he was "kind of a Snooki fan." The buttoned-down former Massachusetts governor continued, "Look how tiny she's gotten. She's lost weight. She's energetic. Just her spark-plug personality is kind of fun."[2]

So the 2012 candidates of each major party, seeking to be the commander in chief of the United States of America, were familiar with this buxom and foul-mouthed reality-show starlet from MTV's *Jersey Shore*. The only philosophy governing Snooki and her friends is "GTL"—gym, tan, laundry. Snooki's exploits are not uplifting or enlightening in any way, but she's a major star—the perfect symbol of the degradation of American culture. She is followed assiduously by entertainment magazines and is known to millions, almost certainly by more Americans than the 28 percent who can name the chief justice of the Supreme Court. A future historian surveying the interests of Americans *circa* 2010 will find Snooki somewhere on the list. But are we really better off with a president who knows who Snooki is?

This question gets at a challenge that has faced American presidents for nearly two centuries: Do they wish to be men of the people or men of higher understanding? Which trait is more helpful for getting elected? Which trait is more helpful for governing? Or can the president simultaneously master both qualities? If he can, how does a president communicate his connection to a partially shared popular culture while also communicating that he has the character to hold the highest office in the land?

How a president responds to this challenge depends on his own predilections and tastes, those of his team, and the particular historical moment in which he lives. How he conceives of himself and popular culture reveals something about the president's intellectual interests, mental discipline, and preparation for the presidency. How a president engages popular culture also tells us about the people who elected him, the changing nature of American politics and society, and the tension between high-, low-, and middle-brow pursuits.

> —▸▸▸ •●• ◂◂◂—
>
> **Presidents John Adams and Thomas Jefferson were among the best-read men on the entire continent. Jefferson, whose personal collection of books became the foundation of the Library of Congress, famously said, "I cannot live without books."**

Ever since George Washington, presidents have struggled to find the right distance for the leader of a republic to keep between himself and the people. Washington himself feared the consequences to his reputation of becoming the president of the newly formed United States. Already venerated as the ideal gentleman who had served when his countrymen needed him, he made no appeals to the vulgar mob to retain his power or to make himself king. The other Founding Fathers may not have been as popular, but they, too, pondered the question of elite leadership. The spectacularly autodidactic John Adams seemed unbothered by the label of Federalist elitism as he studied Cicero and other Roman greats, but his presidency faltered as popular sentiment turned against him.

Appeals to the people changed dramatically with Andrew Jackson, who so naturally connected with the common man. "Old Hickory" exploited this ability to handily defeat the well-educated and well-read John Quincy Adams in 1828. But today there is no massive monument to Jackson in the capital city, perhaps because he was too much defined by his rough and tough ways. The man who best married the common touch with intellectual distinction was Abraham Lincoln. He wanted to connect, and he wanted to achieve. Obsessed with books and himself the author of some of the noblest rhetoric in the English language, he never lost sight of the need to appeal to the common man in his earnest work.

For all the talk of Americans as a common or practical people, this is nevertheless a nation founded on ideas rather than on the ties of race or religion. The United States, more than any other nation, was built on an intellectual vision, but said vision embraces republican and democratic ideals that are occasionally at odds with one another. It is beyond debate, however, that America has long been a home to thinkers. It began with the Founding Generation, a group of extraordinary men who consciously modeled their new republic on ideals they encountered in their considerable reading of history, philosophy, and law. The historian Trevor Colbourn writes, "The Revolutionary leaders were men of substance—propertied, educated. They *read*. And what they read made it easier for them to become rebels...."[3]

> Whether it is Jimmy Carter watching more than four hundred movies in the White House cinema or Barack Obama telling people that the flamboyant killer Omar on HBO's *The Wire* is his favorite character, it is clear that presidents are taking advantage of these varied cultural reference points to communicate to the American public.
>
>

Relatively few cultural pursuits were available to the first presidents—mostly books and theater. Presidents John Adams and Thomas Jefferson were among the best-read men on the entire continent. Jefferson, whose personal collection of books became the foundation of the Library of Congress, famously said, "I cannot live without books." Today, more than two hundred years later, presidents choose from a greater variety of cultural offerings than ever before—books, magazines, films, television, and music. Whether it is Jimmy Carter watching more than four hundred movies in the White House cinema or Barack Obama telling people that the flamboyant killer Omar on HBO's *The Wire* is his favorite character, it is clear that presidents are taking advantage of these varied cultural reference points to communicate to the American public. And they occasionally reveal something important about themselves.

This book is an exploration of how presidents have made use of a multiplicity of cultural pursuits—from the theater-going Abraham Lincoln to the movie-making Ronald Reagan—and how those pursuits have in turn shaped them and the nation. Not all cultural pursuits are of equal value, and there exists an important distinction to be made between popular entertainment and that of intellectual or cultural achievement. The lines between them, however, are not always easily drawn—the most successful presidents have been at home in both worlds.

In the spheres of both entertainment and intellectual endeavor, technology has created a vast array of options for distribution by the creators and for absorption by the recipients. A president's embrace of a new technology has sometimes foreshadowed its penetration of society at large. Woodrow Wilson is supposed to have expressed astonishment at the power of film when he viewed D. W. Griffith's *Birth of a Nation*. When Harry Truman was asked if he would attend the 1947 "Jackie Robinson" World Series, he replied that he would watch some of it on the new technology of television instead.

At the same time, some presidents have appeared to be behind the times. Making small talk at a technology expo in 1992, President George H. W. Bush seemed to be unacquainted with the relatively new technology of supermarket price scanners. The *New York Times* gleefully portrayed the president as out of touch, reinforcing an image that his opponents continued to carefully construct. In America, such an image is costly, and it contributed to Bush's defeat.

The fear of seeming out of touch afflicts almost all politicians. It shapes how they communicate with their constituents, whether it's a candidate memorizing the price of a gallon of milk or the House majority leader, Eric Cantor, keeping up with *People* magazine.[4] President Obama in particular strives to be ahead of the curve, demonstrating his knowledge of the trends and technologies of the moment. In 2011, while trying to outmaneuver House Republicans on a payroll tax cut, he turned to Twitter. The text of his tweet would have been gibberish to earlier presidents raised on the classics and the King James Bible. But it was perfectly clear to the audience whom Obama wished to impress: "Everyone should see what #40dollars means to folks: groceries, daycare, gas, copays. Keep it going. I'll talk abt this tmrw @ 12:15ET.—bo."[5]

In the past, Americans tried to bring the best of European culture to a new land. Now we continually reinvent the world's cultural content and the forms in which it is expressed. Two hundred years ago, Americans' cultural options comprised the theater,

—>·>·>·•·•·<·<·<—

In 2011, while trying to outmaneuver House Republicans on a payroll tax cut, he turned to Twitter. The text of his tweet would have been gibberish to earlier presidents raised on the classics and the King James Bible. But it was perfectly clear to the audience whom Obama wished to impress: "Everyone should see what #40dollars means to folks: groceries, daycare, gas, copays. Keep it going. I'll talk abt this tmrw @ 12:15ET.—bo."

music, books, and pamphlets. Today, presidents and citizens alike face nearly unlimited options—books, films, television, Internet, radio, music, video games, MP3s, podcasts, magazines, and theatrical productions—all available year-round and often twenty-four hours a day. A person molded in this atmosphere will differ from someone raised in a log cabin where he could read only as long as the fireplace remained lit. When the United States was born, it was blessed with a generation of leaders remarkably well-prepared for the task that history presented them. They were immersed in the timeless questions of what makes a just society and how men are best governed. As Leo Strauss observed, the Founders combined the great traditions of Athens and Jerusalem, of reason and revelation.[6] Later, when that system was challenged, it was Abraham Lincoln, grounded in his own deep reading of the Bible, English history, and the works of Shakespeare, who understood what was at stake and fought a terrible and bloody war to maintain the system that the Founders had envisioned.

The history of the United States proves that ideas do have consequences, even if the sources of those ideas are not always as exalted as Shakespeare and the Bible. Ronald Reagan is said to have gotten the idea for his missile defense system from one of his old movies, *Murder in the Air*. At the same time, there was a serious aspect to Reagan's approach. His pursuit of the Strategic Defense Initiative was guided by his optimism about both technology and America itself.[7]

Reagan's predecessor, Jimmy Carter, also immersed himself in the world of movies, but he lacked Reagan's optimism. In a televised address to the nation in 1979, he attempted to draw on the ideas of the scholar Christopher Lasch, whose book, *The Culture of Narcissism*, had made a splash in intellectual circles. The address, which has gone down in history as the infamous "malaise speech," proved a political disaster, sealing Carter's reputation as a gloomy scold and contributing to his defeat the following year.[8]

Ronald Reagan, with his boundless optimism about America, appeared to shape the culture. Or did he simply reflect what was already there? Was John F. Kennedy a visionary who recognized America's opportunities in the space race, or was he simply a creature of his times, reflecting the optimism of his countrymen in poetic phrases like the "New Frontier"? Are presidents simply the pawns of history, as when Jimmy Carter and Gerald Ford got lost in the institutional skepticism and dour outlook of the 1970s? The truth is that presidents are both shaped by the culture and shapers of it themselves.

Looking to the future, we must ask if we are electing leaders who are equipped for the times. The leader of a free and democratic nation must appear to be engaged in his country's culture, but he must do so without letting the coarseness and vulgarity of that culture diminish himself or his office. A further problem is that it becomes difficult to form good leaders in a culture of the sensational, the outrageous, and the vulgar. Too many of today's leaders make us wistful for the generation of the Founding Fathers. Although they lived on the farthest outposts of Western civilization, their formation in the classics, history, and Enlightenment philosophy ensured that they had studied the great questions of human freedom and the just society. As the historian Robert Darnton put it, "Jefferson, Madison, [George] Mason, and their crowd look like American-style *philosophes*."[9] Few of our recent leaders could be mistaken for *philosophes*. "[W]hen compared with today's statesmen," writes Darnton, the Founders "look like giants."[10] Would today's politicians, better versed in popular culture, have served as well at the founding? Or, to turn the question around, does an established polity have less need of a philosopher king than one in its infancy? An understanding of first principles is important, to be sure, but would an understanding of Montesquieu or Locke help a president trying to sort out Medicaid reimbursement or the optimum capital-gains tax rates?

> Without the movies, Ronald Reagan would not have been Ronald Reagan. And yet, at the same time, without Ronald Reagan, would the optimistic and light "popcorn" flicks of the 1980s—from *Rambo* to *Red Dawn* and *Top Gun* to *Back to the Future*—have been the same?

In its insatiable thirst for information, whether important or trivial, about its leaders or its celebrities, the public demands an account of the president's consumption of popular culture. A meaningful evaluation of the president is hardly possible without that information. It is hard to overstate, for example, the extent to which Ronald Reagan was shaped by the movies. Without them, he would have been a friendly ex-lifeguard from Illinois, perhaps a traveling salesman like his father. With them he achieved fame and fortune, worked a lifetime in a world of images and ideas, and ultimately, ascended to the nation's highest office. The movies provided Reagan with the skills he used to excel in politics and to inspire the nation. Without the movies, Ronald Reagan would not have been Ronald Reagan. And yet, at the same time, without Ronald Reagan, would the optimistic and light "popcorn" flicks of the 1980s—from *Rambo* to *Red Dawn* and *Top Gun* to *Back to the Future*—have been the same?

Reagan is the obvious example of popular culture's influence on a president. But the point readily translates to other presidents. The obscure James A. Garfield, whose assassination early in his term left him little time to shape his era, was himself a product of his time, his readings, and his intellectual preparation. Born into poverty, he improved his lot through omnivorous reading and a prodigious memory, becoming a powerful speaker.

These days, however, reading is not the only influence on a president or any other American. We are awash in media, which often appeal to narrowly targeted audiences. In the internet age, in fact, we have few shared experiences and symbols. Only four decades ago such television shows as *All in the Family* and *Happy Days* dominated the national conversation, garnering Nielsen ratings in the low to mid-thirties, corresponding to millions of viewers. These days, ratings for a top-rated show like *American Idol* are in the single digits.[11] Barack Obama understands this cultural fragmentation, and he carefully targets specific audiences on radio, TV, and even podcasts in order to advance his political agenda. Media moguls have become adept at narrowcasting—tailoring programming to a specific demographic and securing advertising for that group, or, conversely, advertising the programming to that particular group. In the future, presidents will need to engage in this micro-targeting as well. Ironically perhaps, the fragmentation of culture has elevated the importance of the presidency, for the president is now one of the few cultural touchstones we all share.

Throughout American history, presidents have tried to use culture and new means of communication in order to project the image of the ideal leader. Over time, those cultural interactions have become less formal, more immediate, and less deliberative. Perhaps these changes have made sense as presidents evolved from founders of the republic to its custodians. But perhaps we have lost a sense of purpose, of grandiosity, and of leadership. This book will demonstrate some of the ways presidents have tried to manage the tensions of political leadership in the face of the realities of our ever-evolving culture.

CHAPTER 1

THE FOUNDERS: READING FOR WISDOM AND VIRTUE

America's Revolution was fought with words as much as with bullets. Ideas spread by the technology of the printing press and transported by ship and by coach united thirteen disparate colonies in an unlikely but ultimately successful rebellion. These ideas were effective, however, not only because they were good. There were also literate and cultured men of character to appreciate them. Despite the enormous differences in technology between the founding era and today, culture—especially popular culture—played as large a role in shaping the views of the Founders and of the early presidents as it does today.

The robust intellectual culture of the British colonies in North America made it possible to disseminate the ideals of liberty among an unlikely group of revolutionaries. After the success of the Revolution, the Founders continued to pursue their interest in the philosophy of politics and in the questions of what makes a great society. Their continuing pursuit of culture, not merely for entertainment but also for inspiration and edification, proved the foundation of the new American Republic.

Above all, the Founders read books. Before the first shot of the war was fired, they had immersed themselves in political philosophy, thinking deeply about how to create a self-governing society, contemplating the consequences of corruption, and pondering the fate of nations. They had a practical bent that enabled them not only to lead a revolution but also to maintain the rule of law in its aftermath. History has rarely produced such an impressive constellation of luminaries at such a critical moment.

Despite their distance from the sources of European civilization, the American colonies boasted a rich literary culture. It would be hard to overstate the importance of reading among the educated classes. "From candle light to early bedtime," wrote Thomas Jefferson, "I read."[1] The *New-York Gazette* and *Mercury* wrote in 1766 that "every lover of his country hath long observed with sacred pleasure, the rapid progress of knowledge in this once howling wilderness, occasioned by the vast importation of *books*; the many public and private libraries in all parts of the country; the great taste for reading which prevails among people of every rank." The Founding Fathers, and particularly the ones who served as our first presidents, were remarkably well-read.[2]

—➤➤➤•●•◄◄◄—

Though perhaps not thought of as a reader—few people are when compared with Jefferson and Adams—Washington had a nine-hundred-book library, considered quite large at the time. The library included biographies, histories, and classics from ancient Greece and Rome, as well as fiction.

While the technology of eighteenth-century communication was limited, the Founders lived in something of an Information Age, thanks to the printing press, faster travel, and expanding freedom. When the flow of information through the more formal channels of newspapers, books, and pamphlets was restricted by the limits of technology or by the government, the colonial populace obtained their news through gossip, rumors, and song.[3] According to Christopher Geist, Americans delighted in "novels and other books for light diversion, cards and card tables, sheet music, children's books and toys, equipment for such outdoor sports as hunting and fishing, and decorative prints such as those produced by William Hogarth."[4]

Colonial Americans, observes the historian Forrest McDonald, were "a remarkably literate people, and they were even more remarkable in the voracity of their appetites for things to read."[5] John Adams, a reliably cold-eyed observer of his fellow man, made the same point in 1765: "A native of America who cannot read or write is as rare an appearance as a Jacobite or a Roman Catholic, that is, as rare as a comet or an earthquake." Literacy rates in the colonies were higher than those in Europe. A clerk on Martinique, Moreau de Saint-Méry, recalled that the American sailors he encountered were so universally literate that they could be counted on to sign the documents he presented to them.[6] In Adams's New England, where the Puritans had attached enormous importance on the individual's reading the word of God, the literacy rate reached as high as 90 percent.[7] McDonald estimates that 50 percent of adult males were regular newspaper readers.[8] This is a remarkable figure, one that we might envy today, when many young people rely on humorous fake news programs such as the *Daily Show with Jon Stewart* or *The Colbert Report*.

> John Adams idolized Cicero from the age of twenty-three. He read the orator aloud in his youth, imitated him throughout his public life, and reread *De senectute* annually after he retired.
>
>

George Washington and the Theatricality of Leadership

The story begins, of course, with George Washington. Though perhaps not thought of as a reader—few people are when compared with Jefferson and Adams—Washington had a nine-hundred-book library, considered quite large at the time.[9] The library included biographies, histories, and classics from ancient Greece and Rome, as well as fiction. Moreover, there is plenty of evidence that Washington's books were put to good use. Ever the autodidact, he had a penchant for practical books on agriculture and for military works.[10]

Washington also borrowed books, although in at least one case the cares of high office seem to have distracted him from his duty to the volumes' owners. The ledger of the New York Society Library indicates that on October 5, 1789, two books—*The Law of Nations* by Emmerich de Vattel and a volume of debates from the House of Commons—were checked out to the president. In 2010, an archivist discovered that the books had never been returned; the fine, adjusted for inflation, amounted to three hundred thousand dollars. Mount Vernon could not find the missing volumes in its collection, but it managed to acquire another copy of *The Law of Nations*, which it handed over to the library. In gratitude, the library canceled Washington's outstanding fine.[11]

Washington and his contemporaries not only read books, they discussed them as well. These discussions sharpened, clarified, and spread the Revolution's ideas. Virginia's George Mason was a key figure in these conversations. A prodigious reader, he owned an impressive library and had written manifestoes on representative government. Mason enjoyed talking about books and ideas with his fellow Virginians Patrick Henry, Thomas Jefferson, James Madison, and Washington, both over meals and in letters.[12]

The art of conversation is difficult to appreciate in a society that communicates through email and Twitter. The dinner table of a gentleman used to be a place for the serious discussion of ideas, politics, and culture. These conversations—more formal and substantive than gossip or banter—were a crucial method of developing policies on the weighty issues of the day. In 1790, for example, the famous "dinner table bargain" between Thomas Jefferson, Alexander Hamilton, and James Madison led to the establishment of the new capital at what is now Washington, D.C. The historian Catherine Allgor has stressed the importance of dinners to the entire founding generation, noting that the Revolution and the founding "unfolded" as part of a series of conversations, many if not most of them of the dinner-table variety.[13]

During his presidency, Washington hosted what he called the Thursday dinners, with a mixed company sitting around a well-laid-out table.[14] The dinners were formal to the point of awkwardness, with Martha serving as hostess. After a meal of many courses, the men retired to the drawing room to drink and discuss matters of consequence. These gatherings were similar in some ways to the famed Georgetown dinner parties of the not-so-distant past. In an age with fewer opportunities for communication, however, social events like the Thursday dinners served a purpose similar to that of today's universities, think tanks, and other institutions dedicated to intellectual discourse.

The Founders were steeped in Roman history and saw in their defense of American liberties a reflection of the defense of the Republic against the tyranny of the Caesars. The heroes of the Roman Republic—Brutus, Cassius, Cicero—were their models. John Adams idolized Cicero from the age of twenty-three.[15] He read the orator aloud in his youth, imitated him throughout his pubic life, and reread *De senectute* annually after he retired.[16] The modern embodiment of the classical hero, of course, was George Washington—with his impressive height, regal bearing, and quiet yet commanding demeanor. The Founders admired in Washington all of the traits that constituted the classical ideal: "restraint, temperance, fortitude, dignity, and independence," in Gordon Wood's words.[17] He was the American Cincinnatus, coming to his country's aid in its hour of peril and then retreating to his plow rather than retaining power.

Re: *Common Sense*

In less than three months, from its publication on January 10, 1776, to the end of March, the pamphlet sold over a hundred thousand copies—one for every twenty-five residents. The equivalent today would be 12.5 million copies, a figure that puts *Common Sense*—a work of political philosophy—in a league with *Peyton Place, Dune*, and *The Bridges of Madison County*.

Washington understood this classical symbolism. He even ordered a bust of Cicero for his Mount Vernon home.[18] He knew he was a symbol to his countrymen, and he understood the importance of theatricality in leadership. He tried to convey a certain image in his dress when on horseback. Jefferson called him "the best horseman of his age and the most graceful figure that could ever be seen on horseback."[19]

Equestrian skills were held in especially high regard in those days because of the practical value and the symbolic importance of the cavalry from the time of Rome until the end of the Middle Ages. Washington's flair for the theatrical may have come, logically enough, from his own love of the theater. According to Myron Magnet, Washington exercised "adroit stagecraft" in his management of the Revolutionary War. He took on the role of stage actor who could skillfully manipulate his audience. He carefully selected his own clothes, recognizing that his impressive military uniform paralleled a costume for an actor playing a character.[20]

Pamphlets and the Spread of Ideas

Ideas fueled the American Revolution, and they spread across the far-flung colonies with astonishing rapidity. The single most powerful expression of these ideas was Thomas Paine's pamphlet *Common Sense*, which demonstrated the ability of the written word to shape events in America.[21] Bernard Bailyn calls it "the most brilliant pamphlet written during the American Revolution, and one of the most brilliant pamphlets ever written in the English language."[22] It sold accordingly. In less than three months, from its publication on January 10, 1776, to the end of March, the pamphlet sold over one hundred thousand copies—one for every twenty-five residents.[23] The equivalent today would be 12.5 million copies, a figure that puts *Common Sense*—a work of political philosophy—in a league with *Peyton Place*, *Dune*, and *The Bridges of Madison County*.[24]

Book collecting was an expensive habit, as most books had to be imported. In 1776, a new copy of Adam Smith's *The Wealth of Nations* cost the modern-day equivalent of $615—roughly the price of an iPad.

As popular as *Common Sense* was, not everyone cared for it. John Adams, who was of a more conservative bent, dismissed Paine's work as "a poor, ignorant, malicious, short-sighted, crapulous mass."[25] Washington, who had a far better sense of public opinion and of the popular mood than Adams, also had a better appreciation of the importance of Paine's work. He praised *Common Sense* as "sound doctrine" and recognized that Paine's work would bolster American morale at a time it was desperately needed.

Paine's pamphlet was the first of the political bestsellers that have shaped the relationship between ideas and practical politics throughout American history. These writings have not always been nonfiction. Harriet Beecher Stowe's *Uncle Tom's Cabin* may have been the most influential novel ever written. America's well-educated populace, its belief in the power of ideas, and the development of publishing technology from pamphlets to tweets have given creative thinkers exceptional influence in the country's political development.

The Best-Read Leaders in History?

Washington would be considered well-read today, and he read more than the amount with which he is generally accredited. Among the Founders, however, he ranks only as a modest reader. The breadth of reading among this group of men was extraordinary, even for that information-hungry age. Thomas Jefferson and John Adams were known for their bibliophilia—"I cannot live without books," Jefferson once wrote to Adams[26]—and collected enormous libraries. Jefferson's father had left a library of forty-two books. The son added to the collection at the rate of twelve a month. In contrast, John Harvard, whose gift of four hundred books to the Puritans' fledgling college in New England was so impressive that they named the institution after him, collected books at a rate of only twelve books per year.[27] Book collecting was an expensive habit, as most books had to be imported. In 1776, a new copy of Adam Smith's *The Wealth of Nations* cost the modern-day equivalent of $615— roughly the price of an iPad.[28]

After the British burned the Congressional Library in 1814, Jefferson offered his collection of 6,487 books to Congress. Despite some reluctance to assume a library of such varied subjects and languages, Congress paid him $23,900 for the collection.

Jefferson, however, was not finished with his acquisitions. He accumulated an additional thousand volumes before he died in 1826. Jefferson's books were lost in a fire at the Library of Congress in 1841, so we cannot peruse his actual collection, but his love of reading did give our national library an important head start.[29]

Adams was even more addicted to the costly printed word and better read than Jefferson.[30] His library comprised over three thousand volumes, including works of Cicero, Plutarch, and Thucydides. He once confessed to his wife Abigail, "I have been imprudent, I have spent an estate in books."[31]

Adams not only read books but actively, even violently, engaged with them.[32] He filled the margins of his books with his reactions, insights, ideas, and—not infrequently—epithets. In his marginalia, he brands Rousseau a "coxcomb," Voltaire a "liar," and Condorcet "a fool," leaving little doubt what he thought of the authors he was reading. And the rate at which he consumed books astonished even Jefferson, who exclaimed in 1816, "Dear Sir, how I envy you!"[33]

What Adams and Jefferson read is even more impressive than how much they read. Their familiarity with both the classics and the philosophical works of their own day is unimaginable today. Jefferson's legal studies gave him a foundation in the natural law tradition harkening back to Plato and Aristotle as well as knowledge of more contemporary legal philosophers such as William Blackstone and John Locke.[34] Familiarity with the classics was not limited to lawyers. Educated Americans at the time knew their Virgil, Cicero, Tacitus, and Thucydides, usually in translation but often in the original Greek or

> —>>>•>—•—•<<<•<—
>
> Adams not only read books, but actively, even violently, engaged with them. He filled the margins of his books with his reactions, insights, ideas, and—not infrequently—epithets. In his marginalia, he brands Rousseau a "coxcomb," Voltaire a "liar," and Condorcet "a fool," leaving little doubt what he thought of the authors he was reading. And the rate at which he consumed books astonished even Jefferson, who exclaimed in 1816, "Dear Sir, how I envy you!"

Latin.[35] Furthermore, many of the less educated and less wealthy were also familiar with Roman history thanks to plays such as Joseph Addison's *Cato*. Many of those who could read but who could not afford to purchase books relied on the innovative subscription library system invented by Benjamin Franklin.[36]

All of this reading was not just a pastime. The Founders soaked up the ideas of the Enlightenment, which were heady ideas indeed and which informed the political system they created. In *The Swerve: How the World Became Modern*, Stephen Greenblatt argues that the discovery of Lucretius's long-lost Epicurean poem *De rerum natura* ("On the Nature of Things") in 1417 was the "swerve" that changed the direction of human history. The West, says Greenblatt, was not marching inexorably into the Renaissance (or into the Enlightenment that followed it) when Poggio Bracciolini, a book hunter and humanist scholar, found the forgotten work on a German monastery bookshelf. Recognizing the importance of his discovery, Bracciolini ordered copies of the book made, some of which survived. The resurrected poem, which introduced the concepts of individual atoms, the lack of an afterlife, and a general skepticism toward received wisdom, ultimately influenced such luminaries as Montaigne, Shakespeare, Galileo, and Newton.[37] Addison, too, read Lucretius, whose ideas can be traced in *Cato*, a work which would have a powerful influence on Washington.

Lucretius' most important influence on the Founders, according to Greenblatt, was through Jefferson, who owned five copies of *De rerum natura* in Latin, as well as English, French, and Italian translations. Jefferson wrote to Adams about his views on matter and motion, key concepts found in Lucretius. Indeed, Jefferson was not coy about his

> Jefferson wrote to Adams about his views on matter and motion, key concepts in Lucretius. Indeed, Jefferson was not coy about his debt to Lucretius; he responded to a question of his personal philosophy by stating, "I am an Epicurean." There is scarcely a more impressive measure of an author's influence on history than the boast that he shaped the thinking of Thomas Jefferson.

—>>>—•—<<<—

The influence of Jefferson's reading on other Founders is perhaps most clearly apparent in his assistance to James Madison in preparing for the Constitutional Convention. In January 1786, Jefferson shipped two trunks of books to Madison in response to Madison's request for reading materials that "may throw light on the general Constitution and *droit public* [public law] of several confederacies which have existed...."

debt to Lucretius; he responded to a question of his personal philosophy by stating, "I am an Epicurean."[38] There is scarcely a more impressive measure of an author's influence on history than the boast that he shaped the thinking of Thomas Jefferson.

The influence of Jefferson's reading on other Founders is perhaps most apparent in his assistance to James Madison in preparing for the Constitutional Convention. In January of 1786, Jefferson shipped two trunks of books to Madison in response to Madison's request for reading materials that "may throw light on the general Constitution and *droit public* [public law] of several confederacies which have existed...." Equipped with the works of authors going as far back as Demosthenes, Madison spent the spring and summer studying this "literary cargo" of more than two hundred books. He distilled his studies into an essay, "Of Ancient and Modern Confederacies," which examined Greece, the Holy Roman Empire, Switzerland, and Holland. The essay guided Madison in the constitutional battles that lay ahead.[39] This remarkable ethos of self-improvement dated from his student days at Princeton, where Madison had studied Hebrew so that he could better understand the Bible.[40]

Ideas among the Non-Readers

John Adams wrote, "The Revolution was in the minds and hearts of the people,"[41] but how did it get there? Not everyone was reading, not even in highly literate New England. The historian David Hackett Fischer recounts an interview that Mellen Chamberlain, then twenty-one, conducted with the ninety-one-year-old Captain

Levi Preston, who nearly seven decades earlier had fought at Concord. "I suppose you had been reading Harrington, Sidney, and Locke about the eternal principle of liberty," Chamberlain asked. Preston's reply: "I have never heard of these men. The only books we had were the Bible, the Catechism, Watts' psalms and hymns, and the almanacs." Looking back on his decision to take up arms against his king, Preston concluded, "Young man, what we meant in going for those Redcoats was this: We had always governed ourselves and we always meant to. They didn't mean we should."[42]

The aspirations of the more learned Founders shine through in the rustic words of old Captain Preston. Not everyone knew Cato but everyone knew Moses, with whom Washington was easily compared. The educated class contributed to a culture in which, through pamphlets, plays, sermons, and books, the idea of liberty made its way to men like Levi Preston, inspiring them to astonishing sacrifice.

> Despite their reverence for the ideas of the Renaissance and the Enlightenment, the Founders were not slavish followers of the European tradition. They were the sons and grandsons of pioneers who had left Europe in search of a better and freer way of life.

Degeneracy and the Case against American Inferiority

Despite their reverence for the ideas of the Renaissance and the Enlightenment, the Founders were not slavish followers of the European tradition. They were the sons and grandsons of pioneers who had left Europe in search of a better and freer way of life. They fought a dangerous revolution to break away from European monarchy, and they were willing to take an intellectual stand against European ideas with which they disagreed.

Apart from these obvious philosophical differences, Americans had to contend with an irritating European trait that persists to this day—the insidious notion of

American inferiority. This prejudice took on a scientific form in the "degeneracy" thesis of Georges-Louis Leclerc, comte de Buffon, the great eighteenth-century naturalist who argued that the harsh conditions of the Americas stunted both its flora and its fauna. Another influential Frenchman, Guillaume Raynal (whom Donald Lutz ranks as the twenty-sixth most frequently cited author by the members of the founding generation[43]), extended Buffon's thesis to the New World's human population of European descent. Thomas Jefferson demolished Buffon's theory of degenerate American wildlife in his *Notes on the State of Virginia*, but he left it to Benjamin Franklin to refute the abbé Raynal. Many years later, Jefferson gleefully recalled how Franklin accomplished that task:

> The Doctor [Franklin] told me ... [h]e had a party to dine with him one day at Passy, of whom one half were Americans, the other half French, and among the last was the Abbé. During the dinner he got on his favorite theory of the degeneracy of animals, and even of man, in America, and urged it with his usual eloquence. The Doctor at length noticed the accidental stature and position of his guest, at table, "Come," says he, "M. l'Abbé. Let us try this question by the fact before us. We are here one half Americans, and one half French, and it happens that the Americans have placed themselves on one side of the table, and our French friends are on the other. Let both parties rise, and we will see on which side nature had degenerated." It happened that his American guests were Carmichael, Harmer, Humphreys, and others of the finest stature and form; while those of the other side were remarkably diminutive, and the Abbé himself particularly, was a mere shrimp. He parried the appeal, however, by a complimentary admission of exceptions, among which the Doctor himself was a conspicuous one.[44]

The story is a delightful illustration of the pragmatic side of the upstart colonists. The book learning of intellectuals like Jefferson and Franklin was perfectly compatible with real-world smarts. They were practical enough to see the implications of a problematic theory like degeneracy—not to mention hereditary monarchy—and knew how to discredit it.

The Americans' willingness to challenge European ideas did not simply arise from personal pique. It was also a result of distance. Being far from the European capitals, they had to think on their own. Ideas did make their way across the ocean, but they took hold in different ways in the New World.[45] Literacy was relatively widespread in the North American colonies, whose leaders were well-read and versed in a variety of genres. And Americans took ideas seriously. The Founders viewed reading not merely as entertainment but as a path to wisdom, virtue, and toward a just society. Ideas transplanted from Europe to the intellectually fertile soil of America yielded a revolutionary harvest.

The Founders "wanted a nation based on the rule of law presided over by deliberative statesmen who were policed by an educated citizenry," writes Matthew Robinson.[46] The part about an educated citizenry was essential. As Jefferson wrote to Washington, "It is an axiom in my mind that our liberty can never be safe but in the hands of the people themselves, and that too of the people with a certain degree of instruction."[47] It was the "instruction" that would protect the nation against demagoguery and populism. Jefferson also warned, more starkly, "If a nation expects to be ignorant and free, in a state of civilization, it expects what never was and never will be."[48] This keenly felt need of an educated populace to sustain American democracy was the impetus for a public education system that was long the envy of the world.

At the same time, the average level of education among the governing class and the relative uniformity of cultural influences on the population were unsustainable. As the nation expanded and prospered, the reach of the elite institutions that had

> The Founders viewed reading not merely as entertainment but as a path to wisdom, virtue, and toward a just society. Ideas transplanted from Europe to the intellectually fertile soil of America yielded a revolutionary harvest.

trained the Founders diminished, and the diversity of influences grew. As immigrants arrived from across Europe and as the nation spread out across the continent, there were more pockets of illiteracy, and it became less likely that even an educated person would be as well versed in the classics as the Founders' generation had been. The changing populace turned to leaders who were less cultivated and more populist. The reading that enabled the Founders to create a new system of government did not help a man get elected in a raucous and growing nation. The problems that the new nation faced were less about the nature and design of a new society and more about the management and development of that society. The preoccupations of the presidents would change as the nation's preoccupations changed.

CHAPTER 2

THEATER AND THE COMMON MAN IN THE NINETEENTH CENTURY

I n the nineteenth century, the stage ruled the visual arts. Theater was the primary form of non-reading entertainment, reaching the broadest range of citizens and touching the lives of every American president. Although reading was of central importance in the founding generation and Americans enjoyed the world's highest literacy rates, literacy was not universal. The stage, however, was accessible to readers and non-readers alike, and it spanned a diverse audience.

Stage productions, both in theaters and presented by touring companies, were widely available throughout the country and proved an efficient means of transmitting cultural developments. They were also a forum for the expression of political ideas, protected in large part by the First Amendment. Plays became politically important and a regular part of the presidents' cultural life. Grover Cleveland even had a son, Francis, who became a Broadway star, playing the role of Sam Craig in *Our Town* in 1938 and working in the theater for the rest of his long life.[1] Presidential patronage, beginning with Washington, bestowed a measure of legitimacy and respectability on the theater in the young nation.

Though more free-wheeling than its European counterpart, nineteenth-century American theater still took its initial cues from across the pond. Theater had a low reputation in England, where it was considered a haven for vulgarity and licentiousness.[2] This attitude prevailed in the colonies as well. As far back as 1682, William Penn wrote that theatrical attendance was "an offense against God [which incited] people to Rudeness, Cruelty, Looseness, and Irreligion."[3] Theater was a long way from attaining its modern reputation as a high-brow haven for literary giants and serious writers.[4]

Theater's poor reputation led the Puritans who long dominated the Massachusetts Bay Colony to ban theatrical productions in 1750. As a result, it took some time for American theater to grow into its own. A man as well-read as Massachusetts's John Adams had never even seen a play until he began his diplomatic service in Europe. Thomas Jefferson, too, picked up an appreciation for theater while abroad. Rhode Island and Pennsylvania passed their own anti-theater laws, and the Continental Congress passed not one but two anti-theater acts, declaring, almost Soviet-style, that going to the theater was a "violation of colonial political goals."[5]

Attending plays was one of George Washington's favorite pursuits, however, and he disregarded this Congressional censoriousness when he had Joseph Addison's *Cato* performed for his soldiers at Valley Forge during the difficult winter of 1777–1778. Written in 1712, *Cato* was the first play in English to be translated into Italian and French.[6] The plot concerns the Roman stoic Cato the Younger, who opposed Caesar and took his own life when resistance to the tyrant became futile. Cato was one of a series of martyred Roman republicans, including Brutus, Cassius, and Cicero, idolized by the Founders.[7] Addison's *Cato* celebrated this ideal. Washington was particularly fond of the play, and he not only showed it to the troops but also quoted from it in his own speeches and in conversation. In one instance, he consoled a demoted and unhappy General John Thomas by paraphrasing the play's line, "Surely every post ought to be deemed honorable in which a man can serve his country." Washington would adapt the line to his own purposes as "'Tis not in mortals to command success."[8] He had first seen *Cato* performed in 1758, when he was a young man in his twenties. Even though the play has a tragic ending—Cato and the Republic itself meet an untimely end—Washington took inspiration from its message that our affairs are not predetermined—that human action can change outcomes.[9]

Washington was not the only Revolutionary leader influenced by the play. Patrick Henry's "Give me liberty or give me death" originated from *Cato*, as did patriot and spy Nathan Hale's famous last words, "I only regret that I have but one life to lose for my country." In *Cato*, the phrase appears as "What a pity it is that we can die but once to save our country."[10] The play's appeal extended to later generations of American leaders in times of trial. After his impeachment by the House of Representatives, President Andrew Johnson had his private secretary read passages from *Cato* to him.[11]

Washington's use of the play at Valley Forge was successful. The troops survived the brutal winter and the Continental Army won the war. But the play may have saved Washington's command as well. Facing a near mutiny in Newburgh, New York, in 1783, he began a speech to his restive officers with a dramatic gesture, reaching for his glasses and remarking,

> Attending plays was one of George Washington's favorite pursuits, however, and he disregarded this Congressional censoriousness when he had Joseph Addison's *Cato* performed for his soldiers at Valley Forge during the difficult winter of 1777–78.

"Gentlemen, you must pardon me. I have grown gray in your service and now find myself growing blind." He then delivered a speech that echoed Addison's lines from *Cato*, and the chastened troops called off the revolt.[12]

Censorship of theater did not survive long amid the Revolutionary fervor. Increasing social and economic diversity also diminished the political influence of religious factions. Anti-theater statutes and sentiments dissolved across the nation, even in Puritan New England.[13] Even in this relaxed atmosphere, however, political pitfalls still awaited the unwary politician—even George Washington. The first president enjoyed Shakespeare—*Hamlet*, in particular—but he also liked the works of the playwright and parliamentarian Richard Sheridan, including the Irishman's somewhat risqué *School for Scandal*. This play involves a scandal-mongering, troublemaking young widow, who is eventually exposed and disgraced, but not before causing much tumult and damage. It is not a subtle work—the villainess is called

Lady Sneerwell, and her henchman and eventual betrayer is dubbed Snake. Washington offended Senator William Maclay of Pennsylvania by inviting him to a performance of Sheridan's play, which Maclay denounced as "an indecent representation before ladies of character and virtue."[14] Washington's reputation for rectitude survived this minor embarrassment, but Maclay's reaction foreshadowed the recurring tension between American culture's occasional taste for barrier-breaking and the president's supra-political role as a moral exemplar for the nation. If a president sticks to what is safe, he risks being seen as conventional, dull, or antiquarian—perhaps a greater liability now than in our more moralistic past but always a problem in a nation as obsessed with the modern as our own. Furthermore, embracing new cultural offerings, especially ones that are racy or have the capacity to offend, can harm a president politically.

The easing of moral qualms and the growing respect for freedom of speech in the early nineteenth century allowed theaters to spread throughout the nation, even to Philadelphia, the second and temporary capital of the United States, where stage productions had been previously banned. Here President Washington enjoyed his theatrical productions, including *School for Scandal*. Washington had also seen *The Child of Nature* in 1797 in Philadelphia, quickly becoming known for a cosmopolitan array of theatrical offerings. Ten years later, the new capital city was ready, but Washington, D.C., was largely deprived of theaters during the presidency of John Adams. The Washington Theater, an unimpressive but permanent structure, opened after Adams's term in November of 1804, at the corner of 11th and C Streets, Northwest. A year later, Jefferson became the first president to attend the theater in the city of Washington, attending a visiting Alexandria company's production of two works by British playwrights—Elizabeth Inchbald's *The Child of Nature* and Thomas Holcroft's *The Tale of Mystery*.[15]

—⟶⟩⟩⟩•●•⟨⟨⟨—

The first president enjoyed Shakespeare—*Hamlet*, in particular—but he also liked the works of the playwright and parliamentarian Richard Sheridan, including the Irishman's somewhat risqué *School for Scandal*.

Getting Out of Washington:
Theatrical Attendance on the Goodwill Tours

Almost every president in the early nineteenth century had at least some interaction with theater. James Monroe, for example, cared little for the theater, but he attended plays while traveling the country on goodwill tours.[16] In July 1817, he took in Charles Dibdin's *The Secret Mine* in Boston, praising it as "superior to any exhibition of the kind which he had ever witnessed in Europe."[17] Monroe, of course, was familiar with European theater, having served as the American minister to France and to Great Britain. While Dibdin himself was English, Monroe's comment about the quality of the production suggests his consciousness of the degree in which the United States was viewed as culturally inferior to Europe. The upstart country continued in its struggle to be culturally relevant in the eyes of the European nations. Monroe's attendance at the play in Boston and his subsequent approval served as a cultural statement. He recognized the symbolic importance of the president's taking on the role of champion for American cultural achievement.

> **But Monroe's attendance at this particular performance was noteworthy because it was almost certainly the first encounter of a U.S. president with a fictional work by an American Jewish author.**

That same year, on the fourth night of a weeklong stay in Charleston, a theatrical center at the time, Monroe also saw the second performance of *Alberti*, by the Jewish playwright and religious reformer Isaac Harby.[18] The play has a Romeo-and-Juliet plot about Florentine lovers kept apart by hatred between their fathers.[19] The play itself is hardly memorable. In fact, the Jewish historian Jacob Rader Marcus dismisses Harby's plays as "not stageworthy."[20] But Monroe's attendance at this particular performance was noteworthy because it was almost certainly the first encounter of a U.S. president with a fictional work by an American Jewish author.[21] These days, when the work of Jewish authors is so prevalent, it bears recalling that while America differed from most other countries in welcoming Jews to its shores, Jews were not welcome universally in this country. It would be another century before a Jew—Sears president Julius Rosenwald—received an invitation to dinner at the White House with William Howard Taft in 1912,[22] a few years after the Jewish playwright Israel Zangwill dined with Theodore Roosevelt for lunch in honor of his play, *The Melting Pot.*

But Monroe had heard from Harby before. Three years earlier, the author had written to then Secretary of State Monroe, complaining about the dismissal of the U.S. consul to Tunis, Mordecai Manuel Noah. Harby had been concerned that Noah was fired because he was a Jew, and it was alleged that Monroe had stated that Noah's religion was "an obstacle to the exercise of [his] Consular function." In Harby's letter, he objected to this very notion, and wrote that it should be "upon the principle of equal inalienable, *constitutional Rights*, that we see Jews appointed to offices...."[23] In hindsight, it is unclear whether anti-Semitism precipitated Noah's firing; nevertheless, there is no doubt that anti-Semitism was prevalent at the time.[24] Regardless of the cause, Monroe's attendance at Harby's play in Charleston could reasonably be interpreted as a gesture of apology.[25]

Harby shared with the president a desire to develop a unique and worthy American culture. He was unfazed when a sarcastic foreign critic declared his play praiseworthy for an "American production." Harby's response to the accusation of being American: "I plead guilty." He added that he was proud of "the accident of birth, which has placed me under the protection of laws that I revere, and in the bosom of a country that I love."[26] America was a striving nation, looking for acceptance but also proudly developing its own political, religious, and cultural traditions. Americans were already building a culture that was more than mere opposition to the European critique (although Europe did not yet recognize it), and Monroe and Harby's actions supported this emerging new culture.

Monroe's successors continued the tradition of attending theatrical productions throughout the country. President John Tyler took in the theater during travels to New York and to Philadelphia in 1843, which included watching a performance of *Jack Cade* with the celebrated Edwin Forrest in the lead. The title character revenges himself on the villainous Lord Say, who has murdered his father, but not before Say stabs him with a poisoned dagger. The hero dies with the democratic words, "The bondman is avenged, my country free!"[27]

Forrest's name is mostly forgotten by history, but that of his archrival is not. In February 1838, President Martin Van Buren saw Junius Booth, the father of the future presidential assassin John Wilkes Booth, in a production of John Howard Payne's *Tragedy of Brutus.* In this tale, Brutus defends the concept of freedom to his son, saying, "This hand should tear this heart from out my ribs, ere it should own allegiance to a tyrant." Less than a month later, Van Buren took in Forrest's performance in *Othello*.[28] For the time, Van Buren's travels and taste for the stage were impressive. He was a serious reader and counted among his friends Washington Irving, whom he introduced to Andrew Jackson. Irving, along with James Fenimore Cooper, was among the first American writers to earn a reputation in Europe, and he encouraged the literary efforts of Nathaniel Hawthorne, Herman Melville, Henry Wadsworth Longfellow, and Edgar Allan Poe.

For the time, Van Buren's travels and taste for the stage were impressive. He was a serious reader and counted among his friends Washington Irving, whom he introduced to Andrew Jackson.

Every American president has attended the theater at least once in his life. For the dour James Buchanan, once was enough. It was in 1833, while serving as Andrew Jackson's minister to Russia, and we don't even know the name of the play he saw.[29] Another one-term president, Jimmy Carter, likewise avoided the theater. *Ain't Misbehavin'* was the first Broadway show he had seen "in fifteen or twenty years."[30] (As we shall see, Carter preferred the movies.) A president's decision to attend or not to attend the theater can tell us more about him than simply how he liked to spend his evenings. It may reveal how he chose to be aware of the sentiments of the people, where he stood on questions of education, elitism, and propriety, and even how hard he worked.

The Theater and Democracy

As America evolved in the nineteenth century, so did American theater. It transformed from a vulgar medium that offended genteel sensibilities to increasingly popular and democratic forms of expression. The Founders envisioned enlightened leaders presiding over an educated and vigilant citizenry. Theater, they hoped, would encourage that citizenry in virtue.[31] But democracy proved to be loud and unruly,[32] and the theater that emerged in nineteenth-century America revealed itself as very different from the vision of the Founders. It was bawdy, raucous, lively, and, above all, democratic.

It was also pervasive, despite the lack of modern technology. The plays and actors were identifiable to ordinary Americans in a way that Hollywood movies and stars might be today. The career of Edwin Forrest, a dominating presence in mid-nineteenth-century theater, provides a good example.

Touring was a regular part of theatrical life in those days, and Forrest toured much of the country in his period of stardom, which lasted from the 1830s to the 1850s. Citizens across the country had seen Forrest, whose fame was by no means limited to New York.[33] His rise also coincided with an increased respectability for the theatrical profession in general. Actors had been frowned upon by polite society from the time of the fall of Rome through the eighteenth century. One consequence of the social stigma attached to the theater was the pervasive use of the title "opera house" instead of theater throughout the nineteenth century. American opera houses rarely staged actual operas, but opera, and music in general, was considered more respectable than drama, which accounts for the misleading nomenclature.[34]

By Forrest's day, however, actors were becoming more respectable. A star like Forrest could mingle in high society and even with public officials.[35] He chose roles that cast him as the common man, fighting for the underdog against more powerful forces arrayed against him. Forrest's star status, coupled with his place on the ideological spectrum, made him a reference point in political debate. In 1858, for example, cartoonists depicted Stephen A. Douglas as Forrest in his famous role of Spartacus. There was even speculation about his running for political office under the Democratic banner. He refused.[36]

Theatrical performances were available throughout the country, even outside the major cities. Americans were introduced to the works of the great playwrights in their schoolbooks, which were likely to include famous monologues, especially from Shakespeare, making the Bard widely known. Politicians such as Abraham Lincoln knew that their audiences would recognize and appreciate Shakespearean references.[37] Virginia's John Tyler loved Shakespeare from an early age and would often quote or allude to him both in public and in private communications. Tyler boasted an elite background. His father had been Thomas Jefferson's roommate at William and Mary. Tyler attended his father's alma mater, beginning at the precocious age of twelve and graduating at seventeen. When he ran for vice president on the "hard cider and log cabins" ticket with William Henry Harrison in 1840, he tried to downplay this upper-class education.[38] But he was well versed in music, poetry, and literature and collected an impressive library of 1,200 books.[39]

Still, Shakespeare remained Tyler's favorite, and he felt comfortable citing Shakespeare, knowing that his audience would understand him. In 1855, after he had moved on from the presidency to the role of "well-read elder statesman," notes Edward Crapol, he gave an important speech on slavery and secessionism to the Maryland Institute. The speech comprised numerous literary allusions. He struck a note of optimism, apparently, by making a reference to Edgar Allan Poe, who had been a household name since the publication of "The Raven" in 1845: "I listen to no raven-like croakings foretelling 'disastrous twilight' to this confederacy...." He also made an adamant stand against secession, doubting that "a

> Tyler could quote *Othello* in a political speech because even his most simply educated countrymen were taught Shakespeare and because so many people went to the theater. Average Americans attended plays far more often than we might imagine. One nineteenth-century Massachusetts man managed to see 102 shows in 122 days.

people so favored by heaven" would "throw away a pearl richer than all the tribe." (His views on this subject would change after the election of Abraham Lincoln in 1860, and he was a member of the Confederate Congress when he died in 1862.) His reference to *Othello* during the central point of his argument reflects his confidence that his listeners would share an appreciation for Shakespeare.[40]

Tyler could quote *Othello* in a political speech because even his most simply educated countrymen were taught Shakespeare and because so many people went to the theater. Average Americans attended plays far more often than we might imagine. One nineteenth-century Massachusetts man managed to see 102 shows in 122 days. Not only must he have been a very determined theater-goer, but he must have had many opportunities. As Heather Nathans observes, "[t]hat he could find 102 opportunities in 122 days to be part of an audience underscores the importance of performance culture in America during this period." The shows themselves were varied, including not just Shakespeare, but also singers, musicals, minstrels, and orators, both professionals and amateurs.[41]

Actors and Audience: Theater in a Democracy

A president's visit to the theater has always been more than an opportunity for his own entertainment or edification. It is an opportunity to influence the audience. Live audiences make the theater an interactive and communal art form. Each performance and each audience is unique. The actors know whether the house is full and whether the material is being appreciated or landing with a thud amidst a disapproving audience. It is a cliché among actors that the energy of the stage performance is radically different from that presented on the big screen.

Nineteenth-century American audiences were infamous for being boisterous and ill-mannered. Frances Trollope, the mother of the novelist Anthony Trollope, immortalized this reputation in 1832 in *Domestic Manners of the Americans*. This memoir of her visit to the United States, which amused her European readers but discomfited

Americans, mocked the habits of American audiences—"the spitting was incessant"—their odors—"the mixed smell of onions and whiskey"—and their volume—"The noises, too, were perpetual, and of the most unpleasant kind." The English visitor found American displays of patriotism particularly painful, complaining that "when a patriotic fit seized them, and 'Yankee Doodle' was called for, every man seemed to think his reputation as a citizen depended on the noise he made."[42] Mrs. Trollope's work continues to be cited by those wishing to present an example of a snooty European deriding American manners.[43]

A filmed performance is the same whether it is screened for a single viewer at home or in a packed cinema, and the actors cannot respond to the audience's reaction. Live theater, by contrast, enables the cast to interact with their audience, an aspect doled out liberally by cast members in the nineteenth century. They can play up particularities a specific audience is more likely to appreciate, and they can ad-lib based on current events or on who is in the house. Needless to say, the presence of the president of the United States changes the theatrical experience for the cast, for the audience, and for the president himself.

Politicians in the nineteenth century frequently attended shows, not only in Washington but also across the country. Andrew Jackson, for example, built his political appeal through his travels, which occasionally included visits to the theater. On a goodwill tour of New York City and Philadelphia in 1819, he saw shows in each city. The Hero of New Orleans's growing popularity was often evident on his travels. In New York, he saw the comic opera *The Poor Soldier*, where the crowds lauded the president whenever the cast ad libbed a reference to their famous guest.[44] In April of that same year, he visited Charleston,

—›››·●·‹‹‹—

Despite Jackson's earthy ways and anti-intellectual airs, he was nevertheless aware of ideas and their power to influence. He was the first president to assemble writers and thinkers to support his campaign, enlisting their help with his speeches and encouraging them to write newspaper articles on his behalf.

where he saw *Julius Caesar* in a packed house of 1,800 people, almost twice as many as had joined Monroe at the theater two years earlier.[45]

Theatrical audiences can be a barometer of popularity when things are going well; they can also be unsparingly brutal in more trying circumstances. Though Jackson emerged a popular war hero, his 1824 race against John Quincy Adams was a titanic struggle—one of the closest and hardest-fought presidential elections in American history. Jackson won a plurality of the popular vote in a four-man race, but since no one received a majority of electoral votes, the election went to the House of Representatives. The election was still undecided on February 7, 1825, when both Jackson and Adams, along with the outgoing President Monroe, attended the Washington Theater for a triple billing of *Damon and Pythias*, *Catherine and Petruchio*, and *The Irishman in London*, with the renowned actor Thomas Abraham Cooper on stage.[46] Two days later, Representative Henry Clay orchestrated an end to the electoral deadlock by throwing his support behind Adams, who, in turn, made Clay his secretary of state—an apparent quid pro quo that Jackson's supporters denounced as the "Corrupt Bargain."

While Adams won the presidency that year, he lost the heart of the populace in the process. Jackson defeated him handily in 1828, served two eventful terms, saw his vice president, Martin Van Buren, elected president—one of only three presidents to do so—and put his stamp on American democracy, transforming the presidency and the nation along with it. This political future boasted a strange foreshadowing when Adams, as president-elect, returned to the Washington Theater. He faced an uncomfortable night as the actors, to the audience's delight, ad-libbed pro-Jackson lines. Congressman

> Adams was understandably appalled when Harvard offered Jackson an honorary degree in 1833. Adams famously complained about the selection to the university's president, his cousin Josiah Quincy III: "I could not be present to see my darling Harvard disgrace herself by conferring a Doctor's degree upon a barbarian and a savage who could scarcely spell his own name."

Louis McLane of Delaware called the awkward scene "an awful knell for the Pres[iden]t-elect—& he felt it." McLane added presciently, "What will he feel, when he hears this shout penetrating every part of the Union?"[47] Many years later, after another disputed presidential election, the defeated Al Gore and his wife attended a performance of *The Producers*. When the audience spotted Gore, they gave him a resounding ovation. While Gore was glad to be applauded, he surely would have been happier to be president.[48]

As for Adams, his cold reception at the Washington Theater stayed with him. Even though he enjoyed the theater, he didn't return to the Washington Theater for two years. He tried to once—to see the comedienne Clara Fisher—but the sitting president couldn't get a ticket.[49]

Several years after Adams had left the White House, the famous British actress Fanny Kemble toured the United States, drawing large audiences wherever she went. While in Boston, she requested an interview with the former president, and the two met on June 11, 1833. Less than a century earlier, theater had been banned in Boston, and now an actress had garnered an audience with the city's most prominent citizen. Adams enjoyed the actress's attention, saying that "As a sort of personage myself of the last century, I was flattered by the wish of this blossom of the next age to bestow some of her fresh fragrance upon the antiquities of the past."[50] Adams told Kemble that "he was a worshipper of Shakespeare," but he criticized *Othello*, *Romeo and Juliet*, and *King Lear*. "The great moral lesson of the Tragedy of Othello," said the former president, "is that white and black blood cannot be intermingled in marriage without a gross outrage upon the law of nature." Three years later, he wrote an essay insisting that we "must look at Shakespeare … in the capacity of a teacher of morals."[51]

Andrew Jackson, in contrast to Adams, rarely attended the theater. In 1833, on a trip to New York, Jackson fell ill after seeing four theatrical performances in New York City, including the play *Fontainbleau*, which introduced the British stereotypical character John Bull. It was the last time he ever attended the theater.[52]

Adams and Jackson:
The Enlightened Leader and the Common Man

The differing attitudes of Adams and Jackson toward the theater reflected more important differences between the two men. Theater, which was once a favorite entertainment of the common man, had now evolved, strangely enough, into the preserve of the cultural elite. This division was already emerging in the 1820s, during the days of Adams's and Jackson's political rivalry. Adams was a literary man who loved the theater. He was one of the few as well as one of the last presidents who actually aspired to be an intellectual rather than a man of the people. At Harvard, he had seriously considered becoming a man of letters. Pressure from his father led him to pursue the family business and to study law in preparation for politics. The senior Adams had mused, "I must study politics and war, that my sons may have liberty to study mathematics and philosophy," but the leisured study for which the father had secured the liberty apparently had to be put off for a later generation.[53]

While studying law, John Quincy Adams was often consumed by depression, which he would combat with a combination of tea, physical activity, and transcribing great works of poetry and plays.[54] As president, he enjoyed poetry, literature, theater, opera, and translating Latin texts. When he left the White House, he had brought thirty-eight boxes and six trunks of books with him.[55] In modern parlance, he might have qualified as an intellectual.[56]

Adams stayed busy after his presidency. In addition to serving in the House of Representatives, he maintained his old intellectual pursuits, including working on a history of the Jewish people. He had a long standing interest in the Bible, and even wrote a series of letters to his son on the Bible's teaching, including his philo-semitic but grim assessment of the Jewish prophets as "messengers, specifically commissioned of [G-d], to warn the people of their duty, to foretell the punishments which awaited their transgressions."[57] Alas, he lost interest in the Jewish history project.[58] However, theater, and particularly Shakespeare, did continue to engage him. In an exchange of letters with the actor James Hackett, he declared *Hamlet* "the masterpiece of the human mind."[59]

Given Adams's intellectual and artistic interests, it is little wonder that he thought ill of the poorly educated rival who vanquished him from the White House, Andrew Jackson. The contrast between their educations and intellectual natures was as sharp as that between any two presidents. The president who followed the superbly educated Adams was ill-educated, poorly-read, and a bad speller. Henry Clay—admittedly not an impartial observer—described Jackson as "ignorant, passionate, hypocritical, corrupt and easily swayed by the basest men who surround him."[60] For Adams to lose to this man, and to lose the support of the people to him, must have been extremely difficult.

Despite Jackson's earthy ways and anti-intellectual airs, he was nevertheless aware of ideas and their power to influence. He was the first president to assemble writers and thinkers to support his campaign, enlisting their help with his speeches and encouraging them to write newspaper articles on his behalf. His literary supporters included James Fenimore Cooper, Horatio Greenough, Nathaniel Hawthorne, George Bancroft, and William Cullen Bryant.[61] Jackson also read some works of policy, including those of Adam Smith, as well as John Taylor's anti-financier *Inquiry into the Principles and Policy of the United States.* He even credited reading a book on the South Sea bubble for his well-documented distrust of banks.[62]

> ━━➤➤➤·●·◄◄◄━━
>
> Polk approached all of his subsequent positions—congressman, governor, candidate, president—with the same brutal determination. In the midst of all this hard work, there was little time for reading, theater, music, or sport, pastimes in which he had no interest in any case.

Still, Jackson is reputed to have read only one work of fiction in his entire adult life, Oliver Goldsmith's *The Vicar of Wakefield.*[63] Adams was understandably appalled when Harvard offered Jackson an honorary degree in 1833. Adams famously complained about the selection to the university's president, his cousin Josiah Quincy III: "I could not be present to see my darling Harvard disgrace herself by conferring a Doctor's degree upon a barbarian and a savage who could scarcely spell his own name."[64] The doctoral diploma conferred on Jackson was in Latin, a language that Jackson barely knew, despite his days practicing law. He showed his common touch in accepting the degree and conversing with the Latin-speaking students afterwards, quipping, "I shall have to speak in English, not being able to return your compliment in what appears to be the language of Harvard. The only Latin I know is E Pluribus Unum."[65] This winning reply demonstrates Jackson's skills as a politician and represents an important shift in the view of the presidency.

After Jackson, presidents would not have to be well-read or well-educated, but they would need to have the common touch. As educated as Adams was, he was ill-suited to the emerging nationalistic and democratic ethos. Jackson, however, proved perfectly suited to this coming age, and he took full advantage of it. In the wake of the Jacksonian ascendance, struggles between enlightened intellectual leadership and an understanding of the common man would firmly be decided in favor of the common man.

James Knox Polk and the Workaholic Presidency

Few nineteenth-century presidents were so priggish as to be opposed to theater; however, James K. Polk, one of our hardest working presidents, was one of them. He dismissed the theater as a "vicious habit."[66] Polk attended the theater only once in his life—in Alabama of all places—for the ballet *Le diable à quatre* by Adolphe Adam. He went not on his own initiative but only because he was invited. He later noted that he was "received with great applause & every demonstration of respect." Nevertheless, he later recalled, "I remained … but half an hour."[67]

Polk was a severe man, a Calvinist who put work above all else, a "tough, no-nonsense, extremely hard-working chief executive…."[68] He remains the only president to declare that he would serve but one term; he would accomplish certain ambitious goals—including the annexation of Texas—and then retire. He did indeed meet his goals in a single term, but only because he put in two terms' worth of energy and focus, often at the expense of his health.

Hard work was nothing new to Polk. Born to an undistinguished family, he received little formal schooling but still managed to attend the University of North Carolina, where he graduated first in his class. Characteristically, after delivering his valedictory address, he collapsed from exhaustion. Polk approached all of his subsequent positions—congressman, governor, candidate, president—with the same brutal determination. In the midst of all this hard work, there was little time for reading, theater, music, or sport, pastimes in which he had no interest in any case.[69]

Polk's single-mindedness was costly for Mexico. He instigated and won the Mexican-American War, gaining California, Texas, and the territory that would become Arizona, Nevada, Utah, and New Mexico. Over the years, historians have gained a renewed respect for Polk. His "virtue of the hedgehog" raises the question of what is the appropriate level of extracurricular activity for a president. For those who insist the superhuman office of the president deserves only superhuman work effort, Polk can hardly be beaten. In recent years, it has become the habit of journalists and opposing partisans to criticize the vacations, golfing ventures, and leisure activities of every president, sneeringly asking how the chief executive has time for the links or a movie when people are unemployed. They couldn't sneer at Polk.

Americans look for a demanding mix of characteristics in their leaders. We want them to be hard-working, but they should not be too stiff or uptight. We want enlightened leadership, but also someone who understands our problems. In the nineteenth century, theater served as a way to convey these different and often contradictory notions regarding presidential leadership. As the reach of theatrical arts expanded, they served as a universal common experience in the pre-television era. The lively and vocal crowds stood ready to give quick approval or disapproval to politicians and plays alike. And the plays themselves conveyed appealing democratic themes to audiences hungry to absorb them. Reading would never disappear as an outlet for presidents, but the nineteenth-century stage presented opportunities to politicians who recognized its potency.

CHAPTER 3

LINCOLN: READING AS A TOOL FOR ADVANCEMENT

As Andrew Jackson proved, the "common man" was now capable of being elected president of the United States. But the question remained what he should do once elected. A democratic instinct was useful, but it was insufficient for exercising the vast responsibilities of the presidency.

No man married the common touch with statesmanlike vision better than Abraham Lincoln. He first raised himself up from exceedingly humble origins with the help of his reading and his intellect. Then he proved that knowledge, attention to facts, persuasive reasoning, and learning, whether garnered through formal or autodidactic channels, could build the essential core of statesmanship. Lincoln had all of these qualities, and he would use them to great effect as president in the nation's moment of crisis.

Lincoln was not the first American to improve his lot through reading. Ben Franklin established the model of the reader who pulls himself up by his bootstraps in his classic autobiography. "From a child I was fond of reading, and all the little money that came into my hands was ever laid out in books," Franklin recalled. As a young man he left his native Boston for Philadelphia. Stepping off the boat, he purchased three puffy rolls for three pennies, consumed one, and "walk'd off with a roll under each arm" to make his way in the world. The model of the voracious reader and the successful striver was one that many Americans, foremost among them Abraham Lincoln, would follow.[1]

Andrew Jackson also contributed to the pattern that Lincoln would follow. Lincoln grew up in a Jacksonian America that admired the common man and in which opportunities were expanding. By the middle of the nineteenth century, books and the ideas they conveyed were no longer reserved solely for the wealthy or the elites. "There is hardly a pioneer's hut that does not contain a few odd volumes of Shakespeare," observed Alexis de Tocqueville.[2]

The spread of books resulted from improvements in paper and printing as well as increasing literacy.[3] American authors and thinkers were emerging, encouraged by the growing audience for their work and by a flow of ideas and culture across the Atlantic that was no longer exclusively east-to-west. Harriet Beecher Stowe's *Uncle Tom's Cabin* (1852), for example, dominated discourse in America and was widely discussed in Europe. As Mary Church Terrell noted in 1911, "this book was read all over the civilized world." And it was read by people who mattered, which was a relatively new development associated with an American work. According to Terrell, "The queen of England read it aloud to the royal family."[4] In the years after the Civil War, Samuel Clemens (better known as Mark Twain) became a phenomenon not only in America but in Europe as well.

> Lincoln grew up in a Jacksonian America that admired the common man and in which opportunities were expanding. By the middle of the nineteenth century, books and the ideas they conveyed were no longer reserved solely for the wealthy or the elites. "There is hardly a pioneer's hut that does not contain a few odd volumes of Shakespeare," observed Alexis de Tocqueville.

As technological developments such as the locomotive, the power press, and the telegraph dramatically increased the flow of information, the ability to sift and discern, to absorb what was valuable and discard what was not, became an essential skill—especially for the self-trained, the striver, the man of humble origins who by sheer determination would make himself literate. The emerging archetype of the self-made man—later immortalized by Horatio Alger—seemed to validate the promise of America. Abraham Lincoln was one of many such men. "America was full of self-made readers," writes Anthony Brandt, "men who had had to struggle to become literate, ambitious men like Abraham Lincoln who were unwilling to spend the rest of their lives splitting rails."[5]

As everyone knows, Lincoln was born poor, yet he found in books a way out of the hardscrabble poverty he saw all around him. In fact, every biography of Lincoln contains an obligatory discussion of his voracious reading; the difficulty he had in securing books; his habit of always carrying a book with him; and his tremendous ability to retain what he read, supplemented by his transcription and memorization of favorite passages or even entire works. Lincoln the reader is as much a part of American lore as George Washington and the cherry tree. Even a century ago, Lord Charnwood noted the proliferating mix of "legends and authentic records of his self-training."[6]

Frequency of Lincoln's Reading

However concealed by legend the details of his reading may be, Lincoln clearly loved books, especially in his youth, and spent a great deal of time so occupied. Reading opened whole new worlds for him, and it became almost an addiction.[7] He looked for books wherever he could find them and carried them with him everywhere.[8] Of course, many youths are bookworms, but his sheer desperation for the printed word set Lincoln apart. The German-born Union general Carl Schurz's description of young Lincoln's bibliomania may now have the feel of romantic overstatement, but it captures his compulsion to read that everyone noticed: "Every printed page that fell into his hands he would greedily devour, and his family and friends watched him with wonder, as the uncouth boy, after his daily work, crouched in a corner of the log cabin or outside under a tree, absorbed in a book while munching his supper of corn bread."[9]

Lincoln's continual and often extraordinary efforts to obtain books were a sign not of idleness but of tremendous industry. The American diplomat Joseph Choate, who had seen Lincoln speak, told a British audience, "He trudged on foot many miles through the wilderness to borrow an English Grammar, and is said to have devoured greedily"—the same term Schurz used—"the contents of the Statutes of Indiana that fell in his way."[10] This constant reading continued, and was noticed by others, even in his peripatetic stages. He was clearly reading heavily during his sojourn in New Salem in his twenties, for it became one of his identifiable characteristics.[11]

What Lincoln read has fascinated historians almost as much as the *quantity* he read. Robert Bray has even compiled "The Definitive Evaluative and Annotated List" in his essay, "What Abraham Lincoln Read." His bibliography evaluates every book Lincoln is known or thought to have read. The list contains some 430 works, each graded on the likelihood that Lincoln actually read it.[12] Given the compulsion with which Lincoln read, he surely read more than 430 books over the course of his life, not to mention newspapers, pamphlets, and magazines, but the list is extremely useful in determining which books he is certain to have read. A given work may or may not have influenced Lincoln, but simply knowing that he read it makes it more interesting to us and raises its historical reputation.

Bray's evaluations, it should be added, are commendably honest. A historian may have prejudices or pet theories that would be vindicated by the knowledge that Lincoln read a certain book. Bray himself hoped to find that Lincoln had read Walt Whitman's *Leaves of Grass*. As many Ph.D. dissertations as such a finding would have generated, the evidence is not there. Bray acknowledges that Lincoln probably did not read *Leaves of Grass*.[13]

Key Works for Lincoln

Many of the books that Lincoln read were among the greatest works of English.[14] Though there are occasional variations in this list, most scholars agree that these essential works included the Bible, Parson Weems's *Life of Washington*, Aesop's fables,

Robinson Crusoe, Pilgrim's Progress, and *A History of the United States*. It was this collection of books that got Lincoln started, opened up his world, and made him hungry for more than a poor, unpedigreed frontier lad could expect to achieve in the early nineteenth century. In a moving and beautiful passage, Charnwood describes how Lincoln consumed these core texts: "These books he did read, and read again, and pondered, not with any dreamy or purely intellectual interest, but like one who desires the weapon of learning for practical ends, and desires also to have patterns of what life should be."[15]

The repetition of reading, the notion that Lincoln read the same few books over and over again, is reminiscent of Saint Thomas Aquinas's warning, "Hominem unius libri timeo" ("I fear the man of a single book"). In a more humorous vein, Irving Kristol allegedly observed—not about Lincoln, of course—that he had no problem with politicians who read books, but that it should not be the same book over and over again.[16] Nevertheless, Lincoln benefitted from reading certain books repeatedly, and it was fortunate that he managed to obtain the particular books that he did. Even rereading these works today, one can see that they encourage a forcefulness of narrative and thought.[17] As Charnwood put it, "There is some advantage merely in being driven to make the most of a few books; great advantage in having one's choice restricted by circumstances to good books...."[18] Choate agreed: "To be shut in with a few books and to master them thoroughly sometimes does more for the development of character than freedom to range at large, in a cursory and indiscriminate way, through wide domains of literature."[19] While reading one book too often may be limiting, immersing oneself in a select

> ───➤➤➤•●•◄◄◄───
>
> In fact, every biography of Lincoln contains an obligatory discussion of his voracious reading; the difficulty he had in securing books; his habit of always carrying a book with him; and his tremendous ability to retain what he read, supplemented by his transcription and memorization of favorite passages or even entire works. Lincoln the reader is as much a part of American lore as George Washington and the cherry tree.

number of true classics can equip one intellectually for life. Lincoln had less than a year of formal schooling,[20] yet he became an educated, if not perfectly rounded, man and leader because of his assiduous love of reading. Instead of college, he had reading, and it served him well.[21]

From the Bible and Shakespeare, he learned a common but elevated language. From Aesop he learned the artful use of anecdotes to make a point. From Weems he gained an appreciation of how a leader can capture the people's hearts.[22] His reading deserves and receives much of the credit for Lincoln's extraordinary evolution from what Choate called "this rough backwoodsman, whose youth had been spent in the forest or on the farm and the flatboat, without culture or training, education or study," to our poet president, enshrined on Mount Rushmore and celebrated for his wit and wisdom.[23] And yet, if you take a hundred, a thousand, or even a million people, and have them read the Bible, Weems, *Robinson Crusoe*, and *Pilgrim's Progress*, over and over and over again—it will not make them into a Lincoln. He was made by his books, but he was also much more than his books. He knew what to make of the education he obtained for himself.[24]

> Lincoln had less than a year of formal schooling, yet he became an educated, if not perfectly rounded, man and leader because of his assiduous love of reading. Instead of college, he had reading, and it served him well.

Lincoln once said of himself, "My mind is like a piece of steel—very hard to scratch anything on it, almost impossible after you get it there to rub anything out."[25] He could recite Aesop's fables by heart. But his prodigious memory also proved useful in politics, allowing him to recall facts, figures, and faces as well as contributing to his success as a speaker in a pre-teleprompter age.[26]

Lincoln was ambitious. He needed to be in order to rise out of the poverty and obscurity into which he was born. Benjamin Franklin's autobiography, which he read in his youth, fueled that ambition. Franklin's story showed him a path forward and assured him that there was more to life than his humble beginnings would lead him to imagine.[27] Ambition requires self-confidence, and Lincoln entered adulthood with the solid self-confidence that overcoming great adversity instills into one's being more effectively than the "self-esteem" lessons that occupy an exalted place in modern education theory.[28] This self-confidence, along with careful practice and his powerful memory, made him a strong speaker who could captivate a crowd.[29] Neither natural gift nor diligent practice could have produced this ability on its own; it was the combination of the two that made him who he was. Lincoln is an example of Malcolm Gladwell's principle that even the highly talented must spend ten thousand hours in practice to become true experts in their field.[30]

There was a tremendously pragmatic aspect to Lincoln's reading. "Year by year his knowledge and power, his experience and reputation extended," said Choate, "and his mental faculties seemed to grow by what they fed on."[31] He read with a purpose, focusing on the works he knew he needed to master to fulfill his ambitions, whether it was Euclid or Blackstone's *Commentaries*. His read like a young man with a goal.[32]

Lincoln also had little interest in novels. "It may seem somewhat strange to say," he once observed, "but I never read an entire novel in my life."[33] That may have been an overstatement, since we know he read *Robinson Crusoe*, and one could argue that *Pilgrim's Progress* counts as a novel. He was at least familiar with the works of Harriet Beecher Stowe and Charles Dickens.[34] Though his tastes ran more to history, his love of poetry and of Shakespeare shows that he did not shun fiction. He may have been pragmatic in his reading, but he was drawn to great works of the imagination.

Uncle Tom's Cabin: Slavery and Abolitionism on the Cultural Battleground

When Lincoln's "moral nature was aroused, his brain developed an untiring activity until it had mastered all the knowledge within reach," wrote Carl Schurz, and the debate over slavery provides the chief example. In the years after the Missouri Compromise, Lincoln learned everything he could about the topic.[35] Slavery turned American literature into a battleground decades before the Civil War turned the country itself into a battleground. Of all the writings on the subject, however, none proved more crucial than Harriet Beecher Stowe's *Uncle Tom's Cabin*.

The book even inspired the phrase "the Great American Novel," a title bestowed on it in 1868 by the journal the *Nation*.[36] Yet its real influence was political, not literary. *Uncle Tom's Cabin* likely exercised more influence on public opinion than any other novel in American history.[37] The book appeared at a crucial moment, when abolitionists had become pessimistic about ever overcoming the entrenched slave interest.[38]

Stowe's story of the Christ-like slave Tom first appeared in serial form in the antislavery *National Era* in 1851. The book, published in March 1852, sold ten thousand copies in the first week and three hundred thousand in the first year. It kept three power presses busy around the clock.[39] *Uncle Tom's Cabin* was the best selling novel of the nineteenth century and the second-best selling book overall, next to the Bible.[40] Sales topped even higher numbers in England, where it sold 1.5 million copies (unprotected by copyright, costing Stowe a fortune in royalties). The novel's appeal was not limited to the English-speaking world. It was eventually translated into thirty-seven different languages, including French, Italian, Spanish, Dutch, German, Russian, and Arabic.[41]

> —➤➤➤•◄◄◄—
>
> **From the Bible and Shakespeare, he learned a common but elevated language. From Aesop he learned the artful use of anecdotes to make a point. From Weems he gained an appreciation of how a leader can capture the people's hearts.**

Hundreds of stage adaptations of *Uncle Tom's Cabin* blossomed, ranging from moralistic tales denouncing slavery to racist comedies mocking the book's African-American characters. At times in the second half of the nineteenth century, more than four hundred productions toured the United States—east and west, urban and rural.[42]

Stowe's novel broke down barriers to the products of American culture. From the degeneracy thesis to critics who faintly praised the fruits of Yankee culture as acceptable "for an American," artists from the United States often had to struggle for acceptance outside the nation's borders. In 1820, the Scottish writer Sydney Smith dismissed American culture with his famous observation: "In the four quarters of the globe, who reads an American book? Or goes to an American play?" Thanks to *Uncle Tom's Cabin* and the subsequent revolution in communications, Smith's question was turned around in the next century. Today our European and Islamic critics ask in dismay, "In the four quarters of the globe, who does not take in American popular culture?"[43]

Not surprisingly, *Uncle Tom's Cabin* even reached the White House. President Millard Fillmore was unpopular with abolitionists because, among other reasons, he had signed the Fugitive Slave Act, which made Northerners feel complicit in what many saw as Southern sin. Given the notoriety of the book and the passions aroused by slavery, one citizen, Mrs. S. M. Greeley, mailed a copy to Fillmore, who was approaching the end of his White House tenure. Fillmore replied with a correct if not warm letter acknowledging receipt of the book. He allowed that he had "only found time to glance at it and see that it is a work of fiction on the 'vexed' Subject of Slavery." He did add that "Mrs. F. however has read some chapters and is much pleased with its Style and interested in its story." As with his support of the Compromise of 1850, Fillmore's compromise position on *Uncle Tom's Cabin*, not reading it himself, but admitting that his wife had done so, did little to cool things down on the book or on the larger issue of slavery.[44] Later, Fillmore's post-presidential personal library at his home would be found to include not one but two copies of Stowe's book.[45]

In the process of touching an entire nation, the book touched ex-presidents as well. In February 1853, Julia Gardiner Tyler, the wife of former president John A. Tyler, responded to an open letter to the women of the South published in a Richmond newspaper from a number of aristocratic anti-slavery British women, who complained about the mistreatment of slaves as described in Stowe's novel. Mrs. Tyler rebuked the foreign correspondents for their presumption and maintained that the working conditions of British laborers compared unfavorably with those of American slaves.

Mrs. Tyler's letter was widely reprinted, and her husband expressed pride at her defense of the South.[46]

Of course, approval of Mrs. Tyler's response was not universal. In April, Frederick Douglass dismissed "the amiable" Mrs. Tyler's "look at home" message. As Douglass powerfully exclaimed, "American Slavery, like every other form of wickedness, has a strong desire just to be left alone; and slaveholders, above all other preachers, to whom we ever listened, insist most strongly on the duty of every man's minding his own business."[47]

As these exchanges and the sales figures suggest, *Uncle Tom's Cabin* had become the must-read book of the mid-nineteenth century. George Sand wrote from France that "it is no longer permissible to those who can read not to have read it."[48] The novel's influence soon became apparent as the abolitionist movement, which had been losing in 1850, strengthened throughout the North.[49] At the same time, attitudes in the South hardened. One of the political losers in this shift of public opinion was Stephen A. Douglas. He failed to understand that the reception of *Uncle Tom's Cabin*, combined with the unpopularity of the Dred Scott decision and John Brown's bloody raid on Harper's Ferry, was turning Northern opinion against Douglas's accommodating approach to slavery.[50]

> Like Lincoln, the leaders of the anti-slavery movement appreciated Stowe's influence. On January 1, 1863, she attended a concert in Boston celebrating the Emancipation Proclamation. The audience, which included Ralph Waldo Emerson, Henry Wadsworth Longfellow, and Oliver Wendell Holmes, honored her presence by chanting, "Harriet Beecher Stowe. Harriet Beecher Stowe. Harriet Beecher Stowe."

Harriet Beecher Stowe herself proved a savvy political promoter. She approached a host of northern politicians and opinion-shapers, such as Salmon Chase, Edward Everett Hale (her niece's husband), and Charles Sumner, and attended political events for the first Republican presidential candidate, John C. Frémont, who lost the 1856 election to James Buchanan.[51]

But the politician who benefited the most from Stowe's work was Lincoln, whose opposition to slavery revived his moribund political career.[52] The Republican Party distributed 100,000 copies of *Uncle Tom's Cabin* in the campaign of 1860.[53] Stowe's readers of the 1850s voted for Lincoln in 1860 and joined his Union army during the Civil War.[54]

As Lincoln admitted, he avoided novels, and Robert Bray judges it unlikely that Lincoln actually read *Uncle Tom's Cabin*. But he was obviously familiar with the book. Stowe visited Lincoln at the

The political philosopher Harry Jaffa has called Lincoln "the supreme advocate of the cause of popular government," and indeed the rail-splitter president was the very embodiment of that ideal.

White House in late 1862, a few weeks before the Emancipation Proclamation.[55] Her visit occasioned Lincoln's famous but apocryphal greeting, "So you're the little woman who wrote the book that made this great war!" There is no record of what they talked about, but Stowe recalled laughing a lot and wrote to her husband of a "really funny interview with the President."[56]

Like Lincoln, the leaders of the anti-slavery movement appreciated Stowe's influence. On January 1, 1863, she attended a concert in Boston celebrating the Emancipation Proclamation. The audience, which included Ralph Waldo Emerson, Henry Wadsworth Longfellow, and Oliver Wendell Holmes, honored her presence by chanting, "Harriet Beecher Stowe. Harriet Beecher Stowe. Harriet Beecher Stowe."[57]

Lincoln: Reader with the Common Touch

In the nineteenth century as well as today, conspicuous book learning could be a disadvantage for a politician. While every president needs a little John Quincy Adams to govern wisely, he needs a little Andrew Jackson to get elected. The common touch was never difficult for Lincoln. His origins—the poverty, the rail-splitting, the one-room schoolhouse—were as humble as they come. But long after he left the log cabin, Lincoln retained an ability to connect with ordinary people despite his impressive intellect and knowledge. An early editor of Lincoln's speeches and writings, Daniel Kilham Dodge, marveled at Honest Abe's ability to expand his horizons while remaining firmly grounded: "[W]hile Lincoln the man remained ever the same, his intellect continually broadened, and his sensibilities were quickened."[58]

> The combination of humble origins and prodigious learning makes Lincoln an irresistibly appealing figure. If Lincoln can do it, politicians and citizens alike may think, *so can I.*

Theodore Roosevelt, who knew something about balancing book smarts and democratic appeal, admired Lincoln's ability to straddle the world of the common man and that of the enlightened leader: "[He] was the statesman who in this absolutely democratic republic succeeded best, was the very man who actually combined the two sets of qualities which the historian thus puts in antithesis."[59] Lincoln honed this skill as a circuit-riding lawyer whose success depended in part on being a good entertainer. Over a century ago, Choate was impressed by Lincoln's sense of courtroom battles as popular entertainment.[60] A good actor, Lincoln knew how to play to his audience. Like Jackson, for example, he made fun of those who wore their Latin on their sleeve. Once, when confronted in court with one of the innumerable legal maxims in that learned tongue, Lincoln responded, "If that's Latin, you had better call another witness."[61]

Lincoln understood the importance of humility in politics. He was one of the most remarkable examples in American history of the man who has pulled himself up by his bootstraps, but he hated drawing attention to his achievement. During his presidential run, he deflected questions about his origins, saying that "it is great folly to attempt to make anything out of me or my early life." When pressed, he simply quoted the famous line from Thomas Gray's "Elegy Written in a Country Churchyard" (1751), "The short and simple annals of the poor," adding, "That's my life, and that's all you or anyone else can make of it." His appeal to the common man more than his opposition to slavery propelled him to the presidency.[62]

The political philosopher Harry Jaffa has called Lincoln "the supreme advocate of the cause of popular government," and indeed the rail-splitter president was the very embodiment of that ideal. The way he lived his life, says the presidential historian Richard Norton Smith, has made him accessible. "In many ways, Lincoln is one of us," says Smith, citing his sense of humor, his difficult marriage, and his personal trials.[63]

This accessibility makes Lincoln admired by politician, scholar, and common man alike. George W. Bush read fourteen biographies of Lincoln during his presidency.[64] Woodrow Wilson believed that Lincoln's rise validated the concept of popular sovereignty.[65] The combination of humble origins and prodigious learning makes Lincoln an irresistibly appealing figure. If Lincoln can do it, politicians and citizens alike may think, *so can I*. Of course, none of his successors has repeated that feat.

The Final Chapter: Lincoln and the Theater

Moving to Washington allowed Lincoln to become an active theatergoer. For most of his life, he had little acquaintance with the theater, although he did take in three plays in Chicago in 1857.[66] The first performance he attended as president was Verdi's *Il Trovatore*, in January 1862, almost one year into his tenure.[67] He was quickly hooked. Theater entertained him, gave him and members of his family comfort in difficult times, engaged his mind on great issues, and at times distracted him from his tribulations.

Shakespeare, says the literary biographer Fred Kaplan, was Lincoln's "secular Bible."[68] His introduction to Shakespeare came early in life through *Scott's Lessons in Elocution*. This childhood introduction instilled in him a love of Shakespeare long before he saw the works come to life on stage.[69]

> —⟶⟩⟩•●•⟨⟨⟨—
>
> The book-loving Abraham Lincoln was an important component of the image of America as the land where one could rise up from poverty to become successful and powerful—and even to become president.

He "read Shakespeare more than all other writers together," according to John Hay, his personal secretary and a future secretary of state.[70] The first performance of Shakespeare that Lincoln saw in Washington was *Henry IV*, Part 1, with James Hackett as Falstaff, in March of 1863.[71] Although Lincoln enjoyed the Bard on stage and saw performances of *Hamlet*, *Richard III*, and *King Lear*, among others, his early love for Shakespeare on the written page continued, and he often read aloud from the plays in the White House.[72]

Nevertheless, performance of Shakespearean works onstage moved Lincoln, and he relished seeing the plays live, as well as enjoying occasional interactions with the actors. In a famous letter to Hackett—which the actor promptly and rudely made public—Lincoln confessed, "For one of my age, I have seen very little of the drama." He added, "Some of Shakespeare's plays I have never read; while others I have gone over perhaps as frequently as any unprofessional reader. Among the latter are Lear, Richard Third, Henry Eighth, Hamlet, and especially Macbeth. I think nothing equals Macbeth. It is wonderful."[73]

Of course, Lincoln liked other plays in addition to Shakespeare's. In October 1863, for example, on his first visit to Ford's Theater, he saw the famous actress Maggie Mitchell perform her best known role, Fanchon in *Fanchon, the Cricket*. The character's dance with her own shadow was an audience favorite.[74]

In March 1865, Lincoln thought of attending a performance of *Still Waters Run Deep* by Tom Taylor. John Wilkes Booth found out about the plan and plotted an attempt on the president's life that day. Lincoln's plans changed, however, and he would not be able to attend the theater until the next month, on Good Friday.[75]

Lincoln went to Ford's Theater on April 14, 1865, to see another play by Taylor, *Our American Cousin*, a well-regarded comedy that poked fun at both backwater Americans and snooty Englishmen. American boorishness had long been a subject for mockery, but by satirizing the snobbishness of the supposedly superior Europeans as well, *Our American Cousin* marked a turning point in the cultural self-consciousness of the New World.

Some of Lincoln's advisors urged him to avoid a public outing that night, but he did not listen.[76] He was not the only one in his family to appreciate the rewards of the theatrical experience. Theater relaxed him and took his mind off his heavy burdens. John Hay observed that Lincoln, who loved reading, "read very little" as president, spending most of each day in meetings and dealing with the favor-seekers who besieged the White House.[77] The lack of time for reading must have been a challenge, one alleviated only to some degree by the outlet of theater. That same evening, his son Tad was at a showing of *Aladdin* at Grover's, another Washington theater. Tad learned that his father had been shot when people burst into the theater with the news, but he did not discover his father's sad fate until the next morning.[78]

The book-loving Abraham Lincoln was an important component of the image of America as the land where one could rise up from poverty to become successful and powerful—and even to become president. Like so many young men on the way up, Lincoln loved the printed word. In Lincoln's case, however, his ascent was about more than his personal fortune. The rise of Abraham Lincoln brought about the end of slavery and the preservation of the Union, and it contributed to an enduring image of America as the land not only of democratic government but also of democratic culture.

CHAPTER 4

THEODORE ROOSEVELT: CULTURE AND DESTINY

The political scientist Richard Neustadt made one of the most famous observations about the American presidency when he declared that its primary power is "the power to persuade." While presidents had always had an outsized ability to shape perceptions in America, the twentieth century bestowed on the president a new capacity for communicating ideas, enabling them to shape, and even reshape, their own images.

Even before the revolution in broadcast media, Theodore Roosevelt had dubbed the presidency a "bully pulpit." While president, he became the first American to send a transatlantic radio transmission.[1] On January 18, 1903, he sent a message to England's King Edward VII that reflected the world's collective amazement regarding the emerging new technology:

> In taking advantage of the wonderful triumph of research and ingenuity which has been achieved in perfecting a system of wireless telegraphy, I extend on behalf of the American people most cordial greetings and good wishes to you and all the people of the British Empire.[2]

Radio existed in its earliest stages under Roosevelt, and the first commercial radio station did not begin broadcasting until 1920, after his death. Roosevelt was therefore one of the last presidents to obtain information primarily through reading. The printed word served as a never-ending resource for Roosevelt. It shaped him as a man and as a politician, and it informed his policies as president. But larger technological forces were at work in early twentieth-century America; between his presidency and that of his cousin Franklin, broadcast technologies would transform the presidency, the culture, and our entire nation.

Theodore Roosevelt: "Reading with Me Is a Disease."

Theodore Roosevelt's rise to power, like Lincoln's, was in many ways shaped by his omnivorous reading. But Roosevelt, unlike Lincoln, came from a wealthy and prominent family, and books were far more varied and easily available in Roosevelt's New York City than they had been in Lincoln's frontier Indiana. His reading was wider and deeper than Lincoln's, and he continued to read books at a prodigious rate even while serving as president.

> The printed word was a never-ending resource for Roosevelt. It shaped him as a man and as a politician, and it informed his policies as president.

Roosevelt got the reading bug—or "disease," as he termed it—at an early age. Like John Adams and Lincoln before him, Roosevelt had a voracious appetite for books; his hunger for them was almost physical.[3] Even before he could read, he would drag David Livingstone's six-hundred-page *Missionary Travels and Researches in South Africa* to adults and ask them to "tell" the pictures to him.[4] As a somewhat sickly child, he developed an intense relationship with books—"Books are almost as individual as friends," he later wrote.[5]

Roosevelt became a reader for the ages. He devotes more than six pages of his autobiography to his childhood reading and travels, noting his predilection for works of adventure and natural history. Recounting his travels to Egypt, Germany, and elsewhere, he carefully notes the books he read during and in preparation for those trips. He would read up on the language, literature, and history of his destination, establishing a habit of reading as preparation, a habit he would maintain throughout his adulthood. He developed a precocious love of the adventure stories of Thomas Mayne Reid. "I was too young to understand much of Mayne Reid," he recalled in his autobiography, "except the adventure part and the natural history part—these enthralled me."[6]

Others noticed the boy's distinctive reading habits. His tutor Arthur Hamilton Cutler noted that "[t]he young man never seemed to know what idleness was," devoting his energy and industry to reading. As Cutler put it, "Every leisure moment would find the last novel, some English classic, or some abstruse book on Natural History in his hand."[7] The stories of his literary consumption are both legion and legendary. As a nineteen-year old, confined for five days with a case of measles, he managed to complete volumes of Horace and Homer as well as Plato's *Apology*.[8]

That pattern of insatiable reading continued for the rest of his days. In 1913, a year after his loss to Woodrow Wilson in the presidential election, Roosevelt set out on a dangerous expedition along Brazil's Rio da Duvida (River of Doubt). While the other expeditionists were trying to figure out how to survive, Roosevelt remained engrossed in a book. Even while suffering from a leg injury that nearly killed him, he still completed all of the many books he had brought along on the trip. The trip was treacherous, and several times the expedition had to discard badly-needed supplies along the way. Roosevelt became desperate to find additional books. He ended up reading his son Kermit's books of French and English verse, although he found them so disappointing that Kermit threatened to confiscate the books if his father would not stop complaining about them.[9] Faced with the horrifying prospect of no reading material, Roosevelt relented.

With all his erudition, Roosevelt at times had to struggle not to appear too full of himself. One flustered geology professor at Harvard had to tell the future president, "Now look here, Roosevelt, let me talk. I'm running this course."[10] But the erudition, as well as his family's wealth, provided him with advantages as well. His first book, *The Naval War of 1812*, which would help him secure a post as assistant secretary of the Navy in the McKinley administration, was published upon his graduation from Harvard. He wrote another six books in the following decade.[11]

Roosevelt's Career: Books as Job Training

Just as his naval history helped Roosevelt obtain his first federal appointment, his endless reading and prolific writing prepared him for each step of his political career. By writing books, he established a name for himself, a strategy that Woodrow Wilson, John F. Kennedy, and Barack Obama would also follow. Through his reading, Roosevelt developed positions and policies on a wide variety of subjects, preparing himself for a meteoric rise from police commissioner to assistant secretary of the Navy to governor of New York to vice president and then, after McKinley's assassination, to president (the youngest ever)—all within less than six years. Roosevelt himself may have emphasized the importance of his impressive experiences, but there is no gainsaying reading's outsized role in his development.[12]

> ——>>➤•●•◄<<——
>
> **Through his reading, Roosevelt developed positions and policies on a wide variety of subjects, preparing himself for a meteoric rise from police commissioner to assistant secretary of the Navy to governor of New York to vice president and then, after McKinley's assassination, to president (the youngest ever)—all within less than six years.**

Through his reading and writing, Roosevelt achieved credibility as an expert on many topics. In fact, the experts themselves were often astonished at his ability to master their own subject and so many others as well. His friend, the naturalist John Burroughs, marveled, "The one subject I do know, and ought to know, is the birds. It has been one of the main studies of a long life. [Roosevelt] knew the subject as well as I did, while he knew with the same thoroughness scores of other subjects of which I am entirely ignorant."[13] It may be more difficult to impress one's own siblings, but when Roosevelt accompanied his sister Corinne to a conference of the Poetry Society of America, she was amazed by how familiar he was with the poets he met there.[14]

Reading helped Roosevelt navigate New York City politics and burnish his credentials as a reformer. In his autobiography, he discusses his closeness with the famed photographer and social reformer Jacob Riis. Even before they met, Roosevelt writes, "I already knew Jake Riis, because his book *How the Other Half Lives*, had been to me both an enlightenment and an inspiration for which I felt I could never be too grateful." Roosevelt went to Riis's office "to tell him how deeply impressed I was by the book, and that I wished to help him in any practical way to try to make things a little better."[15]

Books, however, were not Roosevelt's only guide to the city's politics. He also seems to have had a keen sense of New York's ethnic potpourri. When the anti-Semitic German preacher Rector Ahlwardt visited New York and asked for police protection, Roosevelt made sure to give him an entirely Jewish security detail. As Roosevelt observed, "The proper thing to do was make him ridiculous." He would tell this story often throughout the rest of his career, especially to Jewish audiences.[16]

In his rise from the metropolitan to the national stage, one book in particular shaped Roosevelt's strategic views. In a single consequential weekend in May of 1890, Roosevelt devoured Alfred Thayer Mahan's *The Influence of Sea Power upon History, 1660–1783*.[17] In this first and most famous of his twenty books, Mahan argued that naval might was essential for great powers and that the United States and other nations could use the oceans as a highway for the projection of influence abroad. Mahan even claimed to have coined the term "sea power."[18]

Mahan's thinking would stay with Roosevelt throughout his political career. Even though Roosevelt had fancied himself an expert on American sea power, Mahan's book altered and then crystallized the young politician's thinking. As Edmund Morris puts it, "Roosevelt flipped the book shut a changed man."[19] Roosevelt, characteristically, immediately got in touch with Mahan, explaining, "During the last two days I have spent half my time, busy as I am, in reading your book; and that I found it interesting is shown by the fact that having taken it up, I have gone straight through it." Roosevelt proved himself an accurate prognosticator, adding, "It is a very good book—admirable, and I am greatly in error if it does not become a naval classic."[20] The friendship that Roosevelt thus established with Mahan continued through his presidency.[21] Some historians dispute the influence of that friendship on the rise of American sea power before the First World War. Mahan was the most important naval strategist of the time,[22] widely read among officials in the United States and amongst the other developing sea powers, but Roosevelt was just one actor in this drama. Furthermore, Roosevelt had his own strong views on sea power and the need for modernization of the fleet even before he read Mahan.[23]

In his autobiography, Roosevelt takes up the question "what books a statesman should read." His short answer seems simple: "poetry and novels—including short stories under the head of novels." But he quickly moves on, explaining, "I don't mean that he should read only novels and modern poetry," and adds, "If he cannot also enjoy the Hebrew prophets and the Greek dramatists, he should be sorry." Roosevelt's full answer turns out to be as wide-ranging as his own reading habits. "He ought to read interesting books on history and government, and books of science and philosophy; and really good books on these subjects," he adds, "are as enthralling as any fiction ever written in prose or verse."[24]

> Roosevelt could get lost in books in almost any environment. His lifelong friend Lawrence Abbott, editor of *The Outlook*, found that Roosevelt read whenever he had a spare moment, and even in some moments that others might not consider spare. Dull conversationalists might find the president picking up a book if they did not grab his attention.

Roosevelt could get lost in books in almost any environment. His lifelong friend Lawrence Abbott, editor of *The Outlook*, found that Roosevelt read whenever he had a spare moment and even in some moments that others might not consider spare. Dull conversationalists might find the president picking up a book if they did not grab his attention.[25] He occupied the time waiting for trains or appointments by reading and would not hesitate to open a book at parties and conferences alike. On a train one night after his tenure as president had been completed, Roosevelt went missing. He was found, Abbott recalled, in the lavatory straining to read W. E. H. Lecky's *History of Rationalism in Europe* by the only available light.[26]

So diverse was Roosevelt's reading that it defied characterization, and this was at least in part by design. "I have no sympathy whatever with writing lists of *the* One Hundred Best Books, or *the* Five-Foot Library," he sniffed. He was adamant that "there is no such thing as a hundred books that are best for all men, or for the majority of men, or for one man at all times; and there is no such thing as a five-foot library which will satisfy the needs of even one particular man on different occasions extending over a number of years."[27] Surveying the riches of the world's literature, Roosevelt exclaimed with characteristic enthusiasm: "Why, there are hundreds of books like these, each one of which, if really read, really assimilated, by the person to whom it happens to appeal, will enable that person quite unconsciously to furnish himself with much ammunition which he will find of use in the battle of life"—as perfect a summary of his literary philosophy as one can find.

Roosevelt recognized that "the statesman, and the publicist, and the reformer, and the agitator for new things, and the upholder of what is good in old things,"—that is, men like himself—need the wisdom that comes from good books. Above all, leaders need "to know human nature, to know the needs of the human soul." To accomplish this, he advised readers (and seemingly himself) that "they will find this nature and these needs set forth as nowhere else by the great imaginative writers, whether of prose or of poetry."[28]

Book-Reading Man of the People

Roosevelt's program of reading might be too ambitious for the average man. Still, there were many who admired it, including President William McKinley, who once confessed to Roosevelt, "You make me envious. You've been able to get so much out of books."[29] McKinley's own reading tended toward periodicals rather than books. He might read a dozen papers in a day—five or six from New York and Washington, along with his hometown *Canton Repository*.[30] In his youth McKinley had read a great deal, including David Hume's *History of England* and Edward Gibbon's *History of the Decline and Fall of the Roman Empire*, but he had a particular affinity for magazines, including Horace Greeley's *Weekly Tribune* and his favorite, the *Atlantic Monthly*.[31]

McKinley's childhood affinity for the *Atlantic Monthly* indicates the rising importance of a literary culture in America, as well as the advancing technological means to reach that culture. Founded in 1857, the *Atlantic Monthly* had a circulation of thirty thousand within two years.[32] In the 1890s, when McKinley was president, a host of other, more popular magazines emerged as well, taking advantage of increasing affluence, improved printing capabilities, and faster modes of transportation. These developments also allowed McKinley to maintain his newspaper addiction, an attachment so acute that, even after he was shot following a speech at the Pan-American Exposition in Buffalo in September 1901, he requested a newspaper in order to see how his speech was received.[33]

McKinley's "envy" of Roosevelt's reading, though a compliment, underscored the political danger to Roosevelt of seeming to be an intellectual elitist. Ever since Jackson, the ability to demonstrate the common touch had been essential for winning the presidency. In an increasingly democratic nation in which college attendance remained rare, book learning was not necessarily a political advantage. At the turn of the century, only 6.4 percent of seventeen-year-olds graduated from high school. Roosevelt was not only a college graduate but a Harvard man to boot.[34]

Roosevelt addressed this vulnerability in a number of ways. He worked hard to seem like not only a man of the people but also one of the people as well.[35] First, although he loved books, he never forgot that there were things in life more important than literature. Even in his heavily bibliophilic autobiography, after a lengthy discussion of books and reading, he acknowledges, "Books are all very well in their way, and we love them at Sagamore Hill [his home]; but children are better than books."[36]

Second, he cultivated his image as a tough outdoorsman. "There are men," he writes in his autobiography, "who love out-of-doors who yet never open a book; and other men who love books but to whom the great book of nature is a sealed volume, and the lines written therein blurred and illegible." But love of the outdoors and love of books, he insists, need not be incompatible: "[A]mong those men whom I have known the love of books and the love of outdoors, in their highest expressions, have usually gone hand in hand." For Roosevelt, the two traits were complementary, as "the keenest appreciation of what is seen in nature is to be found in those who have also profited by the hoarded and recorded wisdom of their fellow-men."[37]

Roosevelt's experiences as a naturalist, his boxing skills, his leadership of the Rough Riders in the Spanish-American War, and his travels in the American West in the 1880s all burnished his credentials as an outdoorsman.[38] The Western experience, in particular, compensated for his elite Eastern background. In one of the most famous stories in his autobiography, he tells of a bully who comes into a bar out West—in what was then the Dakota Territory, now situated in Wibaux, Montana[39]—and starts calling Roosevelt "four-eyes." At first Roosevelt ignores the man, but when the bully becomes too confrontational, Roosevelt flattens him with a powerful boxing combination: "As I rose, I struck quick and hard with my right just to one side of the point of his jaw, hitting with my left as I straightened out, and then again with my right." Roosevelt's reputation as a tough guy cemented, the bully slunk out of town.[40] Roosevelt also counted among his friends the two American artists most responsible for creating the popular image of the Old West—his Harvard classmate Owen Wister (grandson of the actress Fanny Kemble), who dedicated his novel *The Virginian* to Roosevelt, and the sculptor and painter Frederic Remington.

> —>>>•●•<<<—
>
> **President William McKinley once confessed to Roosevelt, "You make me envious. You've been able to get so much out of books." McKinley's own reading tended to periodicals rather than books. He might read a dozen papers in a day—five or six from New York and Washington, along with his hometown *Canton Repository*.**

Acutely aware that he read more than others and that this characteristic was not always to be advertised,[41] Roosevelt nevertheless became adept at referring to books that his audiences would appreciate. A reader who did not disdain the cultural choices of those around him, he learned to tailor intellectual points in ways acceptable to any audience. In 1903, for example, he received a delegation from the Jewish service organization B'nai B'rith to discuss the Kishinev pogrom, in which approximately fifty (numbers vary) Jews were murdered in Russia. His response to the group included an expression of sympathy, an acknowledgement that, given America's large Jewish population, a reaction to the atrocity was necessary, and a recitation of some lines from Longfellow's poem "The Jewish Cemetery at Newport." He also recalled Jewish participation in both the Revolution and the Civil War and noted that one of the colonels who fought with him at San Juan Hill was Jewish—"One of the best colonels among the regular regiments who did so well on that day, who fought beside me, was a Jew!" He also informed the group that, as regimental commander, he had promoted five men, one of whom was Jewish.[42]

In general, Roosevelt kept abreast of popular trends, a task in some ways more difficult now. The social scientist Charles Murray recalls Roosevelt's statement that he had no intention of becoming an international "Meddlesome Matty," a universally recognized reference to the eponymous busybody of Ann Taylor's poem, which most Americans knew from McGuffey's *Fourth Reader*. The common culture that made such a reference possible—Americans of every class knew McGuffey's Readers—is vanishing, Murray laments, the victim of the highly individualized cultural consumption that technology has introduced into modern society.[43]

Leisure Activities in the White House Years

While president, Roosevelt maintained his impressive pace of reading in part by seizing every available minute, but he also carved out time to read. He spent the first part of his evenings reading with his wife. After she went to bed at about ten o'clock, he would soldier on, reading with a single good eye at a rate of two to three pages per minute. If busy, he would get through a book a day; when his evenings were free, that number increased to two or even three.[44]

When he was not reading, Roosevelt enjoyed the theater, especially if he could show up unannounced. Occasionally, however, he would plan ahead, as he did in 1908 when he attended Israel Zangwill's *The Melting Pot*. Roosevelt had met Zangwill, a British-born writer of Russian-Jewish extraction, for the first time in 1898, when he was governor-elect of New York. Their conversation made enough of an impression on Roosevelt that he referred to it three years later in a letter to George Briggs Aiton, the editor at the National Encyclopedia Company. Roosevelt explained that he had told Zangwill "it would be a particularly good thing for men of the Jewish race to develop that side of them which I might call the Maccabee or fighting Jewish type." This advice seems to have involved at least some measure of projection onto the Jewish community of his own personal transformation from asthmatic bookworm to rugged outdoorsman. Roosevelt explained this in a way that, while politically incorrect, was not wholly inaccurate. "[N]othing could do more to put a stop to the unreasoning prejudice against them," he wrote, "than to have it understood that not only were they successful and thrifty businessmen and high-minded philanthropists, but also to do their part in the rough, manly work which is no less necessary." That "rough, manly work," in Roosevelt's view, denoted an effective prescription for ethnicities as well as for individuals.[45]

> When *The Melting Pot* ended and playwright Israel Zangwill stepped on stage, Roosevelt shouted out, "It's a great play, Mr. Zangwill; it's a great play!"—an endorsement that Zangwill used to promote the play for years to come.

Roosevelt and Zangwill met again in 1904, when the playwright visited the White House for a discussion about the assimilation of ethnic groups in America. In 1923, after Roosevelt had died, Zangwill revealed that he and Roosevelt had talked in that meeting about "the relation of American Jews to a Jewish autonomous colony." Roosevelt declined to take a position but referred Zangwill to Secretary of State John

Hay, who believed "that it was open to all American Jews, without the faintest imputation on their patriotism, to take part in the foundation of such a colony."[46]

Zangwill, who had married a non-Jewish woman, paid careful attention to Roosevelt's views concerning assimilation. In 1905 he experienced a revelation, seeing "in one vivid flash" the whole of a play about assimilation in America. Originally to be called *The Crucible*, the play examined the question of assimilation and made the case for intermarriage as the solution to ethnic tensions and long-standing hatreds.[47] Zangwill eventually changed the title to *The Melting Pot* (leaving *The Crucible* for a later Jewish playwright, Arthur Miller, to use) and dedicated the work to Roosevelt. In a letter to the president, he wrote that the play "dramatises [sic] your own idea of America as a crucible in which the races are fusing into the future America."[48]

In August 1908, Zangwill invited the president to its opening in Washington. Roosevelt readily accepted. His retinue included Mrs. Roosevelt; Elihu Root, the secretary of state; and Oscar Straus, the secretary of commerce and labor (still one department) and the first Jewish cabinet secretary.[49] Zangwill's wife was a guest in the presidential box, and Roosevelt kept up a running commentary with her about the play. Simon Wolf, another guest, reported that Roosevelt was "most enthusiastic over the lines which advocated the absorption of all classes." When the play ended and Zangwill stepped on stage, Roosevelt shouted out, "It's a great play, Mr. Zangwill; it's a great play!"—an endorsement that Zangwill used to promote the play

> —>>>•●•<<<—
>
> **The communications revolution reverberated in the White House almost immediately. Rutherford B. Hayes was the first president to install a telephone, which Bell himself provided. In 1896, William Jennings Bryan sent William McKinley the first telegraphed concession in a presidential race. We have sound recordings of every president since Benjamin Harrison. (Edison's earlier recording of Hayes's voice was lost, unfortunately.) McKinley was the first president captured by motion picture, and Wilson was the first to watch a movie in the White House.**

for years to come. Two days later, the Zangwills joined Roosevelt for lunch in the White House to discuss and critique the play.[50] In 1914, with Roosevelt's permission, Zangwill dedicated a revised edition of *The Melting Pot* to the former president, who had done so much to make the play a success.[51]

Roosevelt's relations with writers were not always so cordial. After reading Upton Sinclair's best-selling novel *The Jungle**—a gruesome account of unsanitary and inhumane practices in the meatpacking industry in Chicago—he ordered an investigation, which soon led to passage of the Meat Inspection Act and the Pure Food and Drug Act of 1906. As was his custom when particularly impressed by a book, Roosevelt opened a personal correspondence with the author, but this time the result could hardly have been called a mutual admiration society. In fact, Sinclair seems to have powerfully annoyed the president. Unintimidated by Roosevelt's position, he took the presidential overture as an opportunity to agitate for more vigorous action by the government. While Roosevelt was composing a reply to Sinclair, another missive from the author arrived. "Your second telegram has just come," Roosevelt noted dryly, then added, "[R]eally, Mr. Sinclair, you must keep your head." In a letter to the progressive journalist William Allen White, Roosevelt revealed his "utter contempt for [Sinclair]. He is hysterical, unbalanced, and untruthful. Three-fourths of the things he said were absolute falsehoods. For some of the remainder there was only a basis of truth."[52] Sinclair, for his part, was unimpressed by the president, sarcastically calling him "his majesty" in a letter to the novelist Jack London and complaining that Roosevelt had sent him a "three-page discourse upon the futility of Socialism."[53]

Roosevelt was skeptical not only of Sinclair but of the entire cohort of reformist journalists. He rebuked them in April of 1906 in a famous speech comparing them

---

* The scene of Roosevelt reading *The Jungle* over breakfast was immortalized in Finley Peter Dunne's popular "Mr. Dooley" newspaper column: "Tiddy was toying with a light breakfast an' idly turnin' over th' pages iv th' new book with both hands. Suddenly he rose fr'm th' table, an' cryin': 'I'm pizened,' began throwin' sausages out iv th' window … Since thin th' Prisident, like th' rest iv us, has become a viggytaryan."

to the "Man with the Muck-rake" from *Pilgrim's Progress*. This man, Roosevelt reminded his audience, "could look no way but downward," and even when "offered a celestial crown for his muck-rake," he "would neither look up nor regard the crown he was offered, but continued to rake to himself the filth of the floor." These scandal-mongers, Roosevelt meant to suggest, proved too short-sighted to see beyond their own delight in upsetting apple carts. The muckrakers themselves, however, soon embraced the term that had been intended as an insult.[54]

Despite his disdain for the muckrakers, Roosevelt recognized that reform was not only a worthy pursuit but also a useful political tool.[55] His reading was so wide and deep, moreover, that he instinctively drew on it for his political agenda. When a work of literature came along as powerful as *The Jungle*—the most influential novel in American history after *Uncle Tom's Cabin*—Roosevelt recognized its importance and made use of it.

The Last Reading President

Roosevelt may have read more than any other president, but the years he was in the White House were in many ways the gateway to the post-reading era. Baseball cards, the Montgomery Ward catalog, the phonograph—these modern diversions appeared in the first decade of the twentieth century, a trickle of distractions which, as technology advanced, grew into the torrent that swept reading from the leisure hours of most people.[56]

Alexander Graham Bell had his famous first telephone conversation in 1876. Thomas Edison invented the phonograph in 1878 and the "kinetoscope" in 1888. Guglielmo Marconi sent and received radio waves in 1895. The number of patents issued each year grew from twelve thousand in 1871 to seventy-two thousand in 1896.[57] The communications revolution reverberated in the White House almost immediately. Rutherford B. Hayes was the first president to install a telephone, which Bell himself provided. In 1896, William Jennings Bryan sent William McKinley the first telegraphed concession in a presidential race.[58] We have sound recordings of every president since Benjamin Harrison. (Edison's earlier recording of Hayes's voice was lost, unfortunately.)[59] McKinley was the first president captured by motion picture, and Wilson was the first to watch a movie in the White House.

These milestones provide interesting pieces of presidential trivia, but the real story is how the presidents used these new technologies. The first presidency to be documented by the new motion picture technology was Roosevelt's. The Library of Congress has a collection of 104 films capturing Roosevelt in action—and in motion—from 1898 until his death in 1919, making him the most filmed person in history to that time.[60] In his unsuccessful 1912 campaign to become president again, Roosevelt transmitted his voice to American households, not through the nascent technology of radio but via phonograph.[61]

While Roosevelt was exploiting these new media, another emerging medium was exploiting him—advertising. With his larger-than-life persona, Roosevelt became a popular figure for advertisers. Most famously, his image and even his name were used in the creation of the teddy bear. His comment during a visit to Nashville's Maxwell House hotel in 1907 that his cup of coffee was "good to the last drop"

> —→>>→•●•◄◄◄—
>
> **Like Adams and Lincoln before him, Roosevelt had a voracious appetite for books; his hunger for them was almost physical. Even before he could read, he would drag David Livingstone's six-hundred-page *Missionary Travels and Researches in South Africa* to adults and ask them to "tell" the pictures to him.**

became one of the most familiar slogans in advertising history. And as Peter Collier writes, manufacturers of everything from baby powder to cigars freely appropriated the president's image to hawk their wares.[62]

The power of advertising grew as the twentieth century advanced until it became, in Daniel Boorstin's words, "the omnipresent, most characteristic, and most remunerative form of American literature." By the middle of the century, Boorstin noted, "the force of the advertising word and image would dwarf the power of other literature."[63] This would have profound effects on the presidency and on the American people. The comedian Jon Stewart jokes that the average person's exposure to ads increased from "one or two ads a day in 1900 to 5,000 a day in 2010. It wasn't easy for the human brain to process this information, but we found space for it in the cranial regions formerly occupied by our capacity for introspection, wonder, and, of course, joy."[64]

Theodore Roosevelt had the wit and the charisma to take advantage of communications technology even in its infancy. What a man with his gifts might have done at that time with today's technology might be a wonder to behold. But his presidency trailed the end of an era. Mass communications would transform the American presidency in ways that Roosevelt, for all his book learning, could never have imagined.

CHAPTER 5

REFLECTED GLORY

For all his reading, Theodore Roosevelt was an amateur intellectual. Woodrow Wilson, who frustrated his attempted third-party comeback in 1912, was the first and only Ph.D. president thus far. (George McGovern was the only other major-party nominee with a doctorate.) Wilson's ascendancy signaled the "credentialization" of the professions and of intellectual life in America.[1] From now on, professors would have doctorates, physicians would go to medical school, and lawyers would go law school. The presidency, too, became credentialized. Harry Truman was the last president without a bachelor's degree, George H. W. Bush was the last president without a graduate degree, and Ronald Reagan was the last president without a degree from Harvard or from Yale.

Wilson was well-read in political science and in government, his academic field, and wrote an influential book, *Constitutional Government of the United States*, published in 1908. When Lyman Abbott sent Roosevelt an excerpt from Wilson's opus, the president acknowledged that he had not read the book, but he praised the excerpt nonetheless, telling Abbott, "This is a really first-class paragraph."[2]

Wilson's mind found solace and contemplation in academic work, and he had a strong affinity for books. When he served as president of Princeton University, a visitor asked him if he read all of the many books in his office. Wilson's response: "Not every day."[3] As for diversions beyond the ivory towers, Wilson spent relatively little time reading the news or other periodicals. During his presidency, his outside reading leaned heavily to detective novels.

It is possible that Wilson suffered from dyslexia; he did not learn to read until he was ten.[4] But by the time he was an undergraduate at Princeton, his classmate Robert McCarter remembered, he "read a great deal—good books."[5] Wilson wrote in his diary that he skipped class so that he could continue reading Thomas Babington Macaulay's *History of England*, which, he noted, had "all the fascination for me of a novel."[6] He originally intended to study law, but he insisted to his friend Robert Bridges, "I've read all sorts of books besides law books."[7]

> —➤➤•●•◄◄—
>
> **Wilson wrote in his diary that he skipped class so that he could continue reading Thomas Babington Macaulay's *History of England,* which, he noted, had "all the fascination for me of a novel."**

"It is stupid to read any book when you know that you are obliged to read it," Wilson wrote in irritation as an undergraduate.[8] He read *what* he wanted *when* he wanted, allowing no outside force to dictate his reading habits. The news held little interest for him, unlike James Garfield before him and Lyndon Johnson afterward. Wilson "seldom reads the newspapers and gains his knowledge of public affairs largely from the matter brought to his attention, and his general information is gotten from a cursory glance at the Weekly Press," observed his advisor and friend "Colonel" Edward House.[9] A review of Wilson's correspondence during his twenties and thirties, in fact, shows little interest or expertise in the key domestic issues of the day.[10]

As president, Wilson gave little time to serious works. He was known to peruse well-known progressive works such as the English Fabian Graham Wallas's *Human Nature in Politics* and Walter Lippmann's *Preface to Politics*. Like Bill Clinton after him, Wilson loved to escape into a detective novel.[11] After his wife Ellen died in 1914, he plunged into detective stories, lamenting that "books"—by which he presumably meant serious works—"have grown meaningless to me." Instead, he "read detective stories to forget, as a man would get drunk!"[12]

When he was debilitated by a stroke in the fall of 1919, Wilson continued to indulge in mysteries. On a visit to the president's sickbed, his collaborator and subsequent biographer Ray Stannard Baker found him surrounded by a detective book and an old Bible.[13] When it came to mystery book selection, Wilson was quite wide-ranging. In a letter, he wrote "I'm an indiscriminate reader of detective stories and would be at a loss to pick out my favorites. On the whole I have got the most authentic thrill out of Anna Katharine Green's books and Gaboriau's." Green, a ground-breaking detective novelist and one of the first female masters of the genre, showed a willingness by Wilson to break convention in selecting a female detective novelist, providing, of course, that she was a good one. The Frenchman Émile Gaboriau was one of the earliest detective writers, predating even Arthur Conan Doyle.[14]

In 1944, the literary critic Edmund Wilson (no relation) asked in the *New Yorker* "Why Do People Read Detective Stories?" He held the genre in low regard but was "always being reminded that the most serious public figures of our time, from Woodrow Wilson to W. B. Yeats, have been addicts of this form of fiction." Searching for an explanation, he mused that the appeal of the detective story stems from its contrast with the real world, where it proves rarely "conclusively possible to pin down the responsibility." At the end of a detective story, "the murderer is spotted, and—relief!—he is not, after all, a person like you or me." Instead, "He is a villain—known to the trade as George Gruesome—and he has been caught by an infallible Power, the supercilious and omniscient detective, who knows exactly how to fix the guilt."[15] If Edmund Wilson is right, Woodrow Wilson's fondness for the detective novel is the sign of a human need to find a direct causal order to the world—one that presidents rarely see as they grapple with uncertainty in events and personalities.

Whether or not President Wilson was searching for moral clarity in his detective stories, he enjoyed other forms of popular entertainment. He had developed an interest in the theater while a graduate student at Johns Hopkins University, and as president he often took in light musical comedies of the vaudevillian variety.[16] He attended 225 plays while in office, a presidential record.[17] In a later era, Jimmy Carter would watch more movies, but leaving the White House to see live theater, as Wilson often did, required more effort.

Wilson saw two shows the week after his inauguration, including *Mind-the-Paint Girl*, a Cinderella story about a chorus girl falling in love with a viscount. He liked to attend the theater with little fanfare, making a quiet entrance through a side door, and—despite what had happened to Lincoln at Ford's Theater—protected by only a single Secret Service agent.[18] His favorite theater was Keith's, which specialized in vaudeville, and he had his own box there. "I like the theater," Wilson explained, " … especially a good vaudeville show when I am seeking perfect relaxation; for a vaudeville show is different from a play.... [I]f there is a bad act at a vaudeville show you can rest reasonably secure that the next one may not be so bad; but from a bad play there is no escape."[19] At around the same time, a youthful Harry Truman was becoming a vaudeville fan as well.[20]

The president's theater-going continued into his second term, even as America entered the First World War. In contrast to some subsequent presidents, Wilson received praise rather than criticism for his engagement in leisure activities during wartime, under the rationale that it helped maintain employment levels for theater workers. On April 8, 1917, the *Washington Post* even editorialized that Wilson's theatrical attendance "has added dignity to the theatrical profession and has been more keenly appreciated than is generally realized."[21]

In May 1915, Wilson traveled to Baltimore for a Will Rogers show. The cowboy humorist watched the president carefully from the stage and later recalled, "How he did laugh!" Rogers took some friendly shots at Wilson, who proved a good sport. Rogers considered that performance "the proudest and most successful night I ever had on stage." Wilson came backstage after the show and told Rogers, "I want to thank you for all the fun I have had to-night. I am in need of fellows like you." Wilson was so taken with Rogers that he folded many of the performer's lines into his own conversations and speeches.[22]

Later that year, Wilson sat at a breakfast with his advisors when the entertainer Al Jolson came into the room. He announced, "I'm Al Jolson, and I want to see the president." Wilson responded, "I am the president," and added that he had not yet seen Jolson perform. Taking this as his cue, Jolson said, "Wait a minute—you ain't heard nothin' yet," and belted out "You Made Me Love You" for the entire room.[23] Jolson's impromptu performance revealed an astonishing level of comfort for a Jewish entertainer in the presence of a head of state. Given the anti-Semitism of time, it is impossible to imagine such an encounter in any other country. Even in America, it had only been fifty years since General Grant's infamous orders expelling the Jews from his military district during the Civil War, and less than a decade since the first Jewish Cabinet appointee and White House lunch invitation under Roosevelt. Jewish Americans were making great strides in the United States, and presidential validation of Jewish artists was an important gesture of acceptance.

> On a visit to the president's sickbed, Wilson's collaborator and subsequent biographer Ray Stannard Baker found him surrounded by a detective book and an old Bible.
>
>

The presidency became more approachable but less dignified as the communications technology progressed. Motion pictures spread the image of the president far and wide, and radio brought his voice into American homes. Wilson played a role in the development of both of these technologies.

A young Dwight Eisenhower was already taking dates to the movies—now-forgotten silent films like *The Bawlerout* (1913)[24]—when Woodrow Wilson launched the tradition of screening films in the White House with D. W. Griffith's *Birth of a Nation* in 1915. The story behind this historic film goes back to *Uncle Tom's Cabin*. After a theatrical performance of Stowe's anti-slavery tale, the writer Thomas Dixon, a Virginian, felt inspired to create a counter-narrative. The result was *The Leopard's Spots* (1902), *The Clansman* (1903), and *The Traitor* (1909), known as the Klan Trilogy. Dixon explored the same racial themes as Stowe but from a very different perspective, focusing on the injustices that the North and the newly freed African Americans supposedly inflicted on Southern whites after the Civil War.[25]

Griffith based his film on the second volume of the trilogy, *The Clansman*, retitling it *Birth of a Nation*. An enormous success, the production earned ten million dollars in its first year and fifty million by 1949, enormous sums at the time.[26] Dixon, who knew Wilson from Johns Hopkins, invited his old friend to see the film. The president told Dixon that he could not go out to a public entertainment as he was still in mourning for his late wife, Ellen, but that he would be willing to watch the film at the White House. It was reported years later that an astonished Wilson had exclaimed that the film was "like writing history with lightning."[27]

> —>→>·●·<←<—
>
> **He had developed an interest in the theater while a graduate student at Johns Hopkins University, and as president he often took in light musical comedies of the vaudevillian variety. He attended 225 plays while in office, a presidential record.**

It is almost certain that Wilson did not actually utter that line. It has nonetheless taken on a life of its own, becoming perhaps the most famous movie review in history. It is likely that Dixon, who hoped for a presidential endorsement of *Birth of a Nation*, made up the statement, and Griffith used it freely to promote the film. There is some evidence, however, that Wilson liked the film, at least initially. He called it "a splendid production" in a March 1915 letter to Griffith, and only after controversy erupted, with protests in Boston in April, did the president's aides try to distance him from the film. Wilson later declared that he had "at no time expressed his approbation," and in 1918 he called the film "a very unfortunate production."[28]

The *Birth of a Nation* incident pointed to something new in the American presidency—the president's role as chief pitchman, intentional or not, in an increasingly commercial culture. For centuries, of course, artists have sought the patronage and approval of their rulers. And America's tradesmen, as we saw, were eager to associate their wares with Theodore Roosevelt, with or without his knowledge. Israel Zangwill certainly leveraged Roosevelt's endorsement of *The Melting Pot*. But the use of the president to promote a movie distributed throughout the country was a different matter. Zangwill hoped to fill a theater in Washington, while Dixon and Griffith hoped to pack cinemas from coast to coast. They were on to something. Hollywood's appreciation of the value of the First Movie-Goer was never more apparent than at the 2013 Academy Awards—a century after Wilson's unwitting entanglement with Griffith's controversial film—where First Lady Michelle Obama, basking in the adulation of Hollywood's liberal elite, opened the envelope for the Best Picture award.[29]

Endorsement: A Two-Way Street

Just as entertainers now grasped a new way of benefiting from presidential endorsements, new broadcast and motion picture technologies enabled politicians to benefit from having artists endorse them. As far back as the 1820s, Andrew Jackson had sought the endorsement of popular writers and artists.[30] And Franklin Pierce got a campaign biography out of his old Bowdoin classmate Nathaniel Hawthorne.[31] But the most interesting relationship between a president and a celebrity might have been that between the unlikely pair of friends Ulysses S. Grant and Mark Twain.

Grant, not much of a reader,[32] first met Twain at the White House in 1869, before he had become America's most famous author. Twain stood dumbstruck before the short but imposing president, at last stammering, "I—I am embarrassed. Are you?" Grant said nothing, heightening the moment's awkwardness. When they met again ten years later, after the publication of *The Adventures of Tom Sawyer*, Twain, now famous himself, wondered if Grant recalled their earlier encounter. Grant dispelled any doubt when he said to Twain, "I am not embarrassed. Are you?"[33]

Despite this unpromising start, the two men became fast friends, and Twain would frequently visit the former president in his New York home.[34] Grant had run into serious financial problems late in life and was now suffering from throat cancer. Desperate to leave money behind for his family, Grant began work on a memoir with the assistance of Twain, a successful entrepreneur who would publish the work. The project proved difficult. Grant suffered from terrible pain, and no former president had ever published a memoir. With the *New York Times* maintaining a continuous death watch, Grant worked desperately as his condition deteriorated. With Twain's help and the use of William Tecumseh Sherman's memoirs (published a decade earlier) as a model, he managed to finish the job four days before his death on July 23, 1885.[35]

> It was reported years later that an astonished Wilson had exclaimed that *Birth of a Nation* was "like writing history with lightning." It is almost certain that Wilson did not actually utter that line. It has nonetheless taken on a life of its own, becoming perhaps the most famous movie review in history.

The *Personal Memoirs of U. S. Grant* became a huge success, selling over 300,000 copies. The work satisfied his concerns about leaving wealth behind for his family, as his widow, Julia, earned an estimated $500,000 from the book. But beyond the financial success, the book became enormously influential. Its bold, clean opening—"My family is American, and has been for generations, in all its branches, direct and collateral"—is echoed in Saul Bellow's classic novel, *Augie March*, which begins, "I am an American, Chicago-born."[36] Dwight Eisenhower deliberately modeled his own memoirs, written between World War II and his presidency, on Grant's work. Ike particularly liked Grant's "lack of pretension."[37]

Benjamin Harrison was the next president to turn to a literary celebrity for assistance. His old friend Lew Wallace served as a Union general in the Civil War, a member of the military tribunal that tried the conspirators in the Lincoln assassination, and the territorial governor of New Mexico. But he is chiefly remembered as the author of the epic *Ben-Hur*, published in 1880, which surpassed *Uncle Tom's Cabin* as the best-selling American novel, a distinction it held until the appearance of *Gone with the Wind* in 1936. Harrison asked his friend to write a campaign biography for the 1888 election, but Wallace was initially reluctant to take on the task, given its one-month deadline. He did the job, however, and the book, coupled with his friendship with Harrison, led to rumors of Wallace being considered for a cabinet post. The rumors were false, but the biography became the occasion for the press to revive painful accusations that blunders by General Wallace had been responsible for the enormous carnage at the Civil War battle of Shiloh. The historian Victor Davis Hanson observes that this experience of undeserved infamy may have supplied Wallace with his theme for *Ben-Hur*.[38]

The new communications technologies of the twentieth century allowed celebrities to endorse candidates in less onerous ways than composing lengthy campaign biographies. In 1920, Al Jolson wrote and performed a song touting the GOP candidate, Warren G. Harding. "Harding, You're The Man for Us" contained some creaky rhymes—"We think the country's ready, for another man like Teddy" and "We need another Lincoln, to do the country's thinkin'." But Harding could claim the support of the "World's Greatest Entertainer," the sort of endorsement few Republicans have ever obtained. Jolson returned in 1924, along with Will Rogers, to back Calvin Coolidge with a similarly unimpressive song, "Keep Cool and Keep Coolidge."[39]

Broadcasting and other new forms of entertainment allowed presidents to branch out in their search for celebrity endorsers. In fact, the most famous man in America for much of the 1920s and 1930s was neither an actor nor a writer—although he did act and wrote a syndicated column. He was, in fact, a baseball player, George Herman "Babe" Ruth. The legendary slugger met or corresponded with every president from Wilson to Truman and even had his picture taken with the captain of the 1948 Yale baseball team, the young George H. W. Bush.[40] As a number of presidents would learn, interactions with the Babe were prized but also somewhat unpredictable. When the Harding campaign approached Ruth about an endorsement, he first responded, "Hell no, I'm a Democrat." When he subsequently found out there was money involved, he became slightly more receptive, but the endorsement never came off due to scheduling conflicts.[41] Nevertheless, Harding invited Ruth to the White House on a number of occasions and even entertained him in the presidential box on opening day of 1922, when Ruth was unable to play as a result of a suspension.[42]

Calvin Coolidge had a famous but deflating meeting with Ruth on a hot day in 1924. Babe greeted the president by exclaiming, "Hot as hell, ain't it, Prez?"[43] Although he likely meant little by it, Ruth's crack was indicative of the decline in respect accorded to the presidency. The more presidents wanted to be viewed as regular folks, the more they would be treated as such, elevating entertainers and celebrities at the presidents' expense. It is little wonder that a *New York Times* editorial in April of 1925 would argue that "it involves no disrespect to Calvin Coolidge or to Charles W. Eliot [the former president of Harvard] to suggest ... that the Home Run King is the first citizen of the land."[44]

—➤➤➤·●·◀◀◀—

In fact, the most famous man in America for much of the 1920s and 1930s was neither an actor nor a writer—although he did act and wrote a syndicated column. He was, in fact, a baseball player, George Herman "Babe" Ruth. The legendary slugger met or corresponded with every president from Wilson to Truman and even had his picture taken with the captain of the 1948 Yale baseball team, the young George H. W. Bush.

Coolidge's successor suffered even greater indignities at the hands of the great Bambino. In 1928, a rumor went around that Ruth chose to back Herbert Hoover over New York governor Al Smith. When the Hoover team asked to get a picture with Ruth, who in fact backed Smith, he refused. Reporters found out, and the stories of "Ruth refuses to pose with Hoover" threatened to cause trouble for Babe with some of his business interests, notably the Republican papers that ran his syndicated column. Ruth relented and posed with Hoover. But he also posed—along with eight other New York Yankees and their batboy—with the team's home-state governor.[45] Hoover won anyway, securing the privilege of presiding over the Great Depression.

Ruth, in his irreverent way, contributed to the long-standing perception of Hoover as an ineffectual leader. In the fall of 1929, after things had turned sour but before the long-term effects of the Depression had fully set in, Ruth was asked about the disparity of income between himself—who earned $80,000, a staggering amount at the time—and the president, who earned only $75,000. Ruth's famous reply: "Why not? I had a better year than he did." Even though 1929 proved an off year for Ruth—forty-six home runs, and the Yankees failed to make the World Series—Ruth's comment haunted Hoover as the Depression continued and the president's popularity evaporated.[46]

Babe Ruth taught presidents about the dangers of dealing with celebrities, who were a growing force in American culture. The Founders sought wisdom from the cultural leaders of their time, theater-going presidents sought to connect to the common man, and Roosevelt and Lincoln pursued self-improvement. As celebrities became more important, presidents increasingly sought the political advantages of the reflected glory of American superstars of the theater, of the book, or of the baseball diamond. These initial forays into celebrity culture were tentative, as presidents sought to maintain the dignity of their office. As the twentieth century progressed, the outreach to celebrities increased, but the effort to maintain presidential dignity at the same time became increasingly difficult.

CHAPTER 6

FDR: PRESIDENT AS CULTURAL OUTPUT

Radio emerged as a major source of both entertainment and information during the presidency of Franklin Delano Roosevelt, and he made the most of it. He was not the first president to transmit his voice over the radio, but he was the first to make the medium his own. Mass communications continued to transform American popular culture, and the president was going to be an important shaper of that mass culture. Roosevelt proved the original master of this new pop culture, and none of his successors has excelled him.

Woodrow Wilson was the last president to serve before radio became a regular feature of American life. Canada's Reginald Fessenden transmitted his violin rendition of "O Holy Night" on Christmas Eve 1906, the first entertainment broadcast in history. The first commercial broadcast took place in 1920, Wilson's last full year in office, and the first broadcast of a baseball game—the Phillies versus the Pirates— took place on August 5, 1921.[1] Wilson himself did not deliver a radio address until November of 1923. It reached three million people and is the oldest recorded radio address in the National Archives.[2]

Wilson's successor, Warren G. Harding, was the first sitting president to be heard over the radio. His speech at the dedication of a Francis Scott Key memorial reached 125,000 people, twelve times the number of people to whom Andrew Jackson had spoken at his inauguration. Harding's speech had not been composed with the radio in mind, however.[3] The medium was still in its infancy, its powers and economic possibilities—especially for advertising—not yet appreciated. In 1920, the radio pioneer David Sarnoff tried to assemble investors in the wireless "music box;" he failed because no one saw any commercial prospects in his device.[4]

Three months after assuming the presidency upon Harding's death in August 1923, Calvin Coolidge addressed a joint session of Congress. A front-page story in the *New York Times* noted the historic nature of the radio broadcast of the speech. Coolidge's voice, the paper reported, will "be carried over a greater portion of the United States and will be heard by more people than the voice of any man in history."[5] Radio's conquest of politics continued the next year with the broadcast of both major-party conventions.[6] Then, in March of 1925, the nation listened to a ground-breaking live broadcast of Coolidge's inauguration by the pioneering Graham McNamee, who ad-libbed for two hours and frequently dropped his own name.[7] The radio industry started to discover its audience and its political power.

The man known as "Silent Cal" turned out to be adept at speaking to the people over the airwaves. "It is not far-fetched in the least to say that radio re-elected Calvin Coolidge," reported *Literary Digest*. He recognized in radio a friendly medium: "I am very fortunate that I came in with the radio.... I have a good radio voice, and now I can get my messages across ... without acquainting [listeners] with my lack of oratorical ability or without making any rhetorical display in their presence."[8] We may think of him as a stuffy emblem of pre-modern politics, but it was Coolidge, presiding over the Jazz Age, who began the tradition of regular presidential addresses to the American people, preparing the way for Roosevelt and his famous "fireside chats."[9]

Roosevelt: A Career Made by Radio

As the American economy sank into the Great Depression, Herbert Hoover tried and failed to use radio in order to instill confidence. His relations with the press were terrible, giving Franklin Roosevelt a golden opportunity to start over with the American people.[10]

Roosevelt was well-equipped to take advantage of the opportunities that radio offered. He was a great radio speaker. He has been said, in fact, to have had the best radio voice in American politics of his era, better even than that of his 1944 opponent, Thomas Dewey, a trained opera singer.[11] Dewey's good voice did not necessarily lead to good manners. Since 1896, when William Jennings Bryan telegraphed his concession to William McKinley, it had been the tradition for the loser of a presidential election to offer his concession directly to the victor. Dewey instead gave a speech over the radio, saying that he would "wholeheartedly accept the will of the people." An irritated FDR sent Dewey a cutting telegram: "I thank you for your statement, which I have heard over the air a few minutes ago." Privately, FDR thought even less of Dewey's *faux pas*, telling his aides, "I still think he's a son of a bitch."[12] Roosevelt not only had strong views about how he used the radio but also evidently felt strongly about how others used it, too.

Unlike his predecessors, Roosevelt was already practiced in the new medium before becoming president. In his home state of New York, most of the major newspapers were Republican-leaning, and FDR realized that he could use radio to go directly to the people. As governor, he had begun an early version of the fireside chat as early as 1929.[13]

> ─→>>·●·<<←─
>
> **Warren G. Harding was the first sitting president to be heard over the radio. His speech at the dedication of a Francis Scott Key memorial reached 125,000 people, twelve times the number of people to whom Andrew Jackson had spoken at his inauguration.**

Radio had made Roosevelt a national figure. His nationally broadcast speeches at the Democratic conventions had introduced him to the American public in the same way that Barack Obama's televised speech to the 2004 Democratic convention launched him toward the White House. Roosevelt understood that radio required a special rhetorical approach. At the 1924 convention, he put New York Governor Al Smith's name in nomination with a speech that bestowed on Smith a famous sobriquet from Wordsworth, the "Happy Warrior." The line was inserted by the New York

The man known as "Silent Cal" turned out to be adept at speaking to the people over the airwaves. "It is not far-fetched in the least to say that radio re-elected Calvin Coolidge," reported *Literary Digest*. He recognized in radio a friendly medium: "I am very fortunate that I came in with the radio.... I have a good radio voice, and now I can get my messages across ... without acquainting [listeners] with my lack of oratorical ability or without making any rhetorical display in their presence."

lawyer Joseph Proskauer, Smith's campaign manager, over Roosevelt's strenuous objections. "You can't give poetry to a political convention," he complained. Roosevelt and Proskauer fought over the draft for hours before Roosevelt eventually relented. Later, after the speech garnered success, Roosevelt claimed it was his draft, and that he "stuck in" a recommended line of poetry from Proskauer.[14]

The "Happy Warrior" line lived on in part due to radio's growing reach. In 1928, when Roosevelt delivered another well-received speech at the Democratic convention nominating Smith, radio held even more importance. In 1924, only 4.7 percent of households owned radios; in 1928, 27.5 percent of households did. In 1932, the figure reached 60 percent of households, not to mention a quarter of a million cars with radios.[15] Roosevelt tailored that 1928 nominating speech for the radio audience instead of bearing in mind only those listening in the convention hall.[16] There were more staccato pauses than one would typically use when preaching to the true believers. He told his listeners that Smith had "that quality of soul which makes a man loved ... a strong help to all those in sorrow or in trouble ... the quality of sympathetic understanding of the human heart." The speech was a hit; *Time* called it "the most intelligently well-bred speech of either of the big conventions." Roosevelt also accomplished something different from other politicians at the time. As *Time* put it, "Compared to the common run of nominating effusions, Mr. Roosevelt's speech was as homo sapiens to the gibbering banderlog."[17]

As radio grew, Roosevelt recognized that it would allow him to reach many more people than ever before. In 1932, he telephoned his seventy-two-year-old mother to let her know that he had secured the Democratic presidential nomination. But "I had already heard it over the radio in my own home," Mrs. Roosevelt later recalled.[18]

In the spring and summer of 1932, thousands of impoverished World War I veterans and their supporters converged on Washington. Led by the unemployed ex-sergeant Walter W. Walters and calling themselves the Bonus Expeditionary Force, they demanded the early payment of a promised bonus for their services.[19] The protest, known as the "Bonus March," received intense and sympathetic coverage from the press. Douglas MacArthur, then the Army chief of staff, moved in with troops to clear the protesters from their camp, and violence ensued. Radio was there, and Franklin Roosevelt joined the rest of the nation in listening to the reports. Struck by the immediacy of the dispatches, Roosevelt suddenly realized that Hoover was going to lose the election.[20] He saw that radio had brought politics into a new era and that it required its own methods of communication. It was a lesson he would never forget when he was president.

FDR as President

FDR learned from Hoover's experience that more radio did not lead to better results, and he limited his radio appearances for maximum effect. His famous "fireside chats," which began only a week into his presidency, took place at a rate of only two to three chats *annually*. As Roosevelt himself put it, "I ought not to appear oftener than once every five or six weeks. I am inclined to think that in England, Churchill, for a while, talked too much and I don't want to do that."[21]

Roosevelt did, however, put a lot of effort and planning into these addresses. He wore a special false tooth for his radio addresses, as a small gap in his lower teeth created a slight whistle when he spoke. Roosevelt even used a particular type of paper that minimized rustling noises in the background. Every aspect of his presentation—including pauses and emphases—was marked carefully in his text.[22]

The language of the speeches was carefully prepared as well. Roosevelt had speechwriting help from the playwright Robert Sherwood, the author of *The Petrified*

Forest and the winner of three Pulitzer Prizes, two for drama and one for *Roosevelt and Hopkins: An Intimate History.* Sherwood recalled that Roosevelt "disliked long words" and measured each word "not by its appearance in print but by its effectiveness over the radio."[23] He intentionally spoke in the language of the common man over the radio in order to appeal to the widest possible audience.[24] The president closely monitored the response to his radio speeches. His aides analyzed the mail and kept track of the size of the audience and of which radio stations may have been "uncooperative."[25]

Despite the careful planning, some recent evidence implies that the fireside chats may not have been as influential as they are usually depicted. According to George Edwards, a scholar of presidential rhetoric, they rarely addressed legislative initiatives directly before Congress. Even when they did, they were not always successful—his failed court-packing effort received the fireside chat treatment to little avail. Edwards estimates that the chats produced only a tiny 1-percent increase in his approval ratings.[26]

> —➤➤➤·●·◄◄◄—
>
> **Radio had made Roosevelt a national figure. His nationally broadcast speeches at the Democratic conventions had introduced him to the American public in the same way that Barack Obama's televised speech to the 2004 Democratic convention launched him toward the White House.**

Despite the questionable short-term gains, the chats certainly paid off in the way that FDR is so lovingly remembered by journalists and by historians. The image of a family sitting around their radio for one of the fireside chats "remains the most iconic image of 1930s radio listening," in the words of David Suisman and Susan Strasser.[27] Betty Houchin Winfield gushes, "With technology, Franklin D. Roosevelt's public-speaking skill could surpass both Cicero and Demosthenes."[28] Despite her enthusiasm, one doubts that the fireside chats will be read as assiduously as Cicero or Demosthenes a hundred years from now.

However important or overrated the fireside chats may have been, Roosevelt certainly got the larger politics right, winning an unprecedented four national elections.

Some Democrats perceived his 1936 reelection victory as specifically attributable to radio. For example, the party's chairman, James Farley, noted that "[t]he influence of radio in determining the outcome of the 1936 election can hardly be overestimated." Sam Rayburn, later speaker of the House and a canny politician, wrote in a letter to Roosevelt, "It was your nationwide radio speeches in 1936 which carried 46 out of 48 states."[29]

Back in New York, Roosevelt had honed his skills of going over the heads of the press and of rival politicians. "Time after time," he gloated, "in meeting legal opposition, I have taken the issue directly to the voters by radio, and invariably, I have met a most heartening response."[30] After the first fireside chat, about the banking crisis, the *New York Times* recognized the potency of his new tool and skill at wielding it: "His use of the new instrument of political discussion is a plain hint to Congress of a recourse which the President may employ if it proves necessary to rally support for legislation which he asks and which the lawmakers might be reluctant to give him."[31] Roosevelt's embrace of the new technology of radio would provide a model for future presidents with emerging media, including John F. Kennedy and television, and Barack Obama and social media.

The American people noticed Roosevelt's skill with radio. According to the journalist Richard Strout, "you felt he was there talking to you, not to 50 million others, but to you personally."[32] As Strout suggests, radio brought FDR into people's homes in a way that made Americans feel comfortable with Roosevelt, and even at times part of the family. His style would influence budding politicians as well as journalists. When Ronald Reagan began in radio in Des Moines, he modeled his technique on Roosevelt's. Later in life, he would of course switch parties and become a Republican, but he maintained a stylistic debt to Roosevelt. Despite his ideological shift, Reagan never lost that deep respect for the man himself as a leader and a communicator.[33]

The tie that radio established between Roosevelt and the American people was something they remembered for decades. Donald Rumsfeld, a Republican who became the White House chief of staff and secretary of defense, remembers his death: "I had become accustomed to thinking of the president as indomitable. He was the person we listened to on the radio and saw on newsreels, the one who I believed would lead us to victory and keep my father safe." Roosevelt had a unique bond with Americans who grew up hearing his voice over the airwaves: "In my young mind, FDR was tied to my father, his ship, our country, and the war. Now that monumental figure was gone. I cried."[34]

This effect was intentional. Secretary of Labor Francis Perkins, who served the length of the administration, recalled that Roosevelt would picture his audience as he spoke, thinking of "them sitting on a suburban porch after supper on a summer evening" or "gathered around a dinner table at a family meal."[35] Thanks to this approach, Roosevelt became a character in people's homes, just as other famous radio personalities did—the fictional Lone Ranger, the comedian Jack Benny, and the journalist Edward R. Murrow. He became part of the transformation of entertainment from something that people would venture out to see to something brought into the home and enjoyed with family. Television would accelerate this process, advancing to an unimaginable degree in our own time by the individualization of entertainment created by iPads and by home theater systems.

> Roosevelt suddenly realized that Hoover was going to lose the election. He saw that radio had brought politics into a new era and that it required its own methods of communication. It was a lesson he would never forget when he was president.

Roosevelt and the Cult of Celebrity

By mastery of the radio, Roosevelt achieved an unprecedented level of celebrity. While earlier presidents hoped to benefit from the reflected glory of famous writers, athletes, and heroes, Roosevelt had attained stardom in his own right. He and some of his successors would thrive in America's new celebrity culture. Mingling with their fellow stars would bring presidents a host of advantages. Some of their glamour might rub off on the politician, making him a potentially more attractive candidate. Celebrities, usually wealthy, could provide campaign funds and participate in fundraisers. In addition, they could endorse candidates, and their star-power could draw crowds that politicians could not typically reach. Working with celebrities is not risk-free, however. A president who gets too close to celebrities can appear superficial or insufficiently attuned to the needs of the common man. John F. Kennedy recognized this vulnerability and took pains to dole out his celebrity interactions in small doses during the 1960 campaign.[36]

Some presidents have been more at home among celebrities than others. Kennedy, Reagan, and Obama have fitted in with the Hollywood scene in ways that LBJ, Nixon, or Carter did not. But FDR was one of the best presidents at managing his relations with the rich and famous. During the 1932 campaign, Roosevelt traveled to Chicago and threw the first ball in the third game of the World Series between the Yankees and the Cubs. This was the

Roosevelt put a lot of effort and planning into his radio addresses. He wore a special false tooth for the speeches, as a small gap in his lower teeth created a slight whistle when he spoke. Roosevelt even used a particular type of paper that minimized rustling noises in the background. Every aspect of his presentation—including pauses and emphases—was marked carefully in his text.

game in which Babe Ruth, who had frustrated some of Roosevelt's predecessors, perhaps hit the most famous home run of all time—the "called shot" off of the pitcher Charlie Root. In response to taunts by Chicago fans, Ruth apparently pointed to the outfield—the grainy film footage is a bit vague—before sending the ball into the center field bleachers. As Ruth circled the bases, Roosevelt laughed at Ruth's shenanigans, saying, "You lucky bum. You lucky bum." At the same time, Roosevelt needed to be careful not to cheer too loudly, as he wanted to win Illinois's electoral votes the next month, which of course he did. His ability to bask in Ruth's celebrity without getting so caught up in it that he lost sight of the politics of the situation partially comprised his gift in this regard, and it also provided a model for presidents in how to handle their ties with the entertainment world.[37]

In that same campaign of 1932, Roosevelt appeared at the Los Angeles Olympic stadium with Charlie Chaplin, Stan Laurel and Oliver Hardy, Clark Gable, and Boris Karloff. In 1940, the pro-Roosevelt effort became even more official, as the Hollywood for Roosevelt Committee boasted over two hundred members, including Humphrey Bogart, Jimmy Cagney, Henry Fonda, and Katharine Hepburn. The committee sent its members nationwide as speakers in support of Roosevelt.[38]

Throughout his time in office, FDR showed a comfort with celebrities that belied their occasional discomfort with him. In the fall of 1944, for example, Frank Sinatra met Roosevelt, the first of many presidents Sinatra would meet. Despite the singer's reputation for making young girls swoon, it was Sinatra who did the swooning in this case. The meeting with the president left Sinatra "absolutely speechless," according to the comedian Rags Ragland. After Republicans mocked Roosevelt for meeting with the draft-exempt yet apparently healthy Sinatra, the singer changed the words of his song "Everything Happens to Me" as follows:

> Republicans started squawking
> They're mad as they can be
> And all I did was say hello to a
> Man named Franklin D.[39]

FDR's Influence

Franklin Roosevelt revealed himself the most important figure in the transformation of the president into a media star. Part of it was simply timing; he was president when Hollywood's influence on American culture exploded. But his greatest contribution to bringing together the worlds of culture and politics was in the realm of radio. Broadcast technologies, destined to help shape American politics with or without Roosevelt, accelerated because of his efforts and insight. As Bruce Lenthall writes in his book about the rise of mass culture, "Radio, in important respects, made Roosevelt; and he, in important respects, made radio."[40]

Roosevelt, of course, was himself subject to many influences. An avid reader going back to his days at Harvard, he read Mahan's book on naval strategy, like his cousin Theodore, which influenced his views of sea power. He also read and marked up policy books such as *Isolated America* by Raymond Leslie Bull and *Victory in the Pacific* by Alexander Kiralfry, as well as Hitler's hateful *Mein Kampf.* FDR not only read books—he also liked owning them. His collection of fifteen thousand volumes dwarfed those of Adams and Jefferson and may have been the largest book collection of any president. The Roosevelt Library and Museum in Hyde Park still displays his enormous library.[41] As his White House aide Jonathan Daniels recalled, FDR "was fascinated by an attractive volume, the binding, the design, the print and the paper—particularly the rarity."

> **Like Woodrow Wilson and Bill Clinton, Roosevelt loved detective stories. He took fifty of them with him to the 1943 Tehran conference with Churchill and Stalin. At the time of this death in April 1945, he was reading *The Punch and Judy Murders* by John Dickson Carr.**

Like Woodrow Wilson and Bill Clinton, Roosevelt loved detective stories. He took fifty of them with him to the 1943 Tehran conference with Churchill and Stalin. At the time of this death in April 1945, he was reading *The Punch and Judy Murders* by John Dickson Carr.[42] He also enjoyed movies and even took in the Oscar-winning British film *Mrs. Miniver* at the request of none other than Winston Churchill.

Every subsequent president would look to FDR as an example of how to be a media actor as well as a consumer. While previous presidents had highlighted their consumption of the available forms of entertainment in an attempt to convey some of the aspects of the ideal leader, new technologies now allowed them to use the media to broadcast those very characteristics. Thanks to Franklin Roosevelt, the characteristics of the ideal leader would include not only partaking of culture but also using the media of culture to communicate and to lead.

CHAPTER 7

MUSIC AND THE
QUEST FOR COOL

R adio made America modern. It unified the nation by allowing the entire population to experience important events simultaneously. Thanks to radio, a new song could become popular from coast to coast within a matter of days. Politicians could speak directly to the people if they had a good "radio voice" and the ability to speak in sound bites.

Radio's most important product was popular music, which quickly transformed culture and politics. Popular music put politicians—and especially presidents—in a quandary. Embracing it made them seem hip or up-to-date. But if they did not embrace popular music and the culture that went with it, they risked appearing out of touch.

Before radio, music was something that even presidents could take or leave as they pleased. Zachary Taylor loved music and would go out of his way to listen to military bands that played outside the White House on Saturdays in the summer, mingling with his fellow listeners. Chester Alan Arthur, who assumed the presidency after James Garfield's assassination, would play the banjo for fun and to relax. But Ulysses S. Grant, who won two presidential elections by overwhelming margins, once admitted, "I only know two tunes. One of them is 'Yankee Doodle' and the other isn't."[1]

Thanks to radio and the technologies that followed, music is now a constant presence in American homes, cars, stores, restaurants, and even elevators. "We are music-soothed and music-encompassed as we go about our business," observes Daniel

Boorstin.[2] As popular music became ubiquitous, it developed in controversial ways. The cultural old guard—including the presidency—proved slow to catch up. Presidents do not necessarily want to be the first to embrace new trends. And the popular music that emerged after World War II was not only groundbreaking but also subversive. The name of the new musical style—rock and roll—came from African-American slang terms for sex. The new genre's sexual overtones and its African-American origins were enough to keep it out of politics—for a while.

Truman: Piano-Playing President

Harry Truman, the last pre-rock president, loved music. His tastes tended toward the classical. When he was president, he identified his favorite composers as Mozart, Beethoven, and Chopin—an unsurprising list at the time, though a hard one to imagine today.[3] Truman was also an accomplished pianist. In his youth, he practiced two hours a day and contemplated a professional music career.[4] He had the passion but lacked the skill. As he put it in his plainspoken way, "I missed being a musician, and the real and only reason I missed being one is because I wasn't good enough."[5]

Still, Truman's piano playing would come in handy. He would play in the parlor after Sunday dinner with Bess Wallace, his future wife, and her parents.[6] He also played occasionally at official functions or political events. His most famous gig came in early 1945, while still vice president, when he

> —➤➤➤•❿•❰❰❰—
>
> Before radio, music was something that even presidents could take or leave as they pleased. Zachary Taylor loved music and would go out of his way to listen to military bands that played outside the White House on Saturdays in the summer, mingling with his fellow listeners. Chester Alan Arthur, who assumed the presidency after James Garfield's assassination, would play the banjo for fun and to relax. But Ulysses S. Grant, who won two presidential elections by overwhelming margins, once admitted, "I only know two tunes. One of them is 'Yankee Doodle' and the other isn't."

played for eight hundred servicemen at the National Press Club with a young Lauren Bacall perched on top of the piano dangling her long legs. No one would bat an eye at such a stunt today, but at the time it was a scandal. Bacall, only twenty, felt embarrassed and blamed her press agent.[7] Years later she recalled that Truman had played the piano rather "badly."[8] Truman's painfully learned lesson was "I couldn't be Harry Truman and vice president at the same time."[9] His wife, Bess, demanded that he give up playing the piano in public.[10]

Another member of the Truman family—the president's daughter, Margaret—aspired to a musical career, with no happier results. On December 5, 1950, during the Korean War, Margaret gave a concert at Washington's Constitution Hall—"a good one," the president recorded in his diary."[11] Unfortunately, Paul Hume, the music critic of the *Washington Post*, disagreed. "Miss Truman," he wrote in his review, had "a pleasant voice of little size and fair quality," and that was the positive part. She "cannot sing very well," he went on, "is flat a good deal of the time, more last night than at any time we have heard her in past years ... has not improved in the years we have heard her ... [and] still cannot sing with anything approaching professional finish."[12] It was, as the singer's aggrieved father put it, a "lousy review." The secretary of state, George Marshall, agreed, telling Truman, "The only thing [Hume] didn't criticize was the varnish on the piano."[13]

Paternal devotion led the president to fire off a scorching rejoinder to the offending critic—on White House stationery no less.[14] "Some day I hope to meet you," Truman wrote. "When that happens you'll need a new nose, a lot of beefsteak for black eyes, and perhaps a supporter below!"[15]

The president paid a steep public relations price for letting himself be Harry Truman again. The *Post* did not print the letter, but it got around, leading to a public outcry.[16] "How can you put your trivial personal affairs before those of one hundred and sixty million people? Our boys died while your infantile mind was on your daughter's review," wrote one citizen. The harshest response came from a Connecticut couple who had lost a son in Korea. They sent Truman their son's Purple Heart with the rebuke, "One major regret at this time is that your daughter was not there to receive the same treatment as our son received in Korea." Truman kept their letter in his desk drawer as a sobering reminder that he needed to be continually wary of just being Harry.[17]

With the passage of time, Truman regretted sending his letter to Hume, and Hume regretted that it became public. In 1958, the critic came to Kansas City for a Maria Callas concert and visited the former president in nearby Independence. The old enemies ended up playing piano together, and there is no indication that Hume required a new nose after the meeting.[18]

Truman the lover of classical music may have been the first president to express an opinion about rock and roll. At a Veterans' Day event in West Virginia in 1957, he commented, "I was taught to appreciate good music, not this damn noise they play today." The band leader Sammy Kaye objected, finding Truman unqualified to render such a judgment. The former president stood his ground, citing the First Amendment. Every American citizen, he said, has a right "to state a preference of expression in every field of endeavor, and as long as that document is the law of the land, no one can stop him."[19]

Ike, JFK, and LBJ:
Rock Rolls, but Not at the White House

Dwight Eisenhower appeared less expressive about music than Truman, but it is safe to say that he did not spend much time on the cutting edge of popular music.[20] The Eisenhower Library features a list of his favorite songs, which fall into four main categories: popular melodies; sacred music; Christmas music; and semi-classical.[21] "Popular," by the way, does not refer to rock and roll. A phonograph album called *The President's Favorite Music: Dwight D. Eisenhower* was released in 1956, featuring Ike and Mamie on the cover. The selections—including Bach's "Sheep May Safely Graze," the overture to Strauss's *Die Fledermaus*, and "Di Provenza il mar" from *La Traviata*—suggest cultural refinement with a common touch.[22] Perhaps the man who vanquished Hitler did not have to worry about coming across as hip or cool.

In the early 1960s, according to David and Julie Nixon Eisenhower, Ike's grand-daughter Anne would get under the former president's skin by playing certain songs—especially "Runaway" by Del Shannon—again and again on a tiny record player. When Ike learned that Elvis Presley had appropriated two of his favorite melodies, "O sole mio" and "Army Blue," and recorded them as "It's Now or Never" and "Love Me Tender," respectively, he was "shocked" and considered "banishing the music from his range of hearing."[23]

Apparently Elvis did not think much of Ike, either. In August 1956, as the presidential rematch between Eisenhower and Democrat Adlai Stevenson approached, Elvis was greeted at the Los Angeles airport by fans waving "Elvis for President" signs. He refused to take the bait, announcing, "I'm strictly for Stevenson. I don't dig the intellectual bit, but I'm telling you, man, he knows the most."[24] It was rumored, Gail Collins reports, that the Stevenson campaign considered using Elvis in a campaign ad but decided against it. It's unclear whether the King or anyone could have turned things around for Stevenson 1956.[25]

> When Ike learned that Elvis Presley had appropriated two of his favorite melodies, "O sole mio" and "Army Blue," and recorded them as "It's Now or Never" and "Love Me Tender," respectively, he was "shocked" and considered "banishing the music from his range of hearing."

Eisenhower had little interest in musical theater, although he occasionally took a liking to a song from a current hit, such as *My Fair Lady*'s "Get Me to the Church on Time." He took Mamie and Kay Summersby to *Oklahoma!* in 1944, but he attended the theater only twice as president, once each term. In 1953, he and Mamie attended a Metropolitan Opera Company performance of *La Bohème* in New York, and in 1957 they went to see Rex Harrison and Julie Andrews in their record-breaking run of *My Fair Lady*. The president stayed only ten minutes and left before the final curtain. He was no more patient with musicals on the screen. A Secret Service agent, Rufus Youngblood, recalled that when Mamie selected a Gilbert and Sullivan operetta for viewing in the White House movie theater, Ike squirmed through about ten minutes of the production before leaving, complaining to his agents but not to Mamie, "I'll be damned if I can sit through another one of those blasted musicals."[26]

In one of the amusing twists of history, the famous campaign song and slogan for this man who so disliked musicals originated from a musical. In October 1950, Eisenhower attended the opening of Irving Berlin's *Call Me Madam*, a send-up of politics and the tabloids. Berlin sent the general a signed score of the musical's songs, one of which was "They Like Ike." Two years later, Berlin rewrote the song as "I Like Ike" for Eisenhower's presidential campaign.[27] The song was introduced at a rally at Madison Square Garden, and soon "I Like Ike" presented itself the ubiquitous slogan of the winning campaign. Berlin obligingly followed it up in 1956 with "I Still Like Ike" and "Ike for Four More Years." Berlin's ditty is widely considered one of the most effective campaign songs ever written.[28] If the Eisenhower-Stevenson contests of the 1950s are any measure, Irving Berlin beat Elvis Presley—at least in politics—and an old fogey like Ike could still get elected president.

As the new decade of the 1960s opened, the new forms of popular music still seemed subversive, and the musical tastes of presidents John F. Kennedy and Lyndon B. Johnson remained decidedly conventional. Presidents could still be unengaged with popular music, and musical hipness was not yet a requirement. Johnson's favorite songs, for example, did not differ much from Eisenhower's, although they included some more recent Broadway tunes from *The Sound of Music* (1959) and *Hello, Dolly!* (1964).[29] Kennedy was also a "square" in his musical tastes. In fact, he was not a music lover at all. His staff, however, made sure that was a well-kept secret.

Kennedy's reputation as a cultural connoisseur is the result, in large part, of Pablo Casals's famous performance at the White House on November 13, 1961. The legendary cellist had played there in 1904 for Theodore Roosevelt but had not performed in the United States since 1928. The White House invitation for Casals comprised, in part, a conscious effort to portray Kennedy as a patron of the arts. Early in the administration, the historian Arthur Schlesinger Jr., now the court intellectual, wrote a memo instructing the president how to improve the image of the United States abroad. Americans, he observed, were regarded as "materialistic, vulgar, obsessed with comic books and television, hostile to higher cultural and spiritual values." But Kennedy could change that perception. "You are a writer and historian," Schlesinger noted. "Your wife is a patron of the arts. You have appointed intellectuals to positions in your administration. You summoned the leading writers and artists in America to your inauguration." Schlesinger advised Kennedy to build on that reputation by "receiving leading artists and scholars at the White House."[30]

The invitation to Casals came about after an exchange of letters between the president and the cellist in the spring of 1961. Casals praised Kennedy while explaining the political resentment that had kept him away from the United States for so many years. The Spaniard indicated that he would accept a formal invitation if one were extended, which was done in October. Pierre Salinger, the White House press secretary, had a press statement teed up for release as soon as Casals's acceptance arrived.[31]

The White House staff was giddy about the event. Even Mrs. Kennedy lost her trademark sangfroid, gushing to Secret Service agent Clint Hill, "We're going to have a very special after-dinner concert. Pablo Casals, who is perhaps the world's greatest cellist, has agreed to play for us. He hasn't played in the United States in thirty-three years. Isn't that exciting?"[32] The evening did not disappoint. One of the guests, the composer Gian Carlo Menotti, evidently received the intended message, remarking, "English royalty entertains movie stars. Our president entertains artists."[33] Another guest was Alice Roosevelt Longworth, who had been present at Casals's last White House performance, for her father in 1904.[34]

By all accounts, Casals played brilliantly. Kennedy played his part as well, following step-by-step written instructions prepared by the White House social secretary, Letitia Baldridge, telling him to go to the Red Room after the performance and reminding him "(there's an encore)."[35] The press coverage was overwhelmingly positive. The *Washington Post*'s front-page review, written by Margaret Truman's old detractor, Paul Hume, ran with the exultant headline: "Brilliant Gathering at White House Entranced by Fabled Pablo Casals." Hume, won over before the performance even began, reported that "[t]he East Room of the White House has never before seen such a gathering of prominent musicians."[36] The guest list, reported the *Post*'s Dorothy McCardle, "read like a Who's Who among contemporary conductors, composers, musical educators, instrumentalists, and just plain music lovers,"[37] including Aaron Copland and Leonard Bernstein.*

Casals was extremely pleased. "Last Monday night I played with all my heart," he wrote to Kennedy, "and I feel that the results have been rewarding."[38] The results were rewarding for Kennedy as well. Schlesinger helpfully informed Kennedy that the cultural critic John Crosby had written in the *International Herald Tribune*, "President Kennedy is the best friend culture (another dirty word) has had in the White House since Thomas Jefferson."[39]

Kennedy's reputation as an aficionado of high culture was sealed[40]—all according to Schlesinger's plan. The Casals dinner was part of a broader effort to bring class, glamour, and celebrities to the White House for political benefit. It appealed to the country's increasing self-confidence, showing that America had become a cultural power as well as a military and economic one.

As was often the case with John Kennedy, the image did not quite match up to the reality. He was no music lover. His arts advisor, August Heckscher, recalled, "It was not only that he didn't particularly enjoy [music,] but I think it was really painful. . . . It hurt his ears. I really don't think he liked music at all except a few things he knew."[41] Ted Sorenson confessed that Kennedy "had no interest in opera, dozed off at symphony concerts, and was bored by ballet." And Kennedy himself is reputed to have said to a friend, "Pablo Casals? I didn't know what the hell he played—someone had to tell me."[42] This was the reason that Baldridge had to provide such detailed instructions—Kennedy did not even know the proper times to applaud.[43]

---

* The comedian Vaughn Meader spoofed the event in his hit record *The First Family*. As the president and the first lady greet a receiving line of cultural luminaries, each of whom Mrs. Kennedy knows on a first-name basis, the president whispers to his wife, "Jackie, why is it always *your* friends?"

This effort to depict JFK as a sophisticate, forsaking the image of the "common man" that presidents since Andrew Jackson had cultivated, was risky and groundbreaking. It also proved remarkably effective. Kennedy and his team sensed that intellectualism would appeal to American sensibilities at the time.

After Kennedy's assassination, his widow encapsulated the idea of his administration as a highbrow haven with the Camelot metaphor, based on the popular 1960 Broadway musical. The association began with a famous *Life* magazine interview that Mrs. Kennedy gave to the journalist Theodore White, whom she summoned to Hyannis Port, even sending a Secret Service car to pick him up.[44] Mrs. Kennedy told White, "At night, before we'd go to sleep, Jack liked to play some records; and the song he loved most came at the very end of this record. The lines he loved to hear were: 'Don't let it be forgot, that once there was a spot for one brief shining moment that was known as Camelot'." Even in this post-mortem interview, she guarded the image of the highbrow Kennedy: "When Jack quoted something, it was usually classical, but I'm so ashamed of myself—all I keep thinking of is this line from a musical comedy."[45] Still, *Camelot* remained her focus during the interview, and she was quite determined to make sure the concept appeared prominently in the article.

It worked. The Kennedy White House as Camelot took root in the public imagination. The grieving nation embraced the image of "one brief shining moment" in which its dashing leader led it to glory before meeting a tragic end. At a performance of the musical *Camelot* in Chicago, the audience and actors wept as the "shining moment" words were sung. At the 1964 Democratic National Convention in Atlantic City, *Camelot* music accompanied images of JFK shown to the crowd. Camelot has remained the defining image of the Kennedy administration, showing

> As was often the case with John Kennedy, the image did not quite match up to the reality. He was no music lover. His arts advisor, August Heckscher, recalled, "It was not only that he didn't particularly enjoy [music,] but I think it was really painful.... It hurt his ears. I really don't think he liked music at all except a few things he knew."

the power of music to advance mythology, especially when combined with the concept of (benevolent) monarchy.[46]

White willingly collaborated in the construction of this artifice. A journalist with classical training and a nose for public relations, White understood what Mrs. Kennedy intended and played a big role in advancing the desired narrative. In 1978, he wrote that "the epitaph on the Kennedy Administration became Camelot—a magic moment in American history, when gallant men danced with beautiful women, when great deeds were done, when artists, writers and poets met at the White House and the barbarians beyond the walls were held back."[47] Mrs. Kennedy knew what she was doing when she picked White to purvey the Camelot myth.

Kennedy might not have known who Pablo Casals was, but there is at least some evidence that in the right circumstances he could become attached to a song. In Mimi Alford's recollection of her affair with Kennedy, she writes that upon her departure from the White House to return to college (yes, college), Kennedy turned sentimental. He played Nat King Cole's rendition of "Autumn Leaves" on the White House stereo, "making me pay close attention when the lyrics came to, 'But I miss you most of all, my darling, when autumn leaves start to fall.'"

If Kennedy listened to Nat King Cole, there's no reason to think that he might not have listened to the *Camelot* soundtrack in the evening. It seems, though, that he never actually saw the play. After the 1960 election, on a visit to New York City, Kennedy's staff told the press that the president-elect would attend *Camelot* on December 6. He changed his mind, however, and with Mrs. Kennedy's assent went instead to see Gore Vidal's *The*

—➤➤➤·●·◄◄◄—

"Let us first dispose of Camelot," wrote Arthur Schlesinger in 2002 in the introduction to a new edition of *A Thousand Days*. Kennedy knew *Camelot*'s co-creator Alan Jay Lerner from Choate and Harvard, Schlesinger acknowledged, but "during [JFK's] lifetime no one spoke of Kennedy's Washington as Camelot." And if anyone had done so, "no one would have been more derisive than JFK."

Best Man.[48] (Vidal and Jackie shared a stepfather.)[49] Vidal's play was overtly political. Joe Cantwell, one of the two protagonists, is a philandering politician described as a "fancy Dan from the East." The parallels between Kennedy and Cantwell were so obvious that Kennedy, upon seeing the script, even asked Jackie, "Is Gore writing about me?" Despite this concern, he attended the play and sat next to Vidal, surrounded by so many Secret Service agents that *Variety* quipped, "If Abraham Lincoln had had this kind of protection, he would have been around to applaud the final curtain of *Our American Cousin.*"[50] The American president was becoming isolated from the public. Presidents are at their most vulnerable when they try to evade their protective bubbles. At the same time, too tight of a bubble brings vulnerability of the political variety.

"Let us first dispose of Camelot," wrote Arthur Schlesinger in 2002 in the introduction to a new edition of *A Thousand Days.* Kennedy knew *Camelot*'s co-creator Alan Jay Lerner from Choate and Harvard, Schlesinger acknowledged, but "during [JFK's] lifetime no one spoke of Kennedy's Washington as Camelot." And if anyone had done so, "no one would have been more derisive than JFK."[51] Kennedy's secretary,

Vidal's play was overtly political. Joe Cantwell, one of the two protagonists, is a philandering politician described as a "fancy Dan from the East." The parallels between Kennedy and Cantwell were so obvious that Kennedy, upon seeing the script, even asked Jackie, "Is Gore writing about me?" Despite this concern, he attended the play and sat next to Vidal, surrounded by so many Secret Service agents that *Variety* quipped, "If Abraham Lincoln had had this kind of protection, he would have been around to applaud the final curtain of *Our American Cousin.*" The American president was becoming isolated from the public. Presidents are at their most vulnerable when they try to evade their protective bubbles. At the same time, too tight of a bubble brings vulnerability of the political variety.

Evelyn Lincoln, dismissed the myth from a strictly musical perspective: "You know what [the president] would have said about it—'Oh not that trash!' [Jackie] said 'Camelot' was his favorite song. His favorite song was 'Bill Bailey, Won't You Please Come Home?'"[52]

Whatever JFK's musical tastes may have been, the Kennedys understood the power of music in the days before rock and how to use it to their advantage. Everyone acknowledged that classical music was the "best" music, even if everyone could not appreciate it. Broadway was acceptable in both Washington and in proper circles, but it was a second-order indulgence rather than a higher art form. Kennedy himself may have had little interest in either, but he and his aides were able to employ the symbolism of these two musical forms to convey their intended image of him as a leader of godlike refinement who nevertheless cared about the common people. After the Kennedy years, though, music—and its relation to politics—changed completely.

During Queen Elizabeth II's state visit to mark the U.S. Bicentennial in 1976—an occasion for which the cream of American artistic achievement might have been displayed—the Fords inexplicably entertained Her Majesty with the pop duo The Captain and Tennille singing a song called "Muskrat Love."

Nixon and the Rise of the Counterculture

The successfully concocted myth of the cultured Kennedy affected the way his successors would try to use music. As the new forms of popular music secured their grip on American culture, presidents would no longer have the option of ignoring them. Still, it took a while for pop music to gain a foothold in the White House. Jackie Kennedy and Robert McNamara had scandalized Washington by dancing the twist, a rare cultural misstep by the Kennedys.[53] In August 1974, however, the newly installed president Gerald Ford danced at a state dinner to a Jim Croce tune. The journalist Tom DeFrank recalled some raised eyebrows: "I think it's fair to say, Gerald Ford will be the first, the last, and the only president ever to have danced at a state dinner at the White House to a tune called 'Bad, Bad Leroy Brown.'"[54] It was all downhill from there in the Ford White House. During Queen Elizabeth II's state visit to mark the U.S. Bicentennial in 1976—an occasion for which the cream of American artistic achievement might have been displayed—the Fords inexplicably entertained Her Majesty with the pop duo The Captain and Tennille singing a song called "Muskrat Love." As Tennille herself later recalled, a stone-faced Henry Kissinger sat four feet from her during the performance, arms folded impassively across his chest.

In the rock-and-roll era, popular music presented presidents with a choice: ignore it and appear out of touch, or embrace it and risk association with its more subversive and controversial elements. Every president since Nixon has faced this democratic and American dilemma—how to be a regular guy but not too regular, of the people but not demeaned by them.

Even as presidents were pulled into the world of popular entertainment, entertainers became political actors themselves. Casals's boycott of the United States or Elvis's endorsement of Stevenson would pale in comparison with the outspoken political activities of musicians since the 1960s. Celebrities became increasingly identified with the Democratic Party, and most, although not all, displayed hostility toward the Republican Party. This rise of the liberal celebrity has presented challenges and opportunities for presidents of both parties.

Rock and roll's conquest of American popular culture coincided, oddly enough, with the ascendency of Richard Nixon. He came to power at the point at which rock and roll could no longer be ignored. The baby boomers—the generation of approximately seventy-six million born between 1946 and 1964—had been raised on rock and roll. Many of them were now raising their own kids on it, without the resistance their parents had put up to Elvis, the Beatles, and the Rolling Stones. Nixon, of course, was hardly hip to new musical styles. During his famous "Kitchen Debate" of 1959 with Nikita Khrushchev, Nixon had found one point of agreement with his Soviet interlocutor—a dislike of jazz.[55]

By the time he was president, however, Nixon had changed his tune regarding jazz. Perennially jealous of Kennedy, he wanted to throw his own version of the Casals dinner, but he thought it needed to be more "American" and less highbrow. He liked the idea of honoring a black musician, so a dinner was planned in celebration of Duke Ellington's seventieth birthday, shortly after Nixon took office in 1969, at which he would receive the Presidential Medal of Freedom. Nixon instructed his chief of staff, H. R. Haldeman, to invite "all the jazz greats, like Guy Lombardo...."[56] Arthur Schlesinger's autobiography contains two catty comments about this attempt to rival the Casals dinner. He notes Haldeman's "priceless entry" in his diary about Nixon's idea: "oh well!" And he explains that "Lombardo ... was of course the antithesis of Jazz."[57] Ellington was the first black American to have a White House dinner in his honor, but his fête attained nowhere near the cultural resonance of the Casals dinner.[58] The disparity had less to do with the two musicians than with the two presidents. Kennedy had a strategic plan for presenting himself as cultured, and he enjoyed a cultural establishment predisposed to support him. That same cultural establishment disliked Richard Nixon, and he disliked them in return.

Nixon's pop culture odyssey continued the next year when he received Elvis Presley at the White House, perhaps the most famous encounter between an entertainer and an American president. Presley had initiated the meeting, hoping that Nixon would grant him the title of "Federal Agent-at-Large" in the Bureau of Narcotics and Dangerous Drugs. There may have been a mixed motive behind this odd request. Priscilla Presley later claimed that her husband thought the title and badge would allow him to transport prescription drugs and guns without being bothered by law enforcement officials.[59]

Nixon and Presley met, somewhat awkwardly, on December 21, 1970.[60] Presley "dressed in a purple jumpsuit and a white shirt open to the navel with a big gold chain and thick-rimmed sunglasses," reflected Egil "Bud" Krogh, the White House aide who arranged the meeting. Presley complained to Nixon that "the Beatles came over here and made a lot of money and said some un-American things." Somewhat befuddled, Nixon looked at Krogh and asked, "Well, what's this about the Beatles?"[61] While Nixon was dogged by feelings of inferiority to Kennedy, Elvis evidently had issues of his own concerning Britain's Fab Four. Perhaps the president and the King were not as mismatched as we have always thought. Toward the end of their visit, Nixon looked at Elvis's costume and remarked, "You dress kind of strange, don't you?" Elvis's dead-on response: "You have your show and I have mine."[62] The odd encounter was captured in a photograph that has become the most frequently requested document in the National Archives. [63] Elvis received his federal agent's badge at lunch in the White House mess with Krogh.

Despite these efforts, Nixon remained as uncool as ever—worse, really.[64] The image of the uptight Nixon, who wore dress shoes for a photo-op walk along the beach, also had a political context. His administration seemed to highlight the emerging enmity between the entertainment business and the Republican president. Daniel Patrick Moynihan, a Nixon aide, once summarized in a memo to Haldeman and to the domestic policy adviser John Ehrlichman the administration's problems with the cultural elites: "No one writes articles for us, much less books, or plays, or folk songs."[65]

> Nixon, of course, was hardly hip to new musical styles. During his famous "Kitchen Debate" of 1959 with Nikita Khrushchev, Nixon had found one point of agreement with his Soviet interlocutor—a dislike of jazz.
>
>

In the early stages of the culture war, Moynihan recognized that there would be advantages to having celebrities on Nixon's side but that there existed few prospects of getting them. Moynihan had no strategy for attracting celebrity support, and Nixon was too congenitally unhip to have a chance. In fact, Nixon was so disliked that one counterculture figure, Jefferson Airplane's Grace Slick, even tried to drug him, or so she claims. The opportunity arose because Slick was, like Nixon's daughter Tricia, an alumna of Finch College. The Nixons hosted a White House reception for Finch graduates, and Slick planned to attend—with Abbie Hoffman in tow—under her given name of Grace Wing in the hope of spiking the president's tea with LSD. The fun ended when the Secret Service pulled the subversive couple from the line, explaining, "We checked and you're a security risk."[66]

The pop music world hated Lyndon Johnson because of the Vietnam War, but the real battle lines of the culture war were drawn during the Nixon administration. From then on, pop music would be firmly on the side of the Democrats. Some musicians, nevertheless, ended up on the other side of the line. Southern rock and country music, in particular, emerged as conservative strongholds. The Jacksonville band Lynyrd Skynyrd's "Sweet Home Alabama," which Ronnie van Zant wrote in reaction to Neil Young's anti-segregation "Southern Man," is a case in point. The song's most famous line—"Watergate does not bother me, does your conscience bother you?"— played to conservative resentment of liberal double standards. Nixon was a true believer in the reality of the double standard, which has become a core conservative principle.[67]

Country music came to embody the feelings of Nixon's "Silent Majority." Merle Haggard's "Okie from Muskogee" (1969) became "an instant anthem of cantankerous conservatism," writes the journalist and musicologist J. Lester Feder. The song expressed the frustration of many Americans with the hippies, the "long hairs," and the draft dodgers celebrated in so much of the popular culture—especially in the rock and roll of the 1960s and early 70s.[68] The idea for the song came to Haggard, the son of Okie migrants, when his band's tour bus passed a sign for Muskogee and someone remarked, "I bet they don't smoke marijuana in Muskogee." Haggard, who after a troubled childhood had spent three years in San Quentin, found the observation amusing, and composed a list of other things that people in a place like Muskogee would and would not do. A song that began as a joke turned into a huge hit, as Haggard captured the frustrations of Americans whom the cultural left had rendered bewildered and resentful.[69]

"Okie from Muskogee" made Haggard a star, and it attracted the attention of President Nixon, who assiduously courted the country music industry. He invited Haggard to the White House in 1973 and the next year visited the Grand Ole Opry, where he gave a speech extolling the values of country music.[70] "[C]ountry music is American," Nixon told the audience in Nashville. It "isn't something that we learned from some other nation, it isn't something that we inherited." In fact, he observed, "It's as native as anything American we could find." Best of all, the president said, country music expresses Americans' love of country and of religion, two loves that appeared to be in short supply among the countercultural left. He cited country music's appeal beyond the American South, insisting that it stemmed from "the heart of America, because this is the heart of America, out here in Middle America." Nixon showed that political favor could bring country music into the mainstream of American culture.[71] And by highlighting the music's "American" nature, he implied that rock music was something other than American, bespeaking a deepening of the culture war between Nixon and his antagonists within the cultural elite.

Nixon thought country music good for the country and good for him, but he didn't actually listen to it.[72] When he did listen to music, Nixon liked something softer.[73] His dalliance with country music suggests that Nixon tried to use music much as Kennedy had done, but he tailored it to a different audience.

Nixon's musical outreach produced mixed results. Relations with country stars were not always smooth. When Johnny Cash came to the White House, Nixon aides asked him to play the so-called "backlash classics," "Okie" and "Welfare Cadillac." The songs were not in his repertoire, and Cash declined. Some interpreted his

—>>>•●•≪≪—

"Okie from Muskogee" made Haggard a star, and it attracted the attention of President Nixon, who assiduously courted the country music industry. He invited Haggard to the White House in 1973 and the next year visited the Grand Ole Opry, where he gave a speech extolling the values of country music. "[C]ountry music is American," Nixon told the audience in Nashville. It "isn't something that we learned from some other nation, it isn't something that we inherited." In fact, he observed, "It's as native as anything American we could find."

response as a political statement, but it is more likely that that Cash simply was not prepared to play those particular songs.[74]

H. R. Haldeman identified the chief flaw with the Nixon's country music strategy in a diary entry after the "Evening with Merle Haggard" at the White House. "The 'Evening' was pretty much a flop," he wrote, "because the audience had no appreciation for country/western music and there wasn't much rapport, except when Haggard did his 'Okie from Muskogee' … which everybody responded to very favorably, of course." The Nixon White House may have shared certain political views with Haggard and the fans of country music, but they did not share musical tastes.[75]

In a fascinating article in the *Weekly Standard* on Haggard and his appeal to conservatives, John Berlau credits the country star with the kind of pragmatic conservatism that Russell Kirk would recognize. Berlau may be reading too much into "Okie from Muskogee." While Haggard expressed support for Ronald Reagan, he did the same for Bill Clinton and Barack Obama. However one might define Haggard's politics, he is clearly not a conservative intellectual hero.[76]

Nixon's embrace of Haggard inspired a backlash on the Left against country music and against Haggard himself. "There is something utterly sinister about the image of Richard Nixon inviting Merle Haggard to sing at the White House," wrote Richard Goldstein at the time. The president, he said, wanted to "identify with the system of values which country music suggests, which is to say a strongly suburban, strongly conservative, strongly Protestant audience which damned well ought to frighten every long-haired progressive urbanite, and every black man who is not part of it."[77]

Goldstein felt a special discomfort with the Christian background of country music, calling it "the only genuinely Wasp creation in American art forms." His revulsion went deep: "To a New York City Jew there is something intrinsically threatening about the very syntax of country music, not to mention its content."[78] Goldstein could not separate country music from the racist, anti-Semitic, redneck stereotype he bore in his mind. American ethnic groups such as Jews had created new and sometimes subversive forms of culture, but some members of these groups, as critics, opposed the backlash of the old WASP culture to the changes brought on by "long-haired progressive urbanites." Goldstein's overreaction to the conservative strains in country music highlights the breadth of the divide between both sides in the culture war.

Nixon's country music gambit did not save his own political career from ruin. But the "Southern strategy" of which it was a part, and which the Left demonized as racist, helped the Republicans turn a Democratic region into a Republican bulwark, paving the way for the Reagan revolution of 1980 and the Gingrich revolution of 1994. Nixon's insight about the political potency of country music, regardless of his own awkwardness and lack of interest in the genre, proved an important development for a conservative movement buffeted by an increasingly hostile popular culture.

Presidential Music Post-Nixon: Drug Use and Campaign Songs

It is important not to overstate the connection between music and politics. For the most part, the musical world remained separate from politics, and this separation was usually in the interests of both the musicians and the politicians. Yet music has always had a profound influence on culture, as Plato recognized two and a half millennia ago: "This is what Damon tells me, and I can quite believe him; he said that when modes of music change, the fundamental laws of the State always change with it."[79] Or as the Irish liberator Daniel O'Connell put it, "Let me write the songs of a nation, and I care not who makes its laws."[80] For this reason, popular music's ubiquity and its growing influence cannot be ignored.

One example of this influence was the drug culture. The popular music scene has long been more receptive to drug use than the general population. Not so long ago, being caught smoking marijuana would spell the end of a government career. It was only twenty-five years ago that President Reagan withdrew the Supreme Court nomination of Judge Douglas Ginsburg because of reports that the jurist had smoked marijuana during his time as a Harvard faculty member. Now about 40 percent of the population has smoked pot. Three consecutive presidents—Clinton, Bush, and Obama—have effectively admitted using marijuana or stronger drugs with little harm to their electoral prospects. Music had a lot to do with this move toward acceptance.

Musicians have carried the drug culture into many areas where it was once previously unthinkable, including the once impregnable White House. According to David Crosby, of Crosby, Stills & Nash fame, a member of the band lit a joint in the Oval Office during a visit with President Carter in 1977. "It was funny, man," Crosby recalls. "One of us, and I will not say who, lit a joint in the Oval Office just to be able to say he'd done it, you know?"[81] Marijuana returned to the Carter White House when Willie Nelson visited in 1980. He claims to have smoked "a big fat Austin torpedo" on the White House roof. Carter has said that he did not know about Nelson's indulgence, but the singer says the Secret Service was watching.[82]

> Now about 40 percent of the population has smoked pot. Three consecutive presidents—Clinton, Bush, and Obama—have effectively admitted using marijuana or stronger drugs with little harm to their electoral prospects. Music had a lot to do with this move toward acceptance.

These high times in the White House resulted from Carter's eagerness to associate with popular musicians, following Kennedy's playbook but with a Plains sensibility. He entertained Dizzy Gillespie (with whom he sang "Salt Peanuts" on the White House lawn), Sarah Vaughan, and Earl "Fatha" Hines, noting in his diary that he had at one point been "an avid jazz fan."[83] Carter recalled that when he "was in trouble in the White House or needed to be alone, just to relax," he would go into his study and tie flies for fishing while "Willie Nelson's songs played on the hi-fi." He joked, "So all the good things I did or, of course, all the mistakes I've made, you could kind of blame half that on Willie."[84] As these anecdotes show, Carter had the ability as a Southerner, as the supplanter of the hated Nixon, and as a Democrat to mingle with almost any popular musician. The culture war briefly abated.

Carter was vanquished by a man who was himself a product of Hollywood, Ronald Reagan. But most of the good feelings between the White House and the entertainment business came to an end when Reagan moved in. The theme of Reagan's reelection campaign in 1984, "Morning in America," relied on upbeat patriotic images, including Bruce Springsteen's monster hit "Born in the USA." The song became a Republican pep-rally anthem for the go-go 1980s.[85] The president even traveled to New Jersey, the heart of Springsteen country, to make his point. In a speech in Hammonton, he told the crowd, "America's future rests in a thousand dreams inside our hearts. It rests in the message of hope in the songs of a man so many young Americans admire: New Jersey's own Bruce Springsteen."[86]

> —➤➤➤ •●• ◄◄◄—
>
> **Thanks to the baby boomers and their immersion in popular music, the music had become another language politicians needed to master.**

It is extremely unlikely, however, that Reagan was a Springsteen fan or even listened to his music.[87] It was Nixon and Haggard all over again. But the bigger problem was Springsteen's horror of Reagan's appropriation of what the music legend saw as a "working-class troubadour's rejection of Reaganism and rah-rah Americanism."[88] The singer told *Rolling Stone*, "You see in the Reagan election ads on TV, you know, 'It's morning in America,' and you say, 'Well, it's not morning in Pittsburgh.'"[89] Springsteen later called "Born in the USA" the "most misunderstood song since 'Louie, Louie.'"[90]

The lesson for Republicans was that appropriating a pop singer's song for your campaign is an invitation for him to comment on your campaign or policies, so you'd better know what he is going to say. Springsteen's hostility to Reagan was not a secret. He had announced at a concert the day after Reagan's election, "I don't know what you thought about what happened last night, but I thought it was pretty terrifying."[91]

The next Republican president, George H. W. Bush, faced the same hostile music industry. In his 1988 campaign, Bush tried to use Bobby McFerrin's infectious and insipid *a cappella* reggae song "Don't Worry, Be Happy" as an unofficial theme, hoping to link himself to the economic success of the Reagan administration. Once again, a Republican attempt to adopt a popular song backfired. McFerrin loudly announced his opposition to Bush, and the campaign dropped the song.[92]

In 1992, when Bill Clinton adopted Fleetwood Mac's 70s hit "Don't Stop Thinking about Tomorrow," the effect differed entirely. The song resonated with the baby boomers raised on the tune and on other top-forty hits. The campaign played the song so often that the *New York Times'* Caryn James referred to it as Clinton's "endlessly replayed 1992 campaign theme."[93] The song conveyed youthful optimism, emphasizing the contrast between Clinton and his generation-older opponent, George H. W. Bush. As the *Los Angeles Times'* Geoff Boucher wrote, the song "musically encoded both Clinton's baby-boomer target audience and his message."[94] Thanks to the baby boomers and their immersion in popular music, the music had become another language politicians needed to master.

The members of Fleetwood Mac, which had broken up, did not object to Clinton's use of their song—they reveled in it. In fact, the fractious band reunited to perform "Don't Stop" at Clinton's inaugural ball in 1993. In 2012, two decades later, the opening and closing music played for Clinton's speech at the Democratic National Convention was, of course, "Don't Stop." Apart from the singers' political views, their receptivity to Clinton's use of their song could be attributed to Clinton's obvious familiarity with their music, in contrast to Reagan's feigned admiration for Bruce Springsteen. Clinton grew up in a different era than Reagan, and rock and roll was neither threatening nor unusual in his youth. In fact, not only Clinton but his mother, too, enjoyed Elvis's music. As Clinton once recalled, "My mother loved Elvis Presley from the first time she saw him. She thought rock & roll was great for kids."[95]

Clinton used his love of music to great political advantage. He was, as a 1997 documentary described him, a "Rock and Roll president," and he made the most of it. In his 1992 campaign for president, he famously donned sunglasses to play the saxophone on *The Arsenio Hall Show*, "one of the defining moments of that Presidential campaign."[96] This moment was not only defining; it was also groundbreaking. Until then, presidential appearances on non-news shows were rare. But the spectacle of Clinton in shades and appearing as an entertainer violated earlier notions of presidential dignity.

In 2012, the *Weekly Standard*'s Philip Terzian observed that it was "only two decades ago when candidate Bill Clinton blew his saxophone on *The Arsenio Hall Show*, beginning a trend that has yet to play out." He argued that Clinton had broken the "historical model" in which "presidents refrained from granting one-on-one interviews with the press, would never have discussed their religious opinions or personal problems with journalists, and were not expected to make themselves available to the producers of *Late Night with David Letterman* or *The View*." Clinton rejected the tradition of presidents' keeping a "certain statesmanlike distance—mystery, if you will—around their exalted office." At the same time, his actions appealed to generations of voters who had grown up with the culture of mass entertainment.[97] Terzian recognized that some presidents may have found political gain in engaging with pop music, but the presidency lost something in the process.

Still, unlike Kennedy or Nixon, Clinton did not fake his interest in popular music. He and Hillary actually named their daughter after the Judy Collins song "Chelsea Morning." Bill had, writes Caryn James, "a genuine love of music and eclectic taste that includes pop, gospel, jazz, blues and rock." Specific performances served as "markers in his life," including Cass Elliot at Georgetown and Mahalia Jackson at Oxford.[98] He also really knew how to play the saxophone, and the instrument meant something to him. Clinton felt that playing gave him "the opportunity to create something that was beautiful, something that I could channel my sensitivity, my feelings into."[99] He, like many of his fellow boomers, was weaned on rock. Even the artists themselves sensed this. As rocker Joe Cocker gushed in the *Rock and Roll President* documentary, "For a president to be associated with rock and roll is kind of cool."[100]

By the 1990s, rock and roll had become mainstream. Clinton's familiarity with the popular music of the 1960s and 70s was not only unthreatening but even appealing. "Don't Stop" was released in 1977, after all, and anyone old enough to remember the song could vote in 1992. The music that had seemed subversive in the 1960s now appeared safe fare for a political convention. New forms now appeared to replace rock as the subversive music of the moment.

Elvis could shock audiences of the 1950s, but forty years later it took more than a swinging pelvis to do the trick. Rap came along to fill that void. While some forms of rap dated back to the 1970s, its first breakout hit beyond the African-American audience was a 1984 album by Run-DMC, a relatively tame effort. Public Enemy took things down a notch in 1989 with "Fight the Power"—"Elvis was a hero to most / But he never meant s**t to me, you see." By 1991, however, rap had reached a new milestone, which David Samuels described in his groundbreaking cover story on rap in the *New Republic*: "So it was that America awoke on June 22, 1991, to find that its favorite record was not 'Out of Time,' by aging college-boy rockers R.E.M., but Niggaz4life, a musical celebration of gang rape and other violence by N.W.A., or Niggers with Attitude, a rap group from the Los Angeles ghetto of Compton...." The appeal of rap, Samuels wrote, was that it allowed white suburban teenagers to absorb the ghetto experience without facing any of its physical dangers.[101]

This appeal, however, concerned parents, cultural critics, and, increasingly, politicians as the 1992 presidential election approached. Republicans tried to use rap's violence, misogyny, and obscenity as a wedge issue. While NWA and Public Enemy had set the stage, the specific offender in the 1992 campaign was Ice-T and his "gangsta rap" song "Cop Killer." The lyrics—"Cop killer, better you than me / Cop killer, f**k police brutality! / Cop killer, I know your mama's grievin' (f**k her) / Cop killer, but tonight we get even"—seemed to condone or even encourage anti-police violence. In response to the controversy, Ice-T claimed it as merely a song about police brutality, explaining that he was "singing in the first person as a character who is fed up with police brutality. I ain't never killed no cop."[102]

Republicans thought that with "Cop Killer" they could at last turn the Democrats' cozy relations with the music industry against them. Clinton appeared to be in a quandary. If he condemned Ice-T, he risked alienating his deep-pocketed supporters in the entertainment business as well as the indispensible black vote. At the same time, widespread outrage flared up over the song. Faced with this challenge, Clinton used his strong sense of the popular culture to study just how far he could push back on the issue.

Clinton benefited from some plain, old-fashioned luck in the form of a failed rap singer and activist called Sister Souljah. When the policemen whose beating of Rodney King had been captured on videotape were acquitted, rioting broke out in Los Angeles. Sister Souljah told the *Washington Post*'s David Mills, "I mean, if black people kill black people every day, why not have a week and kill white people?" Clinton's opportunity presented itself. In a campaign appearance with Jesse Jackson, he criticized Sister Souljah. "Her comments before and after Los Angeles were filled with a kind of hatred that you do not honor," he told Jackson's supporters.[103] The remark upset Jackson (and Sister Souljah), but it appeared that Clinton was not beholden to his party's special-interest groups and that he shared the concerns of the white working class—Nixon's "silent majority." The columnist Clarence Page cited the debt Clinton owed to Souljah and declared the episode "[t]he most important moment in the 1992 presidential race...."[104]

Later that summer, President Bush—whose personal tastes ran to Broadway tunes and country music—denounced music that glorified violence against the police as "sick," and everyone knew that he was referring to "Cop Killer."[105] The effort proved ineffective. Clinton had already defused the issue with his criticism of Sister Souljah, and he emerged unscathed. Rap remained subversive, even dangerous, for politicians. Rappers would have to wait until Barack Obama's presidency until they were invited to the White House.

In the years following the election of 1992, the game in which musicians gleefully allow Democratic candidates to use their songs but grumpily protest when Republicans do so has continued monotonously. So Tom Petty objects to Michele Bachmann's coming on stage to his "American Girl" and to George W. Bush's use of "Don't Back Down." John Mellencamp, Van Halen, Dave Grohl, and Jackson Browne complain about John McCain's use of their songs. The band Heart throws a tantrum over Sarah Palin's use of "Barracuda." Boston's Tom Scholz demands that Mike Huckabee stop playing "More Than a Feeling."[106] One anonymous internet wag quipped that Republicans "can only use country music or dead people's music...."[107]

In 2003, it looked like Republicans might even lose the safe harbor of country music. As President George W. Bush prepared the invasion of Iraq, Natalie Maines, a fellow Texan and a singer with the Dixie Chicks, told an audience in London that she was "ashamed the president of the United States is from Texas." The remark went over well across the Atlantic, but it shocked many Americans.

Of course no one would have been surprised by a pop star's criticism of a Republican president. But this was a *country* singer. Bush, country music's most prominent fan, had songs by George Jones, Kenny Chesney, and Alan Jackson on his iPod.[108] Many country fans rallied round the president, and a number of radio stations announced a boycott of the Dixie Chicks. Bush responded coolly, telling Tom Brokaw "the Dixie Chicks are free to speak their mind." At the same time, he noted, they have to bear responsibility for their actions: "They shouldn't have their feelings hurt just because some people don't want to buy their records when they speak out. You know, freedom is a two-way street." Finally, he took advantage of the opportunity to make the case for the war. In America, he said, "singers or Hollywood stars" can speak out.

In the years following the election of 1992, the game in which musicians gleefully allow Democratic candidates to use their songs but grumpily protest when Republicans do so has continued monotonously. So Tom Petty objects to Michele Bachmann's coming on stage to his "American Girl" and to George W. Bush's use of "Don't Back Down." John Mellencamp, Van Halen, Dave Grohl, and Jackson Browne complain about John McCain's use of their songs. The band Heart throws a tantrum over Sarah Palin's use of "Barracuda." Boston's Tom Scholz demands that Mike Huckabee stop playing "More Than a Feeling." One anonymous internet wag quipped that Republicans "can only use country music or dead people's music...."

"That's the great thing about America. It stands in stark contrast to Iraq, by the way."[109]

Bush probably came out on top in regards to the Dixie Chicks episode, but his troubles with pop stars weren't over. After Hurricane Katrina devastated New Orleans in 2005, the singer Kanye West appeared in the televised "Concert for Hurricane Relief." West closed a meandering speech accusing George Bush of being a racist who "doesn't care about black people."[110] Bush chose not to respond until he had left office. While promoting his memoir *Decision Points*, he called West's attack "one of the most disgusting moments in my presidency."[111] Despite Bush's anger, few consequences affected West, either critically or commercially. He remains a major star, with eighteen Grammy awards under his belt.

The lesson that entertainers have learned is that they can criticize a Republican president with impunity. Republicans, in turn, have learned that criticism from entertainers is part of the job. The best they can do is to silently uphold the dignity of the office. The pop music business reserves its support almost exclusively for Democrats.

The changes in American popular music since the founding have been dramatic. Popular music is fraught with peril for presidents seeking to take advantage of it. The peril does not deter presidents because the potential advantages it can confer on politicians are enormous. Songs can energize a campaign, and association with particular songs or artists can confer on a president that elusive quality of hipness. Democrats have a huge advantage in this quest, but a certain vulnerability arises as well. Republicans can and do cope without hipness or cool precisely because so few people expect it of them. And pop stars' attacks on Republicans no longer make headlines. They're expected. At the same time, for those presidents—typically Democrats—who can attain hipness, popular music presents a powerful tool for connecting with today's voters. Because of this, and despite the dangers of too close a link with controversial or profane artists, presidents will continue to use music to capture the cool or the hip aspect of voters' mythic presidential ideal.

CHAPTER 8

ALL THE PRESIDENTS' MOVIES: FINDING ARCHETYPAL LEADERSHIP IN FILM

America's love affair with the movies began in Pittsburgh in 1905 when Harry Davis opened the first free-standing theater devoted to projecting moving pictures. He called it a "nickelodeon," a portmanteau word derived from the price of admittance and a Greek word for theater. Although Americans began flocking to these new theaters, it took a while for movie theaters to achieve respectability. "People simply didn't want to crowd into a dark room to look at a flickering light," explains the historian David Nasaw, "and it took nearly twenty years for Americans and motion pictures to embrace each other."[1]

It turned out that being crowded into a dark room with strangers of both sexes was frightening to a lot of people. Theater owners eventually solved the problem by combining the welcoming aspect of a bar with the security of an expensive hotel. A grand exterior, a narrow opening, and uniformed guards—ushers—who ensured the audience's decorous behavior made the cinema seem inviting and safe. To allay the public's concerns about unsanitary conditions, theaters installed early versions of air-conditioning systems, which expelled any befouled air and replaced it with fresh air. A final obstacle to social acceptance was the reluctance of the upper classes to mingle with the riffraff, for which the answer was the by-invitation-only opening night gala.[2]

Even so, it took a while for Hollywood fully to capture the American imagination. The movies' struggle for respectability shows one reason why D. W. Griffith was so eager for President Wilson's endorsement of *Birth of a Nation*. The screening of a motion picture in the White House was a milestone for the nascent film industry. Wilson came to the industry's aid again in April 1918, when he assured the public that it was not inappropriate to go to the movies while the nation was at war.[3]

Because of the movies' winding road to propriety, none of the presidents before World War II grew up on films as the postwar presidents did, but they did enjoy them as adults. Warren Harding hosted screenings after dinner in the White House. Calvin Coolidge once kept a welcoming delegation waiting at Union Station while he finished a film on his train.[4] But the film industry was still in its infancy—talkies did not appear until 1927—and Hollywood's development into a cultural behemoth was still years in the future.

> [JFK] preferred living like James Bond to watching him on the screen. Accordingly, he was rumored to have had flings with such A-listers as Marilyn Monroe, Zsa Zsa Gabor, Marlene Dietrich, Jayne Mansfield, Gene Tierney, Kim Novak, Audrey Hepburn, Sophia Loren, and Angie Dickinson.

An astute observer, nevertheless, could discern how enormously influential this new medium could become. Walter Prichard Eaton, for instance, writing in the *Atlantic Monthly* in 1915, identified the novel power of film: "The smallest town … sees the same motion-picture players as the largest [and] John Bunny and Mary Pickford 'star' in a hundred towns at once." He continued, "At the present time it is almost safe to say that there is not a town of over five thousand inhabitants in the country without its motion-picture theatre…." Eaton estimated that 10 percent of the population—more than ten million Americans—was attending the movies.[5]

A politician with vision would appreciate the political implications of what Eaton was describing. It should come as no surprise that the first president to grasp the political power of the movies was Franklin Roosevelt. Film, he understood, had a unifying effect on the nation. The shared experience of a movie transcended differences of race, age, geography, and class. The consummate politician, Roosevelt would not overlook such an opportunity. Before others were paying attention, Roosevelt had set his sights on Hollywood. His goal was to reflect the glamour of the stars and to enlist them as supporters and campaigners. It worked—he proved better at recruiting and using celebrities than any of his predecessors, and most of his successors.[6]

At the same time that Roosevelt was courting Hollywood's political favor, the filmmakers themselves began to appreciate the power they held in their hands. In 1934, Upton Sinclair, who had run unsuccessfully for office in California as a Socialist, secured the Democratic nomination for governor, to the dismay of Louis B. Mayer and his fellow studio executives. In Hollywood's first foray into politics, Mayer and the film industry raised the money and produced the propaganda to stop Sinclair.[7]

The implications of Hollywood's success in stopping Sinclair were not lost on Richard Sheridan Ames. Writing in *Harper's*, he speculated on the potential of movie studios to shape public opinion in a way no other cultural or political organ could: "[W]hat if Hollywood decides to convert the nation to any of its principles? It has the money, the studios, the talent. It controls the major theaters and can command the best advertising media." Although the anti-Sinclair campaign was a conservative effort, the political tone of Hollywood changed in the decades that followed. The validity of Ames's observations about Hollywood's unique power, however, did not depend on the ideological slant of a particular message. "No amount of books, periodicals, or pamphlets can undo the graphic fidelity of the camera and the effect it produces on the human eye." This unrivaled psychological influence, Ames warned, had important implications for American democracy: "[W]hile our democracy still prides itself on the constitutional guarantee of the right of free speech, no group or faction can talk back to the motion picture."[8] The studios knew that Ames was right, but they saw their political power as an opportunity, not a problem. Hollywood became a mighty engine of propaganda during World War II, and although the messages, as a general trend, have become more subtle over the years, that engine has rarely been left idling.

Roosevelt's outreach to Hollywood, both to the stars themselves and to the increasingly powerful studio heads, proved fantastically fruitful. He dominated the silver screen in ways previously unseen and unable to be replicated since. FDR was depicted in more films—fiction and nonfiction—than any other president.[9] Even his dog Fala took part in the action, starring in a 1943 MGM short that chronicled the first canine's day in loving detail.[10]

An indication of Roosevelt's sway in Hollywood is the fact that during his lifetime he was never portrayed as crippled. In fact, the first portrayal of Roosevelt *as president* in a wheelchair was in 2001, in Michael Bay's *Pearl Harbor.*[11] (*Sunrise at Campobello*, made in 1960, dealt with Roosevelt's struggle to recover from polio before he was president.)

Hollywood's tender treatment of Roosevelt made it easy for him to reciprocate. In 1938, Eleanor Roosevelt affirmed in *Photoplay* that "we Roosevelts are Movie Fans" and mentioned some of the president's favorites, including *Snow White and the Seven Dwarfs* and *I'm No Angel*, the 1933 comedy with Cary Grant and Mae West.[12] Roosevelt included a White House movie theater as part of the East Wing building project in 1942.[13] This theater became a convenient place for presidents to see movies by themselves but also an establishment where one could win political points by inviting others to join them. The theater has also been a boon to historians, as one of the White House projectionists, Paul Fischer, kept careful logs of every movie shown from 1953 to 1986. But the very existence of this theater is testimony to Hollywood's reach. Roosevelt's cinema gave the studios a direct channel to the president.

That channel was less effective when Harry Truman took over after Roosevelt's death. Truman rarely used the White House theater, preferring to entertain himself with a book or music. At "the Little White House" in Key West, he showed films to his guests, but he usually didn't watch them himself.[14] Despite the infrequency of his movie watching, he did have a favorite—the Henry Fonda Western *My Darling Clementine*.[15]

Movies returned to the White House with Eisenhower, who in his youth had found the cinema a convenient place to court. Movies were one of his three favorite recreations, along with playing bridge and, of course, golf. He watched more than two hundred films in the White House screening room, with a decided emphasis on Westerns. The White House Usher J. B. West recalled, "Providing Mr. Eisenhower with enough Westerns became a major task for the Usher's office because he'd seen them all, perhaps three or four times."[16] When Eisenhower was in Walter Reed Army Hospital in 1968, President Johnson, sent him a movie screen, projector, projectionist, and access to the White House library of films.[17]

One of Ike's favorite Westerns, the Gary Cooper classic *High Noon*, boasted a single lawman battling a murderous, revenge-seeking gang while the townspeople cower behind closed doors and shuttered windows. The parallels between Gary Cooper's role and that of the man in the Oval Office have not been lost on the presidents. Several of them, of both parties, have expressed an affinity for *High Noon*, including Ronald Reagan, George W. Bush, and Bill Clinton, who watched it some twenty times.[18]

Eisenhower's grandson David attributed Ike's love of Westerns to his upbringing. "Granddad loved westerns," he wrote, "because he spent his childhood in Abilene, Kansas, and was raised in the lore of the 'old west.'" The future president was born only twenty years after Wild Bill Hickok roamed the streets of Abilene. "The 'big skies' setting of westerns also appealed to him, as did the theme of 'man against nature' prevalent in many western novels."[19]

Eisenhower's own explanation was less romantic. He told Nikita Khrushchev, of all people, that Westerns were just good entertainment. In a September 1960 meeting with the Soviet boss at Camp David, the president admitted, "I know [Westerns] don't have any substance to them and don't require any thought to appreciate, but they always have a lot of fancy tricks. Also, I like horses."[20] Fortunately for Ike, Khrushchev had been trained to watch Westerns. He told Eisenhower that "when

Stalin was still alive we used to watch Westerns all the time. When the movie ended, Stalin always denounced it for its ideological content. But the very next day we'd be back in the theater watching another Western." Khrushchev confessed, "I too have a weakness for this sort of film." "Good," Eisenhower replied, "we'll have some Westerns and other movies."[21]

The Soviet visitors enjoyed Eisenhower's Westerns more than some of his closer allies. After a screening of *The Big Country* at Eisenhower's farm at Gettysburg, it was clear that British Prime Minister Harold Macmillan had found it tedious. The film—"The Great Country or some such name"—had "lasted three hours" and "was inconceivably banal." Eisenhower watched it four times.[22]

> Movies were tedious to Johnson, with one exception—movies about himself. The one he particularly enjoyed was a 1966 documentary by the U.S. Information Agency, narrated by Gregory Peck, *A President's Country*, which was screened eighteen times in the White House, including twelve times in LBJ's presence.

Ike's love of Westerns, like his other hobbies, contributed to his image as a simple man of simple tastes, "often mocked by liberals for his love of golf, poker, bridge, and western novels," as Kim Phillips-Fein puts it.[23] That was the dominant view before Stephen Ambrose and Fred Greenstein launched a revisionist movement among historians. The revisionists argued convincingly that Eisenhower put on a show of simplicity but was effective behind the scenes, keeping the peace during a dangerous stage of the Cold War. The Westerns would have been part of that strategy. Furthermore, Westerns were an especially appropriate genre for the time. As J. Hoberman writes, "Eisenhower's era represented the western's high noon, an era in which the U.S. appointed itself global sheriff and the gunslinger supplanted the cowboy as the archetypal western hero...."[24]

Movies could bring out a side of Eisenhower that was at odds with his genial public persona. After ten minutes of *This Angry Age*, the French director René Clément's exploration of family and repression in post-colonial Vietnam, Eisenhower told his wife, who had selected the film, "You can't choose a movie worth a damn," and stormed out. He also refused to see movies featuring Robert Mitchum. The projectionist Fischer recalled, "When he found out that Mitchum was involved with marijuana, he wouldn't have nothin' to do with any films Mitchum was in." The tough-guy actor was one of the biggest stars of the era, so it was difficult to avoid his films. Fischer tried to sneak some of them past the president, but Ike would leave as soon as he saw Mitchum's name or face on the screen.[25] Nevertheless, the number of movies that Eisenhower watched during his eight years in the White House suggests that he was usually content with whatever Mamie or Fischer selected for him.

The Changing Movie Scene

Like music, motion pictures underwent fundamental change in the 1960s, but the effects of modern technology on the two art forms were different. Broadcast technologies such as radio and later television made popular music more pervasive, despite the development of more controversial content. But those same technologies produced alternatives to the cinema at a time when increasingly controversial content led many Americans to search for different cultural options.

In *Hollywood vs. America*, Michael Medved contrasts the winner of Academy Award for Best Picture of 1965, the family-friendly *The Sound of Music*, with the 1969 winner, the decidedly family-unfriendly—and X-rated—*Midnight Cowboy*, noting that the latter film brought in only one-third the revenue of the former film. Medved presents this discrepancy as an early piece of evidence for his thesis of Hollywood's break with America. After analyzing the box office returns, Medved concludes, "Between 1965 and 1969 the values of the entertainment industry changed, and audiences fled from the theaters in horror and disgust." And the public's revulsion, he maintains, was permanent: "Those disillusioned moviegoers have stayed away to this day—and they will remain estranged until the industry returns to a more positive and populist approach to entertaining its audience."[26]

These changes took place during the Kennedy and Johnson years, but the White House was on the sidelines. The presidency is often one of the last institutions to embrace the cultural shifts overtaking the country. Lyndon Johnson, nevertheless, might have seen them coming. After he left office, he complained about the new style emerging in American cinema. He saw Dustin Hoffman in *The Graduate* with a young Doris Kearns (not yet Goodwin) and asked her, "How in the hell can that creepy guy be a hero to you?"[27]

As different as they were, Kennedy and Johnson shared one important trait—they both lacked the patience for frequent movie-going. Kennedy was more interested in films than Johnson was and certainly tried to appear culturally *au courant*. He seemed to like movie stars—and especially star*lets*—more than the movies themselves. He preferred living like James Bond to watching him on the screen. Accordingly, he was rumored to have had flings with such A-listers as Marilyn Monroe, Zsa Zsa Gabor, Marlene Dietrich, Jayne Mansfield, Gene Tierney, Kim Novak, Audrey Hepburn, Sophia Loren, and Angie Dickinson.[28]

Kennedy preferred dealing with real people rather than images on screen. His national security advisor, McGeorge Bundy, recalled that he "never heard [JFK] talk with real interest on any topic except personalities and politics."[29] Kennedy's college-age mistress Mimi Alford recalled that he would spend nearly every waking moment interacting with other people, averaging over fifty phone calls a day, in addition to holding constant face-to-face conversations. "He was incapable of sitting still," she said, "or of not using a moment of free time to scavenge for information or a good laugh, some form of human connection."[30] Arthur Schlesinger added that "Kennedy was not a great movie fan and tended, unless the film was unusually gripping, to walk out after the first twenty or thirty minutes."[31] In times of stress, however, he could sit through a film. He is known to have watched *Roman Holiday*, starring his "favourite actress of the time, Audrey Hepburn," during the Cuban Missile Crisis.[32] The face-off with the Russians kept the president in meetings until past eleven at night, recalls Alford, who was staying in the White House at the time. "[I] decided to go to bed, [so] I was asleep by the time he finally came upstairs...." With Alford asleep, Kennedy "unwound that night by watching *Roman Holiday* with Dave [Powers]," his long-time friend and aide. "Although our get-togethers were always quite sexually charged," she writes wistfully, "it wasn't to be on this occasion."[33]

Roman Holiday was one of only forty-eight pictures JFK watched in the White House. In keeping with his reputation for youthful vigor, he liked what were known as "red-blooded" movies, including *Spartacus, From Here to Eternity, Bridge on the River Kwai*, and Alfred Hitchcock films.[34] The White House screening of August 16, 1961, however, was an exception to the usual fare. The projectionist Paul Fischer noted that JFK watched Cliff Richard and Laurence Harvey in *Expresso Bongo*, a now-forgotten film about a music business hustler who discovers a budding young star. Of Fischer's over five thousand White House screenings, this is the only one for which Fischer did not note who attended the film with the president. The log book merely indicates "1 guest." While we will never know who the guest was on that night, the mystery does lead to some arch speculation.[35]

Like Kennedy, Lyndon B. Johnson was too impatient for movies. He was too focused on work to be bothered with movies or any other outside interests. Eisenhower even speculated that Johnson "lacked the inner pressure gauge that told him when to relax. He had no hobbies or interests outside of politics."[36] John Connally recalled that Johnson once asked him, "Who is Lana Turner?"[37]

Movies were tedious to Johnson,[38] with one exception—movies about himself. The one he particularly enjoyed was a 1966 documentary by the U.S. Information Agency, narrated by Gregory Peck, *A President's Country*. LBJ and Peck became friendly during the filming, and the president even talked about offering Peck an appointment as ambassador to Ireland in a second full term (which the Vietnam War ensured would never take place).[39] *A President's Country* was screened eighteen times in the White House,

> The second-to-last movie Nixon watched as president was *It's a Wonderful Life*. It's easy to understand the appeal of the Christmas classic about the supernatural redemption of a man facing the possibility of prison.

including twelve times in LBJ's presence.[40] American citizens did not get to see it, however. The film was sent to ninety-eight U.S. embassies but was not released domestically.[41]

When Johnson watched a movie on another subject, "he went right to sleep," observed his aide Jack Valenti, the future head of the Motion Picture Association of America.[42] Movies acted as "a great sleeping pill" for Johnson, said his daughter Lynda Robb. Following his cinematic naps, Valenti remembered, Johnson "would wake up refreshed and want to go back to his office and gather up his assistants and go back to work."[43]

It was Valenti who, four decades before Netflix, arranged for the president to be able to get any film he wanted delivered to the White House. Johnson may not have taken advantage of this great presidential perk, but a number of later presidents did, especially Richard Nixon, Jimmy Carter, and Bill Clinton.

The Rise of the Movie-Loving President

Even though Nixon came from a poor family, and his occasional childhood trips to the movies were, in his words, "a luxury," the movies were a very real part of his upbringing in Southern California. Born in 1913, Nixon grew up with the motion picture. For the members of his generation, movies were not surprising or new. They simply formed part of the landscape.[44]

As a teenager, the young Quaker was moved by *All Quiet on the Western Front* (1930). In law school at Duke, he frequently saw five-cent movies at the student union, including *The Private Life of Henry VIII* (1933), *The 39 Steps* (1935), and *Mutiny on the Bounty* (1935). As a young lawyer courting his future wife, Pat Ryan—who moonlighted as a Hollywood extra—Nixon made regular trips to the theater. In fact, he and Pat heard about Pearl Harbor after leaving a Sunday matinee together. And then, during the war, Nixon saw films while serving in the South Pacific.[45]

Nixon remained a frequent movie watcher in the White House, at Camp David, at San Clemente, and at his Key Biscayne retreat. His favorite companion for a film was his Cuban-American millionaire pal Bebe Rebozo. Nixon watched 153 different movies with Rebozo, including the con caper *The Skin Game* on the night of the Watergate burglary. His communications aide Herb Klein explained that hanging out with his buddy had a soothing effect on Nixon—"It was a time to relax when he was with Bebe and Bebe never tried to bring out discussions of issues."[46] He should have been paying more attention. The second-to-last movie Nixon watched as president was *It's a Wonderful Life*. It's easy to understand the appeal of the Christmas classic about the supernatural redemption of a man facing the possibility of prison.[47]

Nixon's favorite movie, as almost everyone knows, was *Patton*, starring George C. Scott. He watched it five times and urged members of his staff to watch it as well. The portrayal of a brutal and unlovable yet ultimately successful general appealed to Nixon on both a personal and a patriotic level. He enjoyed Patton's success as an American, but he also enjoyed seeing Patton triumph over his detractors.[48]

Nixon watched *Patton* five days before the U.S. invasion of Cambodia, and some have suggested that the film was responsible for the invasion. It appears, however, that Nixon watched the film more for comfort than for inspiration.[49] Still, the story that Nixon invaded Cambodia because he watched *Patton* took on a life of its own, and Nixon felt compelled to deny it in his 1977 interview with David Frost, an interview which itself became the subject of a movie, *Frost/Nixon*. Watching Patton had "no effect on my decisions," Nixon assured the real-life Frost.[50]

John Wayne was Nixon's favorite actor, and his favorite director was John Ford. The two collaborated on more than twenty films. Nixon saw twenty-five John Wayne films and claimed, perhaps implausibly, "I think I've seen virtually all of the one-hundred-forty movies" made by Ford. This reverence for Wayne no longer prevails in the White House. In an interview with the *Chicago Reader* in 1995, Barack Obama observed, "In America, we have this strong bias toward individual action. You know, we idolize the John Wayne hero who comes in to correct things with both guns blazing. But individual actions, individual dreams, are not sufficient. We must unite in collective action, build collective institutions and organizations."[51]

Twenty John Ford movies were shown at the White House during Nixon's tenure, double the number shown for any other president. In a hand-written note to Ford, Nixon told the director that when John Wayne came to the White House, Nixon asked him "who was the best all time Director?" Wayne's response: "John Ford." Nixon wrote, "I agree!"[52] Nixon and Wayne may also have agreed about Fred Zinnemann's *High Noon*, a film that many saw as an allegory about the Hollywood blacklist. Nixon never actually expressed his opinion of *High Noon*—which is conspicuously absent from the list of films he watched in the White House—but Wayne did. He not only turned down the leading role, but he called the film the "most un-American thing I've ever seen in my whole life."[53]

—➤➤➤●◄◄◄—

Nixon watched *Patton* five days before the U.S. invasion of Cambodia, and some have suggested that the film was responsible for the invasion. It appears, though, that Nixon watched the film more for comfort than for inspiration. Still, the story that Nixon invaded Cambodia because he watched *Patton* took on a life of its own, and Nixon felt compelled to deny it in his 1977 interview with David Frost, an interview which itself became the subject of a movie, *Frost/Nixon*.

Nixon's movie selections indicated where he stood in the nation's culture war. His preference was for older movies rather than new releases. "So many of the movies coming out of Hollywood," Nixon explained in a 1973 letter to Jane Wyman, Ronald Reagan's former wife, "not to mention those that come out of Europe, are so inferior that we just don't enjoy them." The older movies reminded Nixon of simpler times, and he found the grimness and moral ambiguity of contemporary pictures discomfiting.[54] Many Americans shared his view, but Hollywood was heading in a different direction. His "whole family has always loved theatre, movies, and music," Nixon told Wyman, and their "favorite relaxation after dinner at Camp David or in Florida or in California was to watch a movie." In 1972, he even joked to a group of actors that keeping hold of the White House screening room was one reason for seeking a second term. But Nixon's view of Hollywood, like that of many of his countrymen, was decidedly mixed.[55]

The tensions between Hollywood and Richard Nixon were personal. In his 1950 Senate race against the one-time actress Helen Gahagan Douglas, Nixon emphasized Douglas's Hollywood ties as well as her leftism.[56] In a tough campaign, Nixon revived an epithet coined by an earlier opponent of Douglas, "The Pink Lady," and she bestowed on him the nickname he could never shake, "Tricky Dick." Nixon won, but the race earned him the undying enmity of the liberal Hollywood establishment, a sentiment he reciprocated, even as he continued to enjoy many Hollywood products.

Jimmy Carter had no such ambiguity about Hollywood. Our most frequent movie-watching president, he watched approximately 480 movies in a single term. His love of movies began "as a farm boy," as he himself put it. Movies "gave me a vision of the outside world," he recalled, including "the first time I saw the White House."[57] His first date with Rosalynn Smith was to a movie, after which he told his mother that he intended to marry her.[58]

In the four busy years leading up to his presidency, Carter did not see many movies. As president, though, he was determined to catch up on what he had missed while campaigning. Carter marveled to communications advisor Gerald Rafshoon about this great perk of the presidency, saying, "Do you know I can get any movie I want?" He then asked Rafshoon to make a list of the movies he most needed to see. Rafshoon eagerly complied, and Carter's 480-film presidency began, starting two days after the inauguration with the film that probably did more than any other to make him president: *All the President's Men*.[59]

The 1976 release of *All the President's Men* was a boon to Carter's presidential effort. By fostering the image of a corrupt Nixon lying to the American public, the film helped contrast Carter—whose signature pledge was "I'll never lie to you"—with Ford, who had succeeded Nixon and pardoned him. Ford needed to put Watergate behind him in order to win, while highlighting the scandal served Carter's interests. *All the President's Men* was a box office hit, and Carter built an early lead during and shortly after the period of the film's appearance. The race tightened and in the end was quite close, but Carter's early lead held, built in large part by national disgust with Watergate.[60]

Carter's White House movie list signals an important historical shift. For the first time, the president's cultural tastes could no longer be described as "old school" but were aligned with those of the cultural elites.[61] Carter's willingness to take in a new kind of film was probably a sign of his acquiescence in what Hollywood was now producing. Early in his presidency, when he expressed a preference for "family-friendly" fare, Paul Fischer told him bluntly, "I got news for you. You're not going to see that many movies that way."[62]

Carter displayed none of the stubbornness that Eisenhower had shown when Fischer tried to sneak in a Robert Mitchum film. Indeed, he was the first—and as far as we can tell the only—president to watch an X-rated film in the White House. To be fair, it was *Midnight Cowboy*, whose X-rating from 1969 was more a reflection of its frank acknowledgment of homosexuality than of explicit images, and its rating was changed to "R" upon its release in 1971.[63]

The president's diary is replete with entries about the movies he watched, and they were by no means limited to Oscar-winners. On September 21, 1977, he notes, "Went to see *The Longest Yard*, a movie, so that we could forget about the day's events."[64] Those "events" were the tribulations of his friend and budget director Bert Lance, who had resigned as chairman of Calhoun First National Bank of Georgia that day in scandal. (He was later acquitted of all charges.)

Another bad day for the administration was May 5, 1979, during the energy crisis, when authorities arrested a drifter who was apparently plotting to kill the president during a visit to Los Angeles. The next day, after returning unharmed to Washington, Carter hosted a hundred people for a screening of Woody Allen's *Manhattan*, a film about a romantic relationship between a middle-aged man (Allen) and an attractive teenager (Mariel Hemingway). Carter was so taken with the film that he watched it again on May 23, demonstrating that whatever the crisis, the Carter attitude towards movies was that "the show must go on."[65]

For someone who devoted so much time to watching movies, Carter failed to understand what those films revealed about American culture and the American psyche. In the same month that he saw *Manhattan* twice, he was given a pre-release screening of *Apocalypse Now*, Francis Ford Coppola's violent and disjointed picture about the Vietnam War. Coppola had not yet decided how to end the film, and he wanted to test his proposed conclusion on the White House audience. The event did not prove successful. At the end of the film, Carter asked "What's wrong back there?" to which Coppola responded: "No, Mr. President. That is the ending." The next day Carter wrote a note to Rafshoon saying, "Jerry, re the movie last night, no comment."[66]

1979 saw the release of another important film about Vietnam, *The Deer Hunter*. Though it is often mentioned in the same breath as *Apocalypse Now*, the two films are quite different. *The Deer Hunter* focuses on the experience of prisoners of war and the difficulty of readjusting to life back home, while *Apocalypse Now* explores the confusion and the ambiguity of combat operations in Vietnam. Jimmy Carter saw *The Deer Hunter* and felt "deeply moved" by it. Ronald Reagan, on the other hand, praised the film as "a story of friendship among young men" that was "unashamedly patriotic."[67] Carter interpreted the film as a dark meditation on the ravages of the Vietnam War, while Reagan took it as a reassertion of American patriotism amid the gloom of the 1970s.

Liberals complained that Reagan misunderstood the film, but he wasn't alone in his interpretation. Writing in the conservative journal *Commentary*, Richard Grenier found *The Deer Hunter* "imbued with a kind of primary patriotism." The picture's

> Carter marveled to communications advisor Gerald Rafshoon about this great perk of the presidency, saying, "Do you know I can get any movie I want?" He then asked Rafshoon to make a list of the movies he most needed to see. Rafshoon eagerly complied, and Carter's 480-film presidency began, starting two days after the inauguration with the film that probably did more than any other to make him president: *All the President's Men.*

131

success demonstrated that "the ardent patriotism it expresses is not so dead a com-modity in today's America as some might have thought."[68] It was this kind of patrio-tism that Americans were seeking, and Reagan's interpretation—like Reagan himself—resonated with the American people. Carter saw movies as an escape, while Reagan understood their ability to shape the American psyche.[69] The contrast between the two men was revealing. Reagan saw that America is more than just a country; it's an *idea*. So he understood how images captivate and transform Americans, who are always dreaming and aspiring. Carter saw art as the depiction of a mechanistic world that needs technocrats to repair it.

Reagan's idealism meant that he was far less interested in the cutting-edge movies of his day than was Carter. The former actor understood the importance of culture in politics, and he liked films of a bygone era, when patriotic, hard-working Ameri-cans strove to make a better life for themselves. The films of the 1970s began to yield dark and morally ambiguous tendencies, calling into question the central aspects of the American character—and even the certainty that the good guys would prevail. When Reagan watched movies, and especially when he talked about movies, he had little interest in such ambiguity. His advice to Paul Fischer was "The golden oldies are the ones."[70] In 1969, a dozen years before his presidency, Reagan admitted to the *Los Angeles Times* that his tastes had not kept up with the motion picture industry: "Call me a square if you want to, but I think the business has degenerated."[71] The Reagans tended to watch films from the 1930 to 1950 timeframe, the time of Reagan's own movie career.[72]

Reagan did not completely ignore contemporary movies. He saw a fair number of them as president, including *Chariots of Fire*, *Gallipoli*, *Breaker Morant*, *The French Lieutenant's Woman*, *The Flamingo Kid*, *Places in the Heart*, *The Purple Rose of Cairo*, *Witness*, and *Continental Divide*. But his aide Mike Deaver's recommendation of the left-wing, homosexual-themed *Kiss of the Spider Woman* was a flop—the president and Mrs. Reagan walked out. The Reagans were not uncomfortable with homosexu-als; as products of Hollywood, they probably knew and were friendly with more homosexuals than any presidential couple up to that point. What likely made *Kiss of the Spider Woman* objectionable to them was its celebration of the sort of leftist revolutionaries that the Reagan administration continued to combat throughout Latin America.

For all the accusations that he conflated movies with reality, Ronald Reagan had a profound understanding of how the American people relate to movies. In his youth, motion pictures were a source of inspiration and pride in America. Reagan's presidency reflected that vision. And he also understood the unifying role of popular culture. Americans disagree about policies, but nearly everyone relates to the popular culture—an insight that contributed to Reagan's effective leadership.[73] He built on the optimism of movies, the idea that the underdog can triumph and that good will overcome evil. He then used those ideas in his political life and succeeded by constantly conveying those themes to the receptive American people.

But many recent movies reflected a different tone, which Reagan rejected. He was not alone. In the 1980s, there was a reaction to the gritty and morally clouded movies of the 1970s. Many of the blockbusters of the Reagan era, including *Rambo*, the films of Arnold Schwarzenegger, *Raiders of the Lost Ark*, and *Back to the Future*, reflected Reagan's vision. When Reagan referenced movies, it was usually the kind that he and the American people, if not the critics, preferred. After a plane hijacking, Reagan joked, "Boy, after seeing *Rambo* last night, I know what to do the next time this happens." Another time, facing a Congressional threat to raise taxes, he borrowed a line from *Dirty Harry*: "Go ahead—make my day." Reagan could pull this off better than anyone else. He quoted movies so often that it never seemed out of character. It was just Reagan being Reagan.[74]

The opportunity to get lost in a film is one of the movies' greatest appeals, and Reagan enjoyed getting lost in a film as much as anyone. In 1983, his chief of staff, James Baker, checked in with the president before an international economic summit at Williamsburg. Baker was dismayed to find the president's briefing book untouched. Reagan's excuse for not completing his homework was, "Well, Jim,

The Sound of Music was on last night." Fortunately, Reagan carried off his role that day without a hitch.[75]

The Sound of Music figured in another controversial episode during the Reagan administration. The president had promised the German chancellor, Helmut Kohl, to visit a military burial ground at Bitburg during a trip to Germany. It turned out that the cemetery contained the graves of forty-nine SS storm troopers, and a dispute arose over whether the president's visit was appropriate. A five-year-old girl in Little Rock, Arkansas, wrote to the president. "I have seen *The Sound of Music*. The Nazis don't look like nice people. Please don't go to their cemetery." The letter was signed Chelsea Clinton. It is unclear whether Reagan saw this letter, which was located in one of his daily mail packets. In any case, it was the kind of argument, spelled out in the language of popular culture, that would have appealed to him.[76]

As Chelsea's letter suggests, movies were an important part of the Clinton household, far more than they were in the home of his predecessor or successor: Bush "41," who liked tennis, golf, and schmoozing, was not nearly the movie fan Reagan had been. Bush "43" was even less interested in movies than his father was.[77]

—➤➤➤•●•◄◄◄—

Bush 43 notes in his memoir that he was a little unsure of what Blair, a "left-of-center Labour prime minister and a close friend of Bill Clinton's," might like. He avoided a replay of Eisenhower and Macmillan by settling on *Meet the Parents*, a comedy with Robert DeNiro and Ben Stiller. After this incident, he recalls, "Laura and I knew the Bushes and Blairs would get along."

Both Bushes, however, saw the political advantages of using movies to connect with people for political reasons. Bush 41 often invited guests to watch movies with him in the White House, a savvy political move.[78] As for 43, the political calculations began with his very first White House screening when he invited Senator Edward M. Kennedy to see *Thirteen Days*, a movie about the Cuban Missile Crisis, part of Bush's successful effort to secure Kennedy's backing for the "No Child Left Behind" education bill. He strengthened his relationship with Tony

Blair, the British prime minister and a key ally in the Iraq war, by watching a movie with him after dinner. Bush 43 notes in his memoir that he was a little unsure of what Blair, a "left-of-center Labour prime minister and a close friend of Bill Clinton's," might like. He avoided a replay of Eisenhower and Macmillan by settling on *Meet the Parents*, a comedy with Robert DeNiro and Ben Stiller. After this incident, he recalls, "Laura and I knew the Bushes and Blairs would get along."[79]

George W. Bush and Bill Clinton were born just a month apart in 1946, but the movies played a much bigger role in Clinton's youth than in Bush's. Growing up in Hot Springs, Clinton admits that he loved movies "almost to the point of compulsion." He told the film critic Roger Ebert, "I saw every movie that came my way when I was a child, and they fired my imagination—they inspired me."[80] In his autobiography, Clinton recalls that he "loved Elvis," both his music and his movies. "Elvis's first movie, *Love Me Tender*; was my favorite and remains so," Clinton writes, "though I also liked *Loving You*, *Jailhouse Rock*, *King Creole*, and *Blue Hawaii*." He wasn't so devoted to the King that he lost his critical distance, however—"After [*Blue Hawaii*], his movies got more saccharine and predictable." [81]

Young Clinton enjoyed epic biblical spectacles of the time, such as *Samson and Delilah*, *The Robe*, *Ben-Hur*, and *The Ten Commandments*, which he watched twice.[82] In the White House, he used the presidential prerogative to see as many movies he could, and took full advantage of his status as first fan. As president he saw movies so varied that they are hard to characterize, including *Midnight in the Garden of Good and Evil*, *Shine*, *Casablanca*, *Shakespeare in Love*, *Billy Elliott*, *Space Jam*, *The Apostle*, *Boyz in the Hood*, *Schindler's List*, *Shadowlands*, *Mrs. Doubtfire*, *American Beauty*, *Three Kings*, and *Sling Blade*. Clinton had seen almost twenty movies at the end of three months as president, while Bush 43 saw only three movies in his first two months on the job. As Clinton's selections suggest, he loved all movies, good and bad, new and old, high-brow and low. As his friend and Hollywood producer Harry Thomason observed, "The president has never seen a film he didn't absolutely love."[83]

One of those movies caused some awkwardness during the Monica Lewinsky scandal, in which Clinton was caught having an inappropriate sexual relationship with a young intern. During the week in which the affair became public, Clinton hosted a screening for *The Apostle*, in which Robert Duvall played an adulterous and charismatic Southern preacher, a profile that some saw as uncomfortably close to Clinton's. It proved an excruciatingly uncomfortable evening for the guests, made worse by the late entrance of the first couple. Upon their arrival, the president and Mrs. Clinton overheard a female guest saying, "I would—wouldn't you?"[84]

Clinton combined the movie habits of other recent presidents. Like Carter, he loved to watch; like the Bushes, he used the White House theater as a political tool; and like Reagan, he understood the importance of popular culture in appealing to the American public. Clinton fit in perfectly as one of the baby boomers, but he also served as a leader for that generation. Speaking the language of the movies had become the twentieth-century way of speaking to the common man, and it was a language Clinton mastered.[85]

> Clinton's success stemmed from his serious engagement with popular culture, yet he managed to avoid being tarnished by Hollywood's excesses. He understood that movies had an escapist quality but that they also allowed America to present an idealized version of itself to the world. Presidents, who must present an idealized version of themselves, have succeeded when utilizing movies to convey their best characteristics to the voting public.

His keen understanding of the movie *Zeitgeist* helped Clinton win two terms as president. He appeared more in touch with the needs of ordinary Americans than George H. W. Bush and Bob Dole, his 1992 and 1996 Republican opponents. Both of these candidates, who were old enough to have served in World War II, pre-dated the pop culture that Clinton and his fellow baby boomers had absorbed. Clinton devoured movies, invited Hollywood stars to screenings at the White House, and discussed films with anyone and everyone. He even appeared on TV with Roger Ebert to discuss his love of movies, prompting critic Stephanie Zacharek to observe that Clinton's movie watching was so wide ranging that he obviously "isn't a guy who limits himself to the new releases rack at Blockbuster."[86] When he left the White House, he recalled, somewhat wistfully, that "[T]he best perk of the presidency is not Air Force One or Camp David or anything else. It's the wonderful movie theater I get here, because people send me these movies all the time."[87]

Clinton's success stemmed from his serious engagement with popular culture, yet he managed to avoid being tarnished by Hollywood's excesses. He understood that movies had an escapist quality but that they also allowed America to present an idealized version of itself to the world. Presidents, who must present an idealized version of themselves, have succeeded when utilizing movies to convey their best characteristics to the voting public.

Watching films in the White House to stay up to date or to reward political allies is commendable, but there's a lot more to political power in the movies than only that. The most astute presidents of the cinematic era, such as Clinton and Reagan, have understood that movies tell stories about themselves and about the country that can reach voters with no interest in political speeches but who hold great interest in what is taking place on the silver screen. More than any other medium, the movies help presidents capture the American imagination.

CHAPTER 9

THE "VAST WASTELAND": PRESIDENTS AND TELEVISION

No means of communication rivals television in its influence on American politics, especially on the presidency. Radio, however, first brought the president into daily contact with the American people, especially in the skilled hands of Franklin Roosevelt. But television does so more powerfully and with more immediacy. It gives the president entrée into America's homes, making him a constant visual presence, as familiar as a relative.

Television shapes how presidents view the world and how the world views them. Since Eisenhower's tenure in office, television has made the president the protagonist in an ongoing social and political drama. Most of us experience television as passive viewers, but for the president, television is very much an active, two-way medium. We can therefore learn as much about the presidents by looking at what they watched as by how they "came across" on TV. We need to consider the relationship of the presidency to television from three vantage points: what presidents have watched on television; how presidents have been portrayed on television, especially in entertainment programming, as opposed to the news; and how presidents project their own image in media.

Fifty years ago, the historian Daniel Boorstin recognized television's unprecedented power of immediacy. In his seminal work *The Image*, he observed that "today can become yesterday; and we can be everywhere while we are still here. In fact, it is easier to be there (say on the floor of the national political convention) when we are here (at home or in our hotel room before our television screen) than when we are there." This magic works in both directions. The president can be here (in our homes) when he is still there (at the White House or wherever he is traveling). Presidents are now a constant presence in our lives in a way they never were before the age of television.[1] They have learned, as a consequence, "to be television stars," observed the historian Roger Butterfield in 1964. "Presidents know, better than most people, that the camera is no longer merely a witness of what goes on at the White House. It has become a major factor in deciding who lives there."[2]

While presidents since the mid-twentieth century have been trying to shape their public image through television, they have had to compete with a host of journalists and entertainers who also try to shape that image. In the ensuing free-for-all, television became a highly democratic medium, plucking individuals from obscurity—like the unknown and inexperienced Illinois state senator Barack Obama—and turning them into celebrities overnight.

The prescient Boorstin saw it coming: "[I]t is possible, by bringing their voices and images daily into our living rooms, to make celebrities more quickly than ever before." At the same time, he wrote, TV-made celebrities "die more quickly than ever." For this reason, Boorstin pointed out, "President Franklin Delano Roosevelt was careful to space out his fireside chats so the citizenry would not tire of him."[3] Ronald Reagan also understood television's power to destroy the celebrities it has made. Following his governorship, he was offered the opportunity to deliver twice-weekly political commentary on the CBS Evening News. His communications advisor, Michael Deaver, was surprised when Reagan opted instead for a daily five-minute nationally syndicated radio spot.[4] "I don't think people will get tired of me on radio," Reagan explained.[5]

The power and prevalence of television rose nearly as quickly as it anointed new celebrities. "Television conquered America in less than a generation, leaving the nation more bewildered than it dared admit," observed Boorstin. Presidents and their

Attending plays was one of
George Washington's favorite
pastimes. In spite of Congressional disapproval, he had
Addison's *Cato* performed
for his troops at Valley Forge.
His library of nine hundred
volumes was quite large for the
time and included an impressive collection of military and
agricultural works.
(Photo: Library of Congress)

Thomas Jefferson, who professed,
"I cannot live without books," was
among the best-read men on the
American continent. His personal
collection became the foundation
of the Library of Congress.
(Photo: Library of Congress)

The Adams dynasty was distinguished for its literary as well as political accomplishments. The literate and cosmopolitan John Quincy Adams was swept from power in Andrew Jackson's democratic whirlwind of 1828, but as John F. Kennedy appreciated, the ideal of the intellectual president has retained its appeal.

(Photo: Library of Congress)

Lincoln's youthful reading included the Bible, Weems's *Life of Washington*, Aesop's Fables, *Robinson Crusoe*, and *Pilgrim's Progress*. "These books he did read, and read again, and pondered," wrote Lord Charnwood, "not with any dreamy or purely intellectual interest, but like one who desires the weapon of learning for practical ends, and desires also to have patterns of what life should be." *(Photo: Library of Congress)*

Stereoscopic view of the Walnut Street Theatre in Philadelphia (opened 1809), the oldest theater in the United States. Jefferson and Lafayette attended *The Rivals* here in 1811. Every president has attended a theatrical production at least once in his lifetime.

(Photo: Mirima and Ira D. Wallach Division of Art)

In serious financial straits and dying of throat cancer, Ulysses S. Grant began writing his memoirs—something no president had done before—with the help of Mark Twain. With heroic effort, Grant finished the work four days before his death. *The Personal Memoirs of U. S. Grant* became a bestseller.

(Photo: Library of Congress)

Rutherford B. Hayes, shown here with his wife, Lucy, installed the first telephone in the White House—provided by Alexander Graham Bell himself.

(Photo: Library of Congress)

"Books are almost as individual as friends," Theodore Roosevelt wrote. He caught the reading "disease," as he called it, early in his sickly childhood.

(Photo: Library of Congress)

Limiting his radio appearances for maximum effect, Franklin Roosevelt delivered only two or three of his famous "fireside chats" a year. "I am inclined to think," he said, "that in England, Churchill, for a while, talked too much, and I don't want to do that."
(Photo: Franklin D. Roosevelt Library)

Ike and Mamie Eisenhower watch the 1952 Republican Convention, a sign of the growing role of television in politics. While twenty-nine million people watched his inauguration the following January, forty-four million tuned in the previous evening for the birth of Little Ricky on *I Love Lucy*.
(Photo: Library of Congress)

During the 1968 campaign, Roger Ailes, the future founder of Fox News, convinced Richard Nixon that "television is not a gimmick." Nixon's famous cameo appearance on *Laugh-In* that September—where he uttered the show's catch phrase "Sock it to me"—was an attempt to promote the relaxed "New Nixon." As the sign at this rally suggests, it worked for a while.

(Photo: Richard Nixon Library)

In one of the strangest encounters between a president and an entertainer, Richard Nixon received Elvis Presley at the White House on December 21, 1970. The King had written to the president offering his services as a "Federal Agent at Large" for the Bureau of Narcotics and Dangerous Drugs.

(Photo: White House Photography)

"No one did more to solidify [President] Ford's unfortunate, and perhaps unfair, standing as the nation's First Klutz than [*Saturday Night Live*'s Chevy] Chase," wrote Mark Leibovich in the *New York Times*. Ford met with Chase at the White House Correspondents' Dinner, where he told him, "Mr. Chevy Chase, you're a very, very funny suburb." *(Photo: Ford Library)*

The 480 movies that Jimmy Carter watched in the White House marked an important cultural shift. The president's tastes could no longer be described as "old school" but were aligned with those of the cultural elites. Carter posed with one of them, Andy Warhol, on June 14, 1977.

(Photo: National Archives)

When Ronald Reagan got his show business start in radio, his model was his political hero Franklin Roosevelt. Though his politics changed, Reagan never lost his respect for FDR as a leader and communicator.

(Photo: Ronald Reagan Library)

It is hard to overstate the extent to which Ronald Reagan was shaped by the movies. As his film career was waning, though, he became the host of the weekly *General Electric Theater* on CBS television, a gig that for eight years took him all over the country and set the stage for his political career.

(Photo: Ronald Reagan Library)

George H. W. Bush jams with his political aide Lee Atwater at an inaugural party on January 21, 1989. The Bush campaign had tried to adopt Bobby McFerrin's infectious but insipid hit "Don't Worry Be Happy" as a theme song, but once again a Republican attempt to appropriate pop music backfired. McFerrin loudly objected, and the campaign dropped the song.

(Photo: White House Photography)

The White House movie
theater became a political
tool in the twentieth century,
and the projectionist Paul
Fischer's logs became a valuable source for presidential
historians. President Obama
and friends watched the
2009 Super Bowl (including
a 3-D commercial) in the
theater.

(Photo: White House Photography)

If you're running for
president, it's good to be
loved by Hollywood—a
matchless source of money
and glamour. The actor
George Clooney—"Obama's
biggest bankroller"—raised
millions for Hollywood's
favored candidate.

(Photo: White House Photography)

staffs have had to adjust and improvise on the fly. TV has redefined the strengths and weaknesses of character and personality for pursuing a political career.[6]

Television transformed the national memory by elevating instantaneous reaction at the expense of persuasion and reflection. "It was no wonder that like the printing press before it," Boorstin writes, "television met a cool reception from intellectuals and academics and the other custodians of traditional avenues of experience."[7] Presidents who watched entertainment programs on TV, therefore, took care in how aggressively and frequently they engaged with the new cultural offerings. Anything the president watched was something that millions of other Americans had also seen and about which they had developed their own opinions. Even an off-hand comment about a TV show risked the disdainful tut-tutting of the smart set who disapproved of TV.

—➤➤➤•●•◀◀◀—

The term "idiot box" apparently dates back to the late 1950s. Versions of it, including "babble box" as well as "babble machine," appear in Robert Heinlein's 1961 sci-fi classic, *Stranger in a Strange Land.*[8]

It's a good thing that the plainspoken Harry Truman didn't have to contend with television as it eventually developed. Television was in its infancy during his epoch. The technology first appeared in the 1920s and 1930s, but the public had to wait for costs to come down and broadcast capabilities to spread.[9] The television, as it initially came to market, was the brainchild of the Russian-born scientist Vladimir Zworykin in 1931.[10] Even so, as late as 1939, only three thousand TV sets were sold in the United States.[11] In 1941, that number had increased to ten thousand, with six commercial stations nationwide. Half of the sets and the stations were located in New York.[12] In that same year, the National Broadcasting Company aired the first television commercial.[13]

World War II temporarily halted the production of television sets, but the numbers took off in the postwar period. In 1948 alone, the number of sets in the United States grew from 102,000 to about 200,000, and a million sets were manufactured by the end of that year.[14] Harry Truman, the first president to have a TV set in the

Over the next few years, TV sales exploded, as forty-one million new sets were manufactured and more than thirty-eight million sold. By 1956, 73 percent of American homes had a television, and 97 percent of homes were in areas capable of receiving TV programming.[18]

White House,[15] was one of the lucky Americans who got to watch the 1947 "Jackie Robinson" World Series on television.[16] The next summer, he watched from the White House as Senator Alben Barkley of Kentucky delivered a rousing speech to the Democratic National Convention. Barkley's speech led Truman to choose him over William O. Douglas as his running mate.[17] Television was already flexing its political muscles.

This penetration redefined the medium and the culture. No longer the novelty of Harry Truman's day, television now provided what Boorstin called a homogenized experience for the entire country and became the make-or-break medium in presidential politics. In fact, when Dwight Eisenhower was inaugurated in 1953, he noted with a mix of sarcasm and displeasure that the country appeared to be paying more attention to the birth of Little Ricky on *I Love Lucy* than to the inauguration of the leader of the free world.[19] That episode of *I Love Lucy* was the first great television "event."[20] Forty-four million viewers—72 percent of households with TV—tuned in, compared with the twenty-nine million who watched Ike's inauguration.[21] The new medium had truly captured the nation.

When Walter Winchell falsely accused Lucille Ball of being a communist, she and her husband-costar, Desi Arnaz, were understandably concerned about the effect on their careers. Desi appeared before the studio audience before the filming of a show and said that "Lucille is 100 per cent an American. She is as American as Barry Baruch and Ike Eisenhower." He also added that "last November we both voted for Ike Eisenhower." (Obviously, this was back in the days when a Hollywood star could admit to voting for a Republican.) Arnaz added that Lucy was his "favorite redhead," although, he joked, "That's the only thing red about Lucy—and even that is not legitimate."[22]

Eisenhower showed that he did not hold a grudge against Lucy for upstaging him. He and Mamie invited Desi and Lucy to entertain at the White House in a celebration of the president's birthday. They were even given a coveted seat next to the president and First Lady. For the actor and actress, the invitation demonstrated a welcome vote of confidence from the White House. Arnaz, relieved to attain the presidential lifeline at a trying time, exclaimed to the crowd, "God bless America!"[23] Winchell eventually retracted his accusation—live and on the air—in September of 1953, and Lucy and Desi left that bump in the road behind them.[24] Sixteen years after Ike's inauguration, Ball later recalled, "President Eisenhower was standing with us outside the El Dorado Country Club and he pointed to my son and said, 'Is that the young man who knocked me off the front pages?'" She was quick to point out that "it wasn't—people were always confusing poor Desi Jr. with the Little Ricky character."[25]

Ike and Mamie took to *I Love Lucy* just like the rest of the country. They watched that show and other network programming so regularly that "the new vogue for television dictated certain aspects of life in the Eisenhower White House," a rather startling revelation by the White House usher J. B. West. Eisenhower's fondness for

This penetration redefined the medium and the culture. No longer the novelty of Harry Truman's day, television now provided what Boorstin called a homogenized experience for the entire country and became the make-or-break medium in presidential politics. In fact, when Dwight Eisenhower was inaugurated in 1953, he noted with a mix of sarcasm and displeasure that the country appeared to be paying more attention to the birth of Little Ricky on *I Love Lucy* than to the inauguration of the leader of the free world. That episode of *I Love Lucy* was the first great television "event." Forty-four million viewers—72 percent of households with TV—tuned in, compared with the twenty-nine million who watched Ike's inauguration. The new medium had truly captured the nation.

Westerns extended to television, and the First Lady often found time for her favorites—afternoon soap operas. This quintessentially 1950s habit became an enduring part of their image. The first couple also watched shows together while they ate their dinner on TV tray tables. These included *Arthur Godfrey's Talent Scouts*, *The Fred Waring Show*, and *The Lawrence Welk Show*.[26]

Although Eisenhower clearly enjoyed TV as a diversion, he did not make use of its full political potential.[27] In fact, television almost derailed his first presidential candidacy before it even got started. In June 1952, he gave a poorly received televised speech in the rain in Abilene, appearing old and gray and lacking the commanding appearance of a war hero.[28] In earlier years, one speech could be written off as an anomaly. In the television era, however, one bad speech could reach the entire nation, and a poor impression was hard to shake.[29]

Realizing what a debacle the speech had been, Eisenhower held a press conference the next day at the Plaza Theater in Abilene, where a good performance superseded the previous day's disaster in the public mind.[30] Eisenhower's aides never forgot that first appearance in Abilene.[31] Nor did he. After his presidency, he lamented, "Probably no televised speech up to that moment was ever delivered under greater difficulties and more uncomfortable circumstances."[32] Whether he was referring to the rain or to his unfamiliarity with TV, the bitter taste of that experience remained with him.

Television remained a problem for Ike throughout that campaign. TV made him look old, and he had trouble mastering the teleprompter. As his aides tried every solution they could think of—more makeup, a sunlamp to highlight the general's features, dropping the teleprompter—the logistics of the campaign seemed to become needlessly complex. Looking over a long memo about a campaign trip, he joked, "Thirty-five pages to get me into Philadelphia. The invasion of Normandy was on five pages."[33]

Television proved no easier for Eisenhower after he became president. In 1953 and 1954, aides brought in the actor Robert Montgomery to improve his television performances. Montgomery had also helped out in the 1952 campaign. The comedian and talk show host Dick Cavett later wrote an entertaining take on this pairing, observing that the "gifted and classy" Montgomery was brought in to help the "marginally articulate" Ike. According to Cavett, "Montgomery transformed the man." Thanks to Montgomery's "seemingly minor adjustments," Cavett wrote, "Suddenly, turgid old General Eisenhower became 'Ike.' A genial, avuncular fellow you might like to have over."[34]

Despite Montgomery's apparent "transformation" of Eisenhower, there remained plenty of hiccups. In March 1957, a reporter at a televised press conference asked about the government helicopters that took Eisenhower to the golf course. The president responded grumpily that he did not "think much of the question." The incident became a topic of conversation, and Ike referred to it as part of the "silly season."[35] It may have affected his view of press conferences, which were usually filmed rather than broadcasted live to allow for necessary editing. Even so, the number of televised press conferences declined from a hundred in the first four years to about fifty in the next four.[36]

Nevertheless, in many ways, Eisenhower's use of television was revolutionary. He understood its power, particularly its entertainment value. Then as now, critics panned the programming on the "idiot box"—a term that dates to the Eisenhower era.[37] It was Eisenhower who first recognized some of the political and cultural potential of the new technology. In contrast to those who would sniff and dismiss TV entertainment, Eisenhower saw it as an admirable expression of American ingenuity and creativity.[38] It is hard to imagine a president talking about television that way nowadays, even if he enjoyed it privately. Barack Obama, for example, enjoys many TV programs, including *The Wire*, *Modern Family*, and *Homeland*. Publicly, however, he tells kids to stop watching *Real Housewives*, lest they fall behind kids in "Beijing and Bangalore."[39]

Ike "got" TV. His best-known speech—and one of the most famous presidential speeches of all time—was his televised farewell address, in which he warned of the dangers of the "military-industrial complex." His presidential "firsts" include the first televised press conferences and Cabinet meetings, as well as the use of an outside consultant with TV expertise.[40] He used television to convey the image of the friendly uncle who understood the people's concerns but who was not a dull technocrat.[41] Other presidents have been better on television, but Eisenhower created the roadmap that other presidents followed and improved on. Still, he came of age in the pre-television era, and his experimentation with the new medium had a forced quality. In the future, the most successful presidents would have a far more natural relationship with the device that was transforming American politics.

Kennedy and Johnson:
Serving in the Age of Saturation

Since the 1960s, American politicians have operated in a country where nearly everyone was watching television. This was a big change even from the beginning of the Eisenhower presidency. TV ownership went from about 30 percent of the population to 70 percent in Ike's first term, and increased to about 90 percent over the course of his second term.[42] Presidents coming to power in this new era had to deal with the enormous influence of television—or risk dangers undreamt of half a decade earlier.

Even presidents who didn't watch *I Love Lucy* needed to pay attention to television. Kennedy and Johnson, who cared so little for movies, didn't care much for television entertainment, either. They certainly did not share the TV obsession that was sweeping the nation, along with the Eisenhower White House. Kennedy turned to television mainly for news rather than entertainment, but he and Jackie did enjoy watching *The Judy Garland Show*, *The Jack Benny Show*, and *Maverick*.[43] Despite their wealth, the Kennedys did not even have a television in their Hyannis Port home before the 1960 presidential debates. In order to watch her husband spar with Vice President Nixon, Mrs. Kennedy rented a sixteen-inch set. She explained to her guests, "I own one in Washington but we don't have one here. I guess I'll have to break down and buy one."[44]

Despite the sparseness of his own viewing, Kennedy understood the power of TV. It transformed him from a junior senator into a celebrity and then into a president. Kennedy and his team carefully managed the 1960 Democratic Convention with television viewers in mind, making skillful use of dimming lights and a slick documentary—*The Pursuit of Happiness*—before an outside audience of forty million. They did with television what Franklin Roosevelt had done with radio.[45] For radio, however, it was sufficient for the steely-eyed and distant Roosevelt to have a rich and emphatic voice. It was still possible to hide from the public his inability to walk. In the television age, poise and physical attractiveness became even more important for a politician—especially a president. And youthful good looks were Kennedy's most outstanding quality. Television elevated these aesthetic advantages at the same time that it minimized the importance of extended persuasive and logical skill. Kennedy's performance in the televised debates against Nixon was crucial to his victory. Eisenhower, who understood television's power, advised Nixon not to debate JFK.[46] But the aggressive Nixon forged ahead, determined to dismantle his young and inexperienced adversary. Television turned the tables on him, as Nixon was at his worst on the screen. His fair skin revealed the barest five o'clock shadow and his propensity to sweat created distracting rivulets—all of which got in the way of his over-rehearsed, encyclopedic responses. It is an established part of American political lore that among those who listened to the debates over the radio, Nixon prevailed, but TV viewers thought that Kennedy, with his charm and relaxed demeanor, walked

Once, when asked about a resolution from the Republican National Committee that deemed his presidency a failure, Kennedy coolly responded, "I'm pretty sure it passed unanimously." When a reporter asked him about Vaughn Meader, the comedian who built his career on his humorous (and by today's standards incredibly gentle) impersonations of Kennedy—the president acknowledged that he had "listened to Mr. Meader's record, but I thought it sounded more like Teddy than it did me." Through it all, the press corps laughed with delight.[47] The public loved it; a president came into their living rooms as if he were a civic-minded—and witty—neighbor.

away the winner. Kennedy defeated him not on the substance but by looking like a man ready to take command.

Kennedy was quick to recognize that television was now indispensible to his presidency. Beyond the debates, and in fact throughout the campaign, he kept up a steady stream of appearances on a variety of shows, including *Meet the Press*, *Person to Person*, *Kraft Television Theater*, and *The Tonight Show* with Jack Paar. After the campaign, he saw a tape of his TV appearances and said, "We wouldn't have had a prayer without that gadget."[48]

As president, Kennedy continued to benefit from television. He held sixty-four live press conferences during his time in office—about one every two weeks. Unlike Eisenhower's press conferences, these appearances were unedited, and fourteen of them were aired live. Kennedy adopted this open approach at the suggestion of White House press aide Pierre Salinger. And in the days before cable and the Internet, Kennedy could be confident that Americans were watching—his first press conference was watched by sixty-five million Americans in twenty-one million households. An astonishing 90 percent of Americans in one poll reported that they watched one of Kennedy's first three press conferences. Unlike today's press conferences, these were not tough grilling sessions so much as opportunities for the young and telegenic president to shine. Even the reporters themselves realized how well Kennedy was using the medium. ABC News' Bill Shadel saw in Kennedy an ability to "use television as FDR used radio, to get the people to go along with his policies."[49]

This plan could not work if Kennedy were just a pretty face. It was his charm, grace, and ease of manner that won over reporters and the public. In his live press conferences, he showed remarkable equanimity, even when faced with a hostile question.

Of course, Kennedy benefitted from a compliant press corps that was in some ways slow to come to grips with the technology that would eventually trim the influence of the country's newspapers. The reporters' laughter was worth millions in campaign advertising. John Barnes notes that out-of-town reporters and editors were "starstruck" at White House luncheons. Even the presumably more jaded Washington reporters fell in line because of their wives' desire to attend a social event with the glamorous Mrs. Kennedy.[50] It is remarkable, from today's perspective, that the press never tattled about Kennedy's sexual escapades. It would take the influence of television to create an appetite—and the financial incentive—for such salacious revelations to come.

Still, no president will ever be fully satisfied with his press coverage. Even though the media treated Kennedy well, he liked television because it let him go around the reporters and appeal directly to the viewers. Daniel Boorstin recognized the importance of these press conferences, which changed the president's relationship with the press: "Newsmen are no longer so important as intermediaries who relay the President's statements." And the format added "a new interest as a dramatic performance."[51]

Kennedy benefitted from media standards that nowadays would be simply unimaginable. NBC executives cut a comedic sketch about the Kennedys from *The Art Carney Show* because, according to a network flack, "we thought it would have been improper to have performers actually portraying the President and his wife." According to the spokesman, the "decision was based on a matter of good taste."[52]

Good taste was guarded a little less rigorously by the fall of 1964, when NBC imported the British parody show *That Was the Week That Was*, starring, among others, David Frost. The show took its share of political shots and would even satirize President Lyndon Johnson, which was unusual at the time. The producers fought with the network censors about the LBJ jokes, and they suspended the satire around the 1964 presidential election. Even then, there was no sense that such jokes were completely off limits, as they had been under Kennedy. The scruples of "good taste" were only a distant memory by the mid-1970s, when Chevy Chase portrayed President Gerald Ford as a bumbling dolt on NBC's *Saturday Night Live*.[53] By 2011, all restraint was gone when HBO's *Game of Thrones*, a Tolkienesque drama, made a politically gaudy use of a severed head that was deliberately made to look like former President George W. Bush.

Friendly media or not, Kennedy dominated the art of sympathetic, even romanticized, television before, during, and after his presidency. In the decade after his assassination, Kennedy continued to dominate the airwaves. In fact, it is impossible to separate that tragedy from television, which brought the assassination into American living rooms. Kennedy had so mastered the medium that the public was familiar with the telegenic young president and his family. When he died, Americans felt as if they had lost a close relative.[54]

The pageantry of Kennedy's funeral was brought home by TV as well. During the three days of memorial coverage, the entire nation seemed to be tuned in—166 million Americans in fifty-one million households watched at least some of the funeral coverage, with an average viewing time of 31.6 hours during the entire period. And the funeral coverage dominated all other coverage at the time. As a National Opinion Research Center study found, "for all practical purposes there was no other news story in America during those four days."[55]

Fifty years after his assassination, Kennedy's influence on television lives on. His chairman of the Federal Communications Commission, Newton Minow, coined an enduring description of American television in a speech to the National Association of Broadcasters, proclaiming it "a vast wasteland." The producer Sherwood Schwartz, in response, named the boat in his sitcom *Gilligan's Island*—presumably a prime example of the "wasteland" fare—the SS *Minnow* after the FCC chairman.

To his litany of horrors, Minow added commercials. Kennedy once complained to Minow about the preponderance of commercials during a TV airing of the movie *PT-109*, about Kennedy's World War II heroics in the Pacific. He was angry that his story was "now selling deodorants, foot powders, and digestive aids." When he got Minow on the phone, he told him, "Why do you let them put so many commercials on? It's cheap! Cheap! Cheap! I want a rule that limits the number of commercials." It's not clear if this outburst influenced Minow, though; one did not need a presidential directive to find TV advertising annoying.[56]

Kennedy did not contact Minow directly about the speech, but his father did. According to Minow, Joseph Kennedy called and said "Newt, good for you. That was the best speech since Jack Kennedy's inaugural address. I talked to the president tonight; he says, you keep it up. Don't let anybody give you any hard time. Anybody does, you call me."[57] One inspiration for the speech might have been the Westerns of which Kennedy's predecessor was so fond. Describing their own programming for his audience of broadcasters, Minow said, "You will see a procession of game shows, formula comedies about totally unbelievable families, blood and thunder, mayhem, violence, sadism, murder, western bad men, western good men, private eyes, gangsters, more violence, and cartoons."[58]

Kennedy's TV image remains with us in other, less obvious, ways as well. According to the critic Paul Cantor, the perennially popular television series "*Star Trek* reflects the political vision of the Kennedy administration, which set out to bring 'the best and the brightest' to Washington in order to administer the country according to the latest scientific principles." There are also similarities between the 'JK' names with definitive middle initials: "John F. Kennedy" and "James T. Kirk," as well as between Kennedy's call for a "New Frontier" and Kirk's quest into the "Final Frontier." Furthermore, in Cantor's view, "Mr. Spock seems to stand for all JFK's brainy advisors from Harvard—a sort of McGeorge Bundy with pointy ears." Although the original series was somewhat short-lived, its spinoffs, sequels, novelizations, and comics—all stemming from that original Kennedy-inspired show—remain with us. Less flatteringly, Cantor finds, the philandering politician on *The Simpsons*, Mayor Diamond Joe Quimby, "speaks with a heavy Kennedy accent, and generally acts like a Democratic urban machine politician." We are now five decades removed from Kennedy's death, and yet, thanks to the powerful and lingering impact of television, the quintessential political image *Simpsons* viewers continue to see is one derived from John Kennedy.[59]

The Simpsons digs notwithstanding, Lyndon Johnson's treatment by the television networks was much less kind than Kennedy's. It wasn't that he didn't pay attention to his TV image. Johnson may not have watched entertainment programs, but he

Being vice president involved embarrassing treatment in the media, such as the "Whatever happened to Lyndon Johnson?" stories. Unsuspecting citizens, asked "Who is Lyndon Johnson?" by *Candid Camera*, couldn't come up with the answer. He must have found the responses—like "astronaut" and "baseball player"—excruciating.[60]

was an obsessive news-watcher and often used the power of television to try to improve his portrayal. But he lacked Kennedy's easy manner, and he suffered under the camera's unforgiving lens.

Johnson was well aware of the power of television. Long before he sat in the Oval Office, he saw the potential for television to derail a political career—in particular, that of Senator Joseph McCarthy of Wisconsin. Johnson had even pushed for the 1954 Army-McCarthy hearings to be shown on TV because he suspected that McCarthy would not wear well under the camera's gaze.[61] Johnson's insight was vindicated when Joseph Welch issued his famous and devastating televised reprimand of McCarthy—"At long last, have you left no sense of decency?"

Johnson's astuteness about the media during his years as Senate majority leader made his diminished standing as vice president so painful. LBJ was so frustrated as vice president that he would refuse to go on TV when invited, even for coveted airtime on shows such as *Today*. As Robert Caro put it, "He couldn't bear to appear on television...." Johnson's press secretary, George Reedy, tired and embarrassed by saying no to media requests, began making up excuses why the vice president of the United States could not appear on TV.[62]

Once he became president, people knew who he was, of course, but his problems with television were only beginning. The famous Johnson intimidation "treatment"—so effective in one-on-one interactions—did not work on television. Johnson and his family understood these weaknesses.[63] Mrs. Johnson herself observed, "Television was not his friend, it was his enemy."[64] And Johnson, after his presidency, lamented his own "inability to establish better rapport with communications media. If I had to do it again, I would try harder." But he didn't take all the blame: "My only stipulation would be an appeal to the news media to try harder also."[65]

Johnson could be obsessed with unflattering press coverage. In fact, criticizing the media proved a recurring theme of his administration. In order to monitor everything said about him, he installed both a teletype and a console with three televisions in the Oval Office.[66] These devices allowed him to monitor the print media and the three major networks—ABC, CBS, and NBC—since they were the primary sources of TV news at the time. He also had three televisions installed in the bedroom and living room of his Texas ranch. Johnson's friend Arthur Krim, the head of United Artists, recalled that the president obsessively listened to the radio while out and about, but he would also "generally manage to get back to the ranch in time to have those three TV sets on, which he would manipulate, because if he was at a console [he would watch] first one channel, then the other, and then the third."[67]

There was a purpose to all this news watching. As Krim recalled, "More often than not, we saw him on those programs and there would be comments about that."[68] Those conversations were often sources of ideas and inspiration, such as the time Jack Valenti and fellow aides Cliff Carter and Bill Moyers watched coverage of the Kennedy assassination on television with Johnson. As the TV "commentators inspected this alien cowboy who was now the leader of the free world," Valenti says, Johnson began to focus on the enormous tasks ahead for all of them: "As we sat glued

More frequently, however, Johnson's reaction to what he saw on television was not so productive. He would often call senior network executives to berate them about critical stories. Sometimes he would even challenge their patriotism. In 1965, after CBS broadcast a report showing a Marine setting a Vietnamese hut on fire with a Zippo lighter, Johnson woke the head of CBS, Frank Stanton, to berate him over the phone for having "shat on the American flag." He also questioned the loyalties of the Canadian-born correspondent Morley Safer. "How could CBS employ a Communist like Safer," Johnson asked. "How could they be so unpatriotic as to put on enemy film like this?"[69]

to the TV set, the new president began to ruminate aloud about his plans, his objectives, the great goals he was bound to attain."[70]

Vietnam exacerbated Johnson's unhappiness with TV, as well as his outbursts. In the winter of 1967, as the war raged, Johnson told NBC News president Bill McAndrew that he thought the networks displayed an anti-administration bias and that he was watching them "like a hawk."[71] Having the president of the United States call and tell the head of a federally-regulated company that he is watching it "like a hawk" is not only disconcerting but pushes the boundaries of propriety and perhaps legality. Johnson's signature hard sell may not have worked with the audience sitting on the other side of the television screen, but he was not shy about trying to employ it on the television executives themselves.

> Obama's knowledge of low quality "reality" television shows is apparently quite extensive. Daniel Halper, writing for the conservative *Weekly Standard*, mistakenly reported that Obama told kids to stay away from the show *Desperate Housewives*, a fictional rather than a reality program.

Of course, berating the network suits at odd hours did not endear LBJ to them or their reporters. It violated the important principle of presidential politics that you can be an occasional critic if you choose your words carefully, but you cannot expect consistent success if you act as a lobbyist or resort to strong-arm tactics. Still, Johnson kept trying. At one point, he complained that NBC deliberately tried to make him look bad by using the wrong take of him speaking. Johnson said he knew it was the wrong shot because his glasses "glistened," giving him a comical and un-presidential look, instead of the cold, piercing stare he imagined he radiated as commander in chief. Yet Johnson, like so many Democrats, took people from the media to work for him, and many of his political people later went into journalism. In 1966, for instance, he brought Robert Kintner, who had been president of both ABC and NBC, to work in his administration. Kintner soon found out what it was like to serve on the other side of the divide, as he fielded frequent complaints from both broadcast and print journalists who griped about Johnson's hypersensitivity.[72]

Johnson's intimidation tactics extended into the entertainment sphere as well. On at least one occasion he also weighed in on behalf of the first lady's TV "boyfriend," Marshal Matt Dillon of *Gunsmoke* (played by James Arness).[73] Lady Bird Johnson loved the show and wrote in her diary of leaving a walk with her husband "because instead I had a date with my favorite Saturday night ten o'clock man—Marshal Dillon."[74] (The first lady was aghast to discover, however, that the series' female lead, Amanda Blake—Miss Kitty—was a Republican.)[75] According to Arness, LBJ told him that when the network was considering dropping *Gunsmoke*, Mrs. Johnson was so unhappy that she made him call the network to complain.[76] The show avoided the ax and stayed on the air until 1975, holding the record as the longest-running fictional television program until *The Simpsons*.

Presidential aides constantly got an earful about how unfair the TV reporters were to their boss. In 1965, a White House Festival of the Arts turned into an embarrassment when some guests used the occasion to protest the Vietnam War.[77] Johnson responded by grumbling about the outsized domestic influence of the "communists." He told his staffers that "the communists already control the three major networks and the forty major outlets of communication."[78] This and other similar pronouncements led biographer Robert Dallek to conclude that Johnson had become "irrational almost to the point of disability."[79]

When Dan Rather of CBS asked to film the White House staff at work, Johnson turned him down cold. In the margin of CBS's letter, the president wrote to his press secretary that "this man [Rather] and CBS are out to get us any way [CBS president] Bill Paley can. Tell him you have much more work than you can handle and these men are workers on routine, not actors." In this case, Johnson's paranoia about television coverage probably served little purpose and may have even proved deleterious, preventing CBS from doing a puff piece about the White House at work.[80]

Johnson may have been peevish with the press and their network bosses, but that doesn't mean he was wrong about their intentions. They gave him a hard time, and not all of it was of his own making. Reporters had enjoyed their close ties with Kennedy, whom they treated more favorably than the hectoring and often undignified

Johnson.[81] As a result, Kennedy was an impossible act to follow, especially after his tragic death. The escalation of the Vietnam War made matters worse, as journalists soured on both the war and on Johnson.[82]

The anti-war bias of TV news reporters came to a head after the Tet Offensive in 1968 and may have cost Johnson his presidency. After the bloody battle, the legendary CBS anchorman Walter Cronkite gave a dour report on the state of the war. Even though Johnson did not see the report live, he is reported to have said in its aftermath, "If I've lost Cronkite, I've lost middle America." Shortly thereafter, Johnson announced in a speech that he would "not seek and [would] not accept" the Democratic nomination for president in 1968. Perhaps this episode could be considered some sort of vindication of his paranoia. Maybe Bill Paley and CBS were indeed after him and did "get him" in the end.

As these incidents show, the network news had a tremendous influence at the time—not merely in the portrayal of the presidency but in how the president saw the world. What is even more amazing is how television allowed small fictions to overwhelm the truth. The consensus of military historians reveals that U.S. forces won the battles surrounding the Tet Offensive, but they lost the battle in the press. And there is considerable debate about whether Johnson actually made the "If I've lost Cronkite" comment. But it is beyond debate that television had become so powerful that a few newscasters could report a victory as a defeat, and the damage could drive a president from office. The opposition to Vietnam may have been too much for a president to overcome in any era, but there is no question that TV made this burden unmanageable for a Johnson ill-equipped, personally and professionally, to use television to persuade the American public otherwise.

Nixon and the Enemies List

Johnson's successor fared even worse with television. Like Johnson, Richard Nixon watched the news and often didn't like what he saw. He didn't share Johnson's obsession, however, and removed LBJ's three televisions from the Oval Office.

Rather than telephoning network executives to complain—perhaps an imprudent tactic but at least straightforward—he was more likely to brood privately over his enemies list.

Nixon began his life as commander in chief by turning on the TV. On the morning after his close-call election in 1968, he woke up at nine o'clock and turned on the television to learn that he had prevailed and was America's president-elect. As Franklin Roosevelt did in 1932, Nixon picked up the phone to notify his family, but this was now the age of television, so they already knew.[83]

Watching TV news would sometimes encourage Nixon's Machiavellian instincts. Charles Colson recalled a day in 1971 when Nixon saw the Democratic senator Edmund Muskie on the news. At the time, Muskie led Nixon in the polls. Nixon suggested to Colson, "Wouldn't it be kinda interesting if there was a committee of Democrats supporting Muskie and busing? Couldn't you arrange that one, Chuck?" Colson noted privately that it was a difficult assignment, but he went ahead with the boss's "suggestion."[84]

Nixon used the television to size up his competition. In August 1972, Nixon and John Connally, who had just stepped down as secretary of the Treasury, were together at the "Western White House" in San Clemente, California, watching delegates to the Democratic National Convention nominate the liberal senator from South Dakota, George McGovern, as their presidential candidate, a process that dragged on until approximately three in the morning—"prime time in Hawaii," as Michael Barone has joked.[87] Nixon remarked that the convention had "the air of a college skit." He began to formulate a plan to defeat McGovern, who he correctly predicted was too far to the left for the American people.[88]

A football fan, Nixon even sent plays to the Washington Redskins' coach, George Allen, one of which contributed to a loss. The humor columnist Art Buchwald quipped, "If George Allen doesn't accept any more plays from Richard Nixon, he may go down in history as one of pro football's greatest coaches."[85] Even so, Nixon insisted, "Except when my favorite teams are playing, I always prefer reading to TV."[86]

The famously secretive Nixon didn't like to admit that he watched television at all. Unlike Johnson, who was quite open about his obsession with what the media said about him, Nixon denied an interest in TV. Nevertheless, he watched at least some entertainment programming, including the detective show *Kojak* and various sports.

Even in private, Nixon didn't like to admit to watching television. In June 1974, as the Watergate scandal churned toward its climax, he told Colson that his daughter Julie had appreciated Colson's interview with ABC's Howard K. Smith. Colson, however, suspected that it was not just Julie who had watched. "Nixon would never—even to me—admit to watching television," Colson wrote in his memoir, "but [Nixon's valet] Manolo [Sanchez] later told me he'd wheeled a television set into Nixon's office so the President could view this one."[89] Nixon's shyness about TV watching likely had two causes: he wanted to appear to be a highbrow reader as his old rival Kennedy seemed, and he also may not have wanted to admit that he was paying attention to what the hated media were saying.

When confronted with unfavorable treatment in the press, Nixon didn't complain, he got even. The chief offenders, in his view, were *Time*, *Newsweek*, the *New York Times*, the *Washington Post*, and CBS.[90] (One wonders why NBC and ABC were spared.) Getting more specific, he compiled a famous "enemies list" of individuals. The list became public, as these things inevitably do, during the 1973 Watergate hearings. CBS's Daniel Schorr, who was number seventeen on the original list of twenty, read the list on the air and was surprised during his recitation to find his own name on it. A longer version included four of Schorr's TV colleagues, from both CBS and NBC. After the initial shock, Schorr reveled in his making the list. For the rest of his life, he boasted that it made his lecture fees go up.[91] Such is the power of the presidency in popular culture that one fight can simultaneously degrade the status of the man in the Oval Office while elevating his target to new and lucrative heights.

Schorr may have laughed off the enemy list later in life, but presidential displeasure could be dangerous. More than once, Nixon contemplated going after the stations that made him unhappy. He tried to have the FCC refuse to renew the licenses of offending stations and suggested using antitrust law to break the networks into smaller entities. Nixon's attitude was, "If the threat of screwing them is going to help us more with their programming than doing it, then keep the threat [sic]. As far as screwing them is concerned, I'm very glad to do it."[92] The hardball tactics backfired. They not only made Nixon more hated but helped extinguish any semblance of a conservative presence in increasingly liberal Hollywood.[93] The lesson for politicians is never pick a fight with the people who own the megaphones. Nixon's experience also serves as a reminder to politicians that journalists are the only people on the planet more sensitive to criticism than the politicians themselves.

During the Nixon years, as the president's relations with both the news and the entertainment sides of television soured, the entire medium went the way of popular music: largely hostile to Republicans and largely friendly to Democrats. Even Nixon's friends in the television business couldn't defend his hostile posture toward their medium. They were driven deeper underground as liberal voices achieved dominance. Hollywood money and support flowed to the Democrats. More importantly, however, the liberal viewpoint determined editorial and artistic decisions as well. According to the conservative TV analyst Ben Shapiro, "[W]hen blue-collar workers vote Reagan and Nixon, Hollywood despises them and focuses instead on upper-class elites; when blue-collar workers vote Carter, Hollywood loves them and paints them as ignorant heroes."[94]

The classic example of what Shapiro is talking about is the blustery, blue-collar Archie Bunker, brilliantly portrayed by Carroll O'Connor on the most popular television series of the Nixon era, Norman Lear's *All in the Family*. The show exemplified a new style of hyper-political and aggressively liberal television. Nixon recognized *All in the Family*'s political impact, even while he loathed the construct of the show, in which a liberal son-in-law, played by Rob Reiner, regularly faced off against Bunker, his closed-minded and cantankerously behind-the-times father-in-law.[95] In a taped conversation with Haldeman and the domestic policy advisor John Ehrlichman, Nixon criticized the program for promoting homosexuality, launching into a tirade about homosexuality. "Do you know what happened to the Romes,

Romans? The last six Roman emperors were fags. The last six. Nero had a public wedding to a boy."[96]

These comments represent Nixon's well-known dark side, but it was not the only side. There was a time, in fact, when television rescued his political fortunes. Dwight Eisenhower selected Nixon as his running mate in 1952, but after word about a secret Nixon slush fund emerged, Eisenhower let the young California senator twist in the wind while he decided whether to keep him on the ticket. With his career on the line, Nixon took to the new medium of television and went straight to the American people with his case. On September 23, he defended himself in a heartfelt speech, concluding with a sentimental flourish. Supporters had given him a dog that his daughters named Checkers. "And you know, the kids, like all kids, love the dog," he told the nation, "and I just want to say this right now, that regardless of what they say about it, we're gonna keep it."[98]

> —➤➤➤•❮❮❮—
>
> **Re: comedy of Ford Press Secretary Ron Nessen**
>
> **Once, when pressed about the status of the just-deceased Generalissimo Francisco Franco, whom Nessen had earlier said was "stable," Nessen said: "I didn't say that he wasn't dead. I just said that he was stable."**[97]

It's easy to look back on that speech now and sneer. "The very term 'Checkers speech,' reducing the whole broadcast to its saccharine doggy-passage, is a judgment in itself," writes Garry Wills. At the time, however, the public was still unused to having politicians in their living rooms, and the response was overwhelmingly favorable. The speech worked, notes Wills—"that broadcast saved Nixon's career, and made history."[99]

The Checkers success stayed with Nixon and gave him confidence that TV was one more tool to be used to his advantage. He agreed to the televised debates with Kennedy in 1960 only because of his earlier successes with the Checkers speech. Even Nixon's failures in those debates were the result of his own mistakes—inadequate preparation, for example, and his refusal of makeup—rather than the hostility of the television business.

A different story occurred in 1968. The television-savvy Nixon campaign—immortalized in Joe McGinnis's *The Selling of the President 1968*—started early with Nixon's appearance on the *Mike Douglas Show* in 1967. "It's a shame a man has to use gimmicks like this to get elected," Nixon complained. Douglas's twenty-eight-year-old producer, Roger Ailes, retorted, "Television is not a gimmick." Nixon ended up hiring Ailes—the future creator of the Fox News Channel—who helped craft the new media strategies that got Nixon elected.[100] Part of this campaign included Nixon's appearance on the popular comedy *Rowan & Martin's Laugh In*. The appearance only lasted long enough for Nixon to say the show's catchphrase "Sock it to me!" but it did the job, helping to generate stories about a more at ease and relaxed "new Nixon."[101] Donald Rumsfeld recalls, "The fact that Nixon was willing to appear on the show demonstrated to many of his critics that he was able to take himself less seriously and have a little fun."[102] Nixon's *Laugh-In* gig represents another lesson of pop culture. The main value of new media for a politician is to humanize him. Nixon saw this, and he created a White House television office staffed by two television pros from Los Angeles.[103]

Nixon's openness to TV didn't last. This president and the television industry were destined for a collision. Television news coverage of the administration, which irritated him from the beginning, only got more hostile with Watergate. As for television's entertainment programming, four seconds on *Laugh-In* was not enough to counteract the direction in which the medium was going, and it was not a direction Nixon liked.

Nixon resigned from the presidency in August 1974, but his negative image continued to linger. Other presidents might do better or worse on camera, but Nixon remained a target on television for more than a decade. "Gerald Ford's sin was pardoning Richard Nixon," wrote Peter Rollins and John O'Connor, but "Richard Nixon's sin was being Richard Nixon." As late as 1998, *Saturday Night Live* was still socking it to the thirty-seventh president in skits and jokes. But by then, Nixon wasn't alone. As Gerald Ford would learn, TV and comedians combined to become a potent force in defining public perception of presidents and the presidency.[104]

Presidents in the Comedy Sketch Era

The placid and decent Gerald Ford did not create his own problems with television through insecurity or paranoia as Nixon and Johnson had done. He was a victim of circumstances beyond his control. He rose unelected to the highest office in the land at a time when Vietnam and then Watergate had poisoned the relations between the White House and the press. Ford came along as the imperial presidency gave way to the imperiled presidency.

Perhaps the strangest sign of the hard times on which the American presidency had fallen was the media's portrayal of a maladroit Ford. The former starting center for the University of Michigan may have been the finest athlete ever to become president. His Wolverines won two national titles, and Ford turned down at least two offers to play professional football.[105] Nevertheless, after what the *New York Times* described as a "few ill-timed episodes of camera-range clumsiness, like stumbling down the steps of Air Force One in Austria, wiping out on the slopes in Vail, Colo., and getting zonked on the head by a passing chairlift," the image of Ford the klutz proved irreversibly established.[106] He became a living, breathing warning to all future presidents about the remorseless brutality of the television camera.

Ford soon realized that there was little he could do about the clumsiness caricature, and although it was painful, he rarely complained about it, says his press secretary, Ron Nessen. He mentioned it to Nessen only once, at a Christmas retreat at Ford's vacation home in Vail. The still nimble president—a skillful golfer, skier, and tennis player—remarked that the reporters who mocked him got "most of their exercise on the bar stool."[107] Years later, Ford recognized that the media image contributed to his loss in the 1976 election. The athletically graceful Ford reminisced slightly bitterly: "[E]very time I stumbled or bumped my head or fell in the snow, reporters zeroed in on that to the exclusion of almost everything else.... [This] helped create the public perception of me as a stumbler. And that wasn't funny."[108]

Perhaps not, but people were laughing. And politicians who realize when a gag works are much more likely to respond swiftly and effectively. Ford might have survived politically if only journalists ridiculed his supposed clumsiness. The real damage came when the joke migrated to the entertainment side of television, thanks to the ground-breaking comedy show *Saturday Night Live*, one of the hottest shows on television in the late 1970s and still on the air today. Its creator, Lorne Michaels, became incredibly wealthy, as did many of the stars he discovered. As a pop-culture force, the show remained unrivaled until Comedy Central's *The Daily Show with Jon Stewart* and *The Colbert Report* entered the scene.

Presidents had been imitated on television before—most notably Vaughn Meader's impersonation of JFK. But it was Chevy Chase's crude bumbling-and-stumbling performances of an inept Gerald Ford—in which Chase did not even try to look like the president—that redefined presidential humor. In a devastating parody of Ford's debates with Jimmy Carter, Chase responded to a question with a plaintive "It was my understanding that there would be no math." The jibes were frequent and unrelenting, and the sketch—which often opened the show—comprised the subject of Monday water-cooler conversations across the country.[109] As Mark Leibovich wrote in the *New York Times*, "No one did more to solidify Mr. Ford's unfortunate, and perhaps unfair, standing as the nation's First Klutz than Mr. Chase."[110] Donald Rumsfeld, who served as Ford's chief of staff, recalled in his memoir that "Chase's popular parody ... did damage to the president's image throughout his presidency."[111]

Ford tried a number of responses to the *Saturday Night Live* problem, none of them very effective. He appeared on the dais with Chase at the Radio and TV Correspondents' dinner, one of the Washington events that Laura Bush would later call the "Washington ritual of roasting the president."[112] Ford acknowledged Chase's act to begin with, intentionally acting like a klutz by dropping some papers. Then he directly confronted Chase, albeit in a playful way, turning one of the comedian's signatures lines on him: "Good evening, I'm Gerald Ford and you're not." He also told him, "Mr. Chevy Chase, you're a very, very funny suburb."[113]

Ron Nessen, a genuinely funny guy in his own right,[114] went on *Saturday Night Live* himself in an attempt to play along, but the gesture was doomed from the start. Rosie Shuster, one of the show's writers as well as the producer's wife, urged her colleagues,

"The President's watching. Let's make him cringe and squirm." It's hard to imagine such venomous treatment of a Democratic president by a respectful, if opinionated, conservative like William F. Buckley on *Firing Line*. The television rules had changed. "Looking back," says Nessen, "it's obvious that my attempt to smother the ridicule of Ford by joining the laughter on *Saturday Night* was a failure."[115]

For Chase and the *Saturday Night Live* team, the Ford parodies proved a lucrative gambit. For American presidents, they showed that there are some fights you cannot win by laughing *with* someone who wants to laugh *at* you. Chase himself betrayed his own prejudices when he told a reporter, "Ford is so inept that the quickest laugh is the cheapest laugh, and the cheapest is the physical joke."[116] The performances became a standard for other comedians. When Tina Fey was criticized for her devastating yet spot-on impression of Sarah Palin in 2008, she responded, "No one ever said it was 'mean' when Chevy Chase played Gerald Ford falling down all the time."[117]

After Ford lost the 1976 election in a close race, there was a clear sense that TV had romantically created and buried one president, Kennedy. It then exposed another president, Johnson, as a charmless strong-arm artist you didn't want in your home. Television then targeted the insecure and paranoid Nixon in a struggle neither could let go of. And finally, it toppled his successor through ridicule, forever linking Gerald Ford the varsity athlete to Chase's primitive imitations.

Jimmy Carter was determined to change the paradigm. In the presidential campaign of 1976, Carter made a brilliant move. He ran an "open" campaign, with multiple daily appearances, in contrast to Ford's "Rose Garden" strategy, which limited his appearances to once a day. Carter gave the appearance of letting a little sunlight into post-Watergate politics, and the American people responded.[118]

Ford and Carter also revived the televised debates that we now take as a matter of course in presidential campaigns, but which had been in abeyance since their first appearance in the Nixon-Kennedy contest of 1960. In doing so, they unknowingly released a new, powerful, and unpredictable force in presidential politics—the verbal blunder now universally referred to as the debate "gaffe." In his second debate with

Carter, Ford told an astonished nation that "there is no Soviet domination of Eastern Europe and there never will be under a Ford administration." It was bad enough that the president of the United States should make such a preposterous assertion, but it was endlessly replayed on television, magnifying the misstatement and engraving it on the public consciousness. Nixon's disadvantage in his debates with Kennedy had been cosmetic. Ford revealed an even greater danger of televised campaigning. There was now no such thing as a "momentary" lapse of judgment. Television ensures that a gaffe, like a diamond, is forever.

Television, then, created the Carter presidency. The new medium had come into Carter's life in 1952, when he bought his first television set at age twenty-eight.[119] This serves as a reminder of the technology's youth. Not until Bill Clinton and George W. Bush did America have presidents who had watched TV as children.

A sense of national exhaustion took root after the media savagery of the Nixon-Ford years, and Carter enjoyed a honeymoon when he took office. Even *Saturday Night Live* treated him with a light touch.[120] The new president took advantage of the good feelings by continuing his openness to the news media, and he was an adroit participant in televised press conferences.[121] As the election of 1980 approached, Carter got lucky again when his formidable opponent self-destructed on national television. In November 1979, Senator Edward Kennedy, whose older brother had a magic touch with TV, was poised to announce a challenge to the faltering incumbent of his own party for the presidential nomination. He sat for an interview with CBS's Roger Mudd, who asked him an obvious and simple question: Why did he want to be president? The senator appeared to freeze at first; his eventual response was meandering and utterly meaningless:

> The reasons I would run are because I have great belief in this country, that is—there's more natural resources than any nation in the world, there's the greatest educated population in the world. It just seems to me that this nation can cope and deal with the problems in a way it has done in the past … and I would basically feel that it's imperative for the country

to either move forward, that it can't stand still or otherwise it moves backwards.

Mudd later called this ramble "almost a parody of a politician's circumlocution," adding that if Kennedy had been a Southerner, the answer could have come from the mouth of the comic radio character Senator Beauregard Claghorn.[122] The incident not only helped Carter defeat Kennedy, but it also stuck with Kennedy for the rest of his life. In his posthumously published memoir, Kennedy accused Mudd of having blindsided him, a claim Mudd dismissed as a "fantasy."[123] Kennedy's experience was another lesson for politicians in the television age. No candidate should ever again be caught off guard by the "Roger Mudd question."

Carter's ideology provided some insulation from media hostility, but it couldn't insulate him from the news of the world, which got gloomier as his term progressed. When the American embassy staff were taken hostage in Iran, ABC began broadcasting a nightly report on the crisis anchored by Ted Koppel. The broadcasts eventually

---

Another Reagan favorite was *Family Ties*, whose lead character, played by Michael J. Fox, proved unique on network TV in being identified as a Republican. The program's creator, Gary David Goldberg, an outspoken liberal, intended Alex Keaton to be a caricature of conservatives. The scheme backfired, however, as Alex became one of TV's most beloved characters, especially among Republicans.[124] The *Family Ties* example revealed that conservatives are often better able to laugh at themselves. Reagan in particular was one of those Republicans who could laugh at himself. He even offered to make an appearance on *Family Ties,* but Goldberg and company ignored it.[125] This tendency persists today. After more than two decades of comedy and hosting *The Tonight Show*, Jay Leno has said, "The interesting thing is, I have found that the Republicans respond much more to jokes about themselves than the Democrats do."[126]

---

took the permanent form of the news show *Nightline*. The nightly reminders that the humiliating crisis was dragging on with no resolution in sight eroded Carter's support, and it revealed itself a major contributor to his defeat in 1980. Television had made Jimmy Carter's presidency, and television would cripple it.[127]

After getting past Ted Kennedy's challenge in the primaries, Carter faced the consummate television pro in the general election: Ronald Reagan. Democrats liked to dismiss the former actor as an "amiable dunce," but the "dunce" knew how to use television to communicate his idealistic message. The defining moment of the campaign was the lone televised debate. In his closing remarks, Reagan looked at the camera and asked the voters, "Are you better off now than you were four years ago?" He broke away in what had been a close race, and one week later he defeated Carter in a landslide.

Reagan probably watched more entertainment programming on television than any president since Eisenhower. In the early 1950s, when Reagan and Nancy were still dating, he often watched programs with her.[128] As governor, Reagan would finish work at six, exercise, eat with Nancy, and watch television or read.[129] He followed a similar routine in the White House as much as possible. In the absence of other social obligations, he would exercise, and even get into his pajamas and robe by six, as would Mrs. Reagan. He would then read or watch TV in their living room until ten-thirty or eleven o'clock, when they went to bed.[130] They particularly liked *Jeopardy!* and *Murder, She Wrote*.[131] Reagan's fondness for *Murder, She Wrote* was so well-known that after the Iran-Contra affair, Johnny Carson even joked that Reagan had issued new instructions that "he must be awakened from his nap whenever there's an arms deal. Before that, the only thing you could wake him for was nuclear war and 'Murder, She Wrote.'"[132]

Reagan often found consolation in TV. In 1981, while the president recuperated from John Hinckley's assassination attempt, Nancy went to England without him to attend the wedding of Prince Charles and Diana. Reagan never liked to be without Nancy, and he was disappointed to miss the wedding of the century. He did find some comfort on the tube, however, remaining at home watching reruns of *The Waltons*.[133]

All of his preparation paid off. By the time he entered politics, Reagan was far more at ease with broadcast audiences than any of his rivals. In 1967, for example, he sparred with Robert F. Kennedy (and a panel of hostile international students) in a curiously forgotten debate on CBS. After Reagan easily bested him, a flummoxed Kennedy complained to his staff, "Who the f— got me into this?"[134]

Toward the end of his administration, the *New York Times* ran a story, citing unnamed aides, that Reagan was depressed in the wake of the Iran-Contra affair. "All he wanted to do was to watch movies and television at the residence," the paper reported. The White House spokesman, Marlin Fitzwater, dismissed the broader story but made no comments about Reagan's TV habits.[135]

Reagan also watched TV for more than just entertainment. He was a frequent consumer of TV news, and it often shaped his actions. In October of 1981, he watched in horror as the Libyan dictator Muammar Gaddafi gloated over the assassination of Egyptian president Anwar Sadat.[136] Gaddafi's rejoicing over the death of a man whose sin was forging a peace agreement with Israel no doubt remained on Reagan's mind when he made the decision to have U.S. jets bomb Libya in 1986. Earlier that year, Reagan watched the explosion of the space shuttle *Challenger*, and his watching—as well as the nation's—made it into his remarks on the event: "On the day of the disaster, our nation held a vigil by our television sets. In one cruel moment, our exhilaration turned to horror; we waited and watched and tried to make sense of what we had seen."[137] That speech was one of the best remembered and most moving of his presidency.

He and Nancy also liked watching the Sunday talk shows, especially *This Week with David Brinkley*.[138] He responded to those shows as well. After watching Margaret Thatcher defend him on *Face the Nation* in 1987, Reagan wrote in his diary, "Margaret Thatcher on 'Face the Nation' was absolutely magnificent." Later that week, he even took a call from her during a cabinet meeting, telling her how much he appreciated her remarks on the show. Then he added, "Well, I'm here with a bunch of my cabinet secretaries, and they'd all like to do the same and express their thanks for your support of our administration."[139]

A skilled and experienced performer, Reagan always presented himself well on TV. He knew what to do, and he always hit his marks. An anonymous aide said of his former boss, "He's an actor. He's used to being directed and produced. He stands where he is supposed to and delivers his lines, he reads beautifully, he knows how to wait for the applause line."[140]

Reagan had decades of success in front of the camera by the time he became president. He started out as a radio announcer, became a Hollywood star, and then had his own TV show, *General Electric Theater*, from 1954 to 1962. These experiences gave him an indispensible insider's understanding of the media—and more importantly, of the American audience. His understanding of the media was one reason that he counted Franklin D. Roosevelt among his political heroes. Even after Reagan switched parties, he continued to emulate Roosevelt as a communicator.[141]

As even his opponents recognized, Reagan understood what Americans needed at the time. Chris Matthews, who, as an aide to the Democratic speaker of the House Tip O'Neill often came out on the losing side in political battles against Reagan, said that Reagan and his people understood that "the presidency is ideally suited for the television age, because it is one person, there is all the *People* magazine aspect—what is he like, what is Nancy like?" Matthews betrayed frustration with how this "*People* magazine aspect" aided the presidency at the expense of Congress: "It is amazing how the monarchy translates so well into the television age and legislatures do not."[142] From the more neutral historian's perch, Gil Troy offers a less cynical view, arguing Reagan more than able to "captivate America's collective psyche" with his winning TV persona, mixing relentless optimism and amusing homespun stories.[143]

Other TV professionals were also frustrated by Reagan's success on television. David Burke, a former aide to Ted Kennedy, once whined that he could not "explain why [Reagan] hasn't been as vulnerable to the onslaught of the American press as some previous Presidents." Revealing his loyalties, Burke, who later became an ABC

News executive vice president, added, "It is a hard subject for me."[144] Even *Saturday Night Live*, the scourge of President Ford, could hardly lay a glove on the "Teflon president." The show tried six different actors, but the best they could do was depict Reagan as a genial man in public and a hard-charging and tough manager behind the scenes—not exactly a devastating portrait.[145]

Reagan succeeded on TV, but he did not do it alone. He had a talented and aggressive staff that included Mike Deaver and David Gergen. Deaver, in particular, devised the "message of the day" strategy, which the disciplined White House communications team enforced relentlessly on a press corps hungry for good material and compelling images.[146] Deaver emphasized the importance of visuals over content, and he was on to something. Once, when CBS's Lesley Stahl tried to do an anti-Reagan piece about budget cuts, her negative voiceovers were paired with images of Reagan at the Special Olympics and at an old-age home. Stahl thought the piece would hit the administration hard, but she found that the White House saw it as a positive piece.[147] As Stephen Weisman wrote in the *New York Times Magazine* in 1984, Reagan and his team took full advantage of what they saw as "the built-in tendency of television to emphasize appearances and impressions more than information."[148] Visuals, as Deaver argued, would always trump content. Ultimately, however, even the best staff is selling a product, and Reagan was an attractive product. His campaign press secretary James Lake praised him as "the ultimate presidential commodity … the right product."[149]

Reagan's vice president and successor, George H. W. Bush, initially appeared to have acquired at least some of Reagan's TV know-how. One of the most important moments in Bush's presidential quest took place in January 1988, when he appeared on a five-minute segment with CBS's Dan Rather, who had planned an ambush over the Iran-Contra affair. Bush, however, had planned an ambush of his own. Roger Ailes had insisted on Bush's behalf that it be a live interview. CBS did not like the condition but had no choice if it wanted Bush. *Time* reported that Rather had three one-hour prep sessions for the interview, in which he "was coached as if he were a candidate preparing for a debate or a pugilist preparing for a fight, rather than a journalist going into an interview." Bush's team was right to question Rather's motives.[150]

Bush prepared for the interview too, and he was ready when Rather came at him. Pressing the Iran-Contra issue, Rather "crossed the line between objectivity and emotional involvement," in *Time*'s estimation. Bush, with Ailes in the room nearby, countered with the most memorable line of the exchange. "How would you like it if I judged your career by those seven minutes when you walked off the set in New York? Would you like that?" Rather was caught off guard and the round went to Bush, who shed the unfair "wimp" label. In the process, he also galvanized conservatives. Afterward, with his microphone still on, Bush gloated: "The bastard didn't lay a glove on me.... Tell your goddamned network that if they want to talk to me to raise their hands at a press conference. No more Mr. Inside stuff after that."[152]

Cantor notes that the "single funniest political line in the history of *The Simpsons* came at the expense of the Democrats. When Grandpa Abraham Simpson receives money in the mail really meant for his grandchildren, Bart asks him: 'Didn't you wonder why you were getting checks for absolutely nothing?' Abe replies: 'I figured 'cause the Democrats were in power again.'"[151]

The Rather exchange was a high point for Bush with respect to television. Although he received largely positive press in his 1988 campaign for president, Bush did not have Reagan's skills before the camera. Who did? Always an avid outdoorsman, he never watched much television and may have missed the way TV was evolving.[153] By the early 1990s, television had become more important than ever for the leader of a global power. TV was the fastest way to get information on rapidly changing global developments, and even Bush occasionally felt that it was his obligation to watch.[154] He was not the only one. CNN's founder, Ted Turner, bragged that Margaret Thatcher, François Mitterrand, Nancy Reagan, and Fidel Castro were all big fans of his all-news network.[155] This new need for watching TV in order to keep up with world events was brought home by the collapse of the Berlin Wall and the first Gulf War, both featured 24/7 on CNN.

In a hyper-modern, television-centric world, Bush seemed a relic of an earlier era, one of proper manners, handwritten notes, and no TVs on during dinner. His administration even engaged in some high-profile fights with the TV industry, including, most memorably, Vice President Dan Quayle's spat with the producers of *Murphy Brown*, whom Quayle accused of viewing single motherhood as "just another lifestyle choice." The attacks failed in the short run. The Bush-Quayle ticket lost its reelection bid against the much more culturally savvy Bill Clinton. Quayle, however, was rewarded not long after the loss with a cover story in the *Atlantic Monthly* entitled "Dan Quayle Was Right."

In that long article (in which, interestingly, Quayle's name is mentioned only once), Barbara Dafoe Whitehead examines the growing problem of family structure and the role that our cultural institutions played in promoting the breakup of the traditional family. "Madison Avenue and Hollywood," she writes, "did not invent these behaviors, as their highly paid publicists are quick to point out, but they have played an influential role in defending and even celebrating divorce and unwed motherhood." What's worse, she notes, "They have taken the raw material of demography and fashioned it into a powerful fantasy of individual renewal and rebirth."[156] It was a declaration that, at the very least, culture was *not* reinforcing the ideals of marriage and family.

The Whitehead interpretation of the Quayle argument became the conventional wisdom on the subject. Eighteen years after the controversy, *USA Today*'s Jim McKairnes noted that the show abandoned the baby boy—trivia alert: his name was Avery—almost immediately after he was born. Apparently, Avery proved more a ratings goose than the fulfillment of a true maternal need. This kind of treatment was what Quayle had seemed concerned about in the first place, and his concerns were not at all unfounded. As McKairnes put it, "Dan Quayle, seems to have been, gulp, *right*. And maybe today more than ever."[157]

For his part, President Bush sidestepped the controversy, saying, "I'm not going to get into the details of a very popular television show." After the subject came up at a press conference with the Canadian prime minister, Brian Mulroney, Bush told a baffled Mulroney off camera, "I told you what the issue was. You thought I was kidding."[158]

Bush and his family did take on another popular show, and it was as dismal a failure as the *Murphy Brown* gambit. Along with conservative culture warriors such as Bill Bennett, the Bushes criticized the animated phenomenon *The Simpsons*. The cartoon, which had started as a feature on the *Tracy Ullman Show* in 1987, became a series in its own right in 1989. In doing so, it became the *Saturday Night Live* of the 1990s, a must-watch skewering of presidents and everyone else.[159]

The Bushes did not think much of the show. After its first season, Mrs. Bush told *People* that it [*The Simpsons*] was "the dumbest thing I've ever seen." This elicited a written response from *The Simpsons'* animated matriarch, Marge. Mrs. Bush was chastened by Marge's letter and apologized for her "loose tongue." The Bushes, however, didn't learn the lesson of avoiding a fight with someone that, to adapt an old saying, "distributes photons by the megapixel." In 1992, President Bush pined for an America "closer to the Waltons than the Simpsons."[160] (As Ben Shapiro observes, *The Waltons* was created by a liberal, actually, and "consistently promoted liberal messages of tolerance for everyone (including many criminals).")[161] Once again, the Simpson family got the better of the exchange. On a subsequent episode, Bart Simpson referred to the economic slowdown, saying, "Hey, man, we're just like the Waltons. Both families are praying for an end to the depression." After Bush lost the 1992 election, an entire episode of *The Simpsons* was devoted to mocking him, concluding with the president spanking an exasperatingly annoying Bart.[162]

Presidents Who Grew Up with TV: Clinton, Bush, and Everyone to Come

Naturally, the liberal Bill Clinton fared better on *The Simpsons* than Bush did. "[T]he show was surprisingly slow to satirize President Bill Clinton," observes Paul Cantor. "On balance, it is fair to say that *The Simpsons*, like most of what comes out of Hollywood, is pro-Democrat and anti-Republican."[163] Clinton received better treatment from the rest of Hollywood as well. Richard Nixon, who had an unexpectedly good relationship with Clinton, grumbled that TV comedy shows gave Clinton a far easier ride than Nixon had received as president, as well as after he had left office.[164]

Clinton benefited even more from active promotion by Hollywood than from soft handling. *The West Wing*, a series that began in 1999, seemed like one long tribute to the greatness of Democratic presidents, Clinton in particular. Martin Sheen, who played President Josiah Bartlet, told PBS's Charlie Rose, "I think if you took three presidents that I happen to admire very greatly and put them all together, you'd have the fantasy of Bartlet and that would be John Kennedy, Jimmy Carter, and Bill Clinton."[165] Aaron Sorkin, one of the series' creators, acknowledged that they made "a conscious decision not to include" the Clinton scandals, particularly the one involving Monica Lewinsky, on *The West Wing*. It was "too bad," he mused, "because there's actually, you know, there's some great stories you can get out of scandals."[167] Because of the show's pro-Clinton approach, the *Atlantic*'s Chris Lehmann called it "a sort of higher-minded, conscience-haunted upgrade of the Clinton White House," emblematic of "the selective (yet ever didactic) liberal retreat into political fantasy." Clinton, of course, loved the show.[168]

While *The West Wing* presented America with a sanitized, non-philandering version of Clinton, the news side of the television business aired his foibles more openly.[169]

"Monica-gate" changed Clinton's television-viewing habits. His fundraiser and friend Terry McAuliffe writes of an excruciatingly awkward Park City vacation with the Clinton family at the height of the Lewinsky drama. Bill, Hillary, Chelsea, and McAuliffe tried to watch TV together but had trouble finding a station not featuring the scandal. "It was a bizarre, surreal experience sitting there with them, but none of us said anything. Hillary just kept clicking until she ended up on ESPN, not her favorite, but the President and I were happy and at least they weren't whacking the Clintons."[166]

The media began reporting on what became known as the "bimbo eruptions" as far back as the 1992 campaign. He and Hillary appeared together in a famous interview on *60 Minutes*—another one of Reagan's favorite shows—to refute the charges that he had an affair with nightclub singer Gennifer Flowers. Hillary Clinton infamously insisted that she was not "some little woman standing by her man like Tammy Wynette." The interview worked—Clinton became the Democratic nominee and won the presidency—but the "bimbo eruptions" would return.

Bill Clinton proved a savvy manipulator of television. He donned sunglasses and played the saxophone on *The Arsenio Hall Show*, a flash of hipness from a baby boomer in the twilight of his youth. Of course, it wasn't hard to look hip when you were running against George Bush, but Clinton still gave it all he had. He had received his first TV set in 1956, at the age of ten, and he was the first president to have grown up with a television. He liked watching Elvis, but "what really dominated my TV viewing that summer," Clinton recalled, "were the Republican and Democratic conventions. I sat on the floor right in front of the TV and watched them both, transfixed." Just as Daniel Boorstin described the new experience of television, young Clinton was "here" (at home in Hot Springs) but watched and imagined what it would be like to be "there" (at the convention). Less than four decades later, he would indeed be there, as millions of people looked at Clinton and imagined what it would be like for them to be "there." When Adlai Stevenson appeared reluctant to accept the Democratic nomination for a second time, Clinton remembered, "even then I couldn't understand why anyone wouldn't want the chance to be president."[170]

As president, Clinton tried to circumvent the media and reach voters unfiltered through television. He brought in the former Reagan White House aide David Gergen, who taught Clinton to follow Reagan's model of carefully staged events designed to capture the day's news.[171] Clinton and company took the lessons to heart, and they implemented Mike Deaver's message-of-the-day technique for emphasizing their chosen themes in the press.[172]

In the few years since the Reagan administration, however, television news had moved to twenty-four-hour-a-day coverage, and the new cable networks had broken the three-network monopoly of American television news. Clinton's communications staff responded by bringing campaign tactics into the White House, setting up a "war room" to ensure that no charge—of which there were many—would go unaddressed within a twenty-four-hour news cycle.[173] In 1998, the all-consuming Lewinsky scandal put Clinton's media strategy to the test. Twenty-four-hour news coverage kept public figures on screen all the time.[174] Therefore, when there was a scandal, it would be a round-the-clock affair. Nevertheless, Clinton's aggressive approach allowed him to survive an enormously taxing scandal that would have toppled almost any other president.

"Monica-gate" changed Clinton's television-viewing habits. His fundraiser and friend Terry McAuliffe writes of an excruciatingly awkward Park City vacation with the Clinton family at the height of the Lewinsky drama. Bill, Hillary, Chelsea, and McAuliffe tried to watch TV together but had trouble finding a station not featuring the scandal. "It was a bizarre, surreal experience sitting there with them, but none of us said anything. Hillary just kept clicking until she ended up on ESPN, not her favorite, but the President and I were happy and at least they weren't whacking the Clintons."

McAuliffe's story shows how presidents have to consume what they produce on television. Clinton's White House debauchery not only tarnished his office but also polluted the news that came into every American living room. The president who enjoyed *The West Wing*'s glowing fictional representations of himself had to endure the graphic on-air descriptions of his lubricious private recreations. McAuliffe does not seem to have spent much time pondering the poetic justice of the situation. He was just trying to survive the trip. At one point on the vacation, when the White House steward offered to bring some wine, both Bill and Hillary refused. McAuliffe responded: "You bet. And leave the bottle right here for me."[175]

After he left the White House, Clinton made less news but continued to enjoy TV. In 2007, he told television advertisers that in addition to continuing to watch basketball, he also liked *24* (produced by a known Republican), *Grey's Anatomy*, and *Boston Legal*, as well as reruns of *All in the Family, I Love Lucy, The Andy Griffith Show,* and

Bonanza on TV Land, a cable network where old series spend their afterlives. He explained all this TV-watching by saying, "As you know, my wife is away [running for president], so I'm home alone a lot." As a result, he was "particularly grateful to TV Land for giving [him] something to do at night." Nevertheless, he insisted that all the television did not interfere with his work on climate change, hurricane and tsunami relief, AIDS, and childhood obesity.[176]

These remarks were classic Clinton: He was continually self-revealing, pop-culture referential, and aching to be the center of attention. He acted this way while running for office, as president, and as ex-president. It was reminiscent of his famous 1994 MTV town hall, in which he answered the invasive "boxers or briefs" question: "usually briefs." Clinton was clearly a master of pop culture, but he also gave ammunition to critics who thought he took it too far. In the continuing struggle to be a man of the people and maintain presidential dignity, dignity was often relegated to second place, or worse.

George W. Bush also grew up in the TV era, but the medium played a different role in his life. While he did watch sports on television, he relied little on TV for news or entertainment. When Barack Obama's advisor David Axelrod started to tell Bush how he had praised the outgoing president for how his staff had handled the transition, Bush cut him off, saying, "I don't watch television."[177] He read multiple newspapers and watched ESPN regularly, but he had little interest in TV's entertainment offerings.[178] In 2005 the *Los Angeles Times* ran an article about the shows Bush had *never* seen, including *The Daily Show with Jon Stewart* and *Desperate Housewives*. It also noted that he had not seen *Saturday Night Live*'s parody of Jenna and Barbara, the Bush daughters. "They put an off button on the TV for a reason," said Bush in a 2005 interview. "Turn it off."[179]

In contrast to Johnson and Nixon, Bush didn't spend time watching TV news. In March 2003, soon after U.S. warplanes began bombing Iraq, a reporter asked Bush's press secretary Ari Fleischer if the president had been "busy watching bombs fall on the Iraqi capital?" "The President doesn't need to watch TV to find out what's going on in the war," Fleischer responded dismissively. Unlike his father, who had followed the progress of the first Gulf War on CNN, the younger Bush was confident that the U.S. government had sufficient sources of information to keep him up to date.[180] The media interpreted this to mean that he was uninterested and dubbed him "Uncurious George," perhaps demonstrating how beholden they themselves were to TV as a source for all information. Bill Clinton always made sure that the media knew he needed them. Bush was confident and did not. In a world where the media's political influence is overwhelming, Clinton's course seems to be the wiser one.

Even during the agonizing five-week electoral recount fight of 2000, Bush rarely followed events on television.[181] But he was watching TV on December 12, when the Supreme Court ruled in his favor on the Florida recount, handing him the presidency. The problem was that different networks reported the *Bush v. Gore* decision differently, leading to some confusion between Bush and his top advisor, Karl Rove. The two men spoke by phone and Rove said, "I'm watching NBC, and it's good news." Bush replied, "I'm watching CNN, and it's bad news." Rove's reasonable—and, as it turned out accurate—reply: "Well, then watch NBC."[182]

The contrasting network stories ended up informing much of the Bush administration's approach toward the media. In addition to highlighting the confusion that reigned during the recount, the discrepancy in the reports revealed that different stations could present the same news in remarkably different ways. Conservatives had long criticized the networks for being biased against them. There was certainly a case to be made for this, but many in Washington found the uniformity of network views comforting. If the networks represented only one point of view, that upset the existing sense of order and meant that the phrase "conventional wisdom" no longer had any real meaning. Yet for conservatism, the prospect of the end of the network monopoly on news presented a real opportunity. The development of successful TV news alternatives such as Fox News, as well as new outlets for conservative voices in the form of talk radio and the blogosphere, exposed both the bias and the diminishing dominance of the three big networks. Consequently, the Bush White House no longer treated them with the same deference as had previous administrations, feeding scoops to Fox News or the blogosphere rather than the less friendly networks.

The mainstream media noticed Bush's cold shoulder. As the *New York Times*' Amy Chozick put it, "George W. Bush and his aides liked to say they ignored the Fourth Estate...."[183]

The left developed their own programs as well; the reliably liberal MSNBC became for the Democrats what Fox News was for the Republicans. This put a squeeze on the supposedly neutral CNN, as well as CBS, ABC, and NBC. With Fox and MSNBC, most viewers could now get their news in the flavor that appealed to them. Fast-food options had now come to TV news.

The big three networks did not go away, of course. In fact, they often tried to assert their relevance. One of these attempts backfired on CBS's Dan Rather during Bush's 2004 reelection battle against the Democratic challenger, Senator John Kerry. The aging correspondent—who apparently had not learned his lesson in his tangle with the elder Bush—produced documentation that the young Bush had not fulfilled his National Guard obligations during the Vietnam War. To the embarrassment of Rather and his network, however, an incredulous blogosphere quickly showed the document to be a forgery. Rather's eager effort to recover his journalistic relevance backfired spectacularly; he lost his anchor position and was later fired by CBS News.

Bush's belief that he could largely ignore TV had costs as well. The late-night comics regularly portrayed him as a dimwit, which he decidedly was not. Furthermore, Bush's relatively infrequent TV appearances let others define him. Bush had never spoken on television from the Oval Office until after the September 11, 2001, terrorist attacks, and he waited for a month after 9/11 to hold a prime-time press conference.[184] The strategy of favoring Fox News made it harder to take his case to people disinclined to be supportive of him. Bush's approach was ultimately a mixed success. He won reelection in 2004, but he had a poor second term, in which his troubled media relations contributed no small part to his woes. Bush's approach would also have long-term implications, showing that a president who is not beholden to TV could liberate himself from TV's power to control the agenda. Bush may not have succeeded in this regard, but one of his successors could potentially employ such a strategy to his benefit.

Whether or not modern presidents have enjoyed watching television for hours on end—and no president had time to watch the staggering thirty-four hours a week of the average American[185]—all of them have had to deal with the new medium. The rapid emergence of TV as an essential tool of modern political life meant that those who could master it would thrive. Those who couldn't are still entertaining voters in old and embarrassing YouTube clips. But the technology and content of television is constantly changing, as are Americans' viewing habits. Presidents who look solely to their predecessors for how to deal with TV will inevitably and forever be left behind.

CHAPTER 10

READING AND THE MODERN PRESIDENT

Technology has advanced at a dizzying pace since the Founders inscribed the Constitution of their new republic on parchment and disseminated copies of it by riders on horseback. Yet there remains one constant: the written word. Thomas Jefferson pored over his costly and laboriously collected books by candlelight. Barack Obama flicks through blogs on an iPad that would hold Jefferson's entire library a hundred times over. But the act of reading—the encounter of one human mind with another through the written word—is essentially the same.

The difference, however, is in the vast explosion of options of reading material. A quarter-million new titles are published in the United States every year, a figure that would have been unimaginable to the Founding Fathers. The presidents who grew up in the twentieth century enjoyed an unprecedented choice of books, magazines, and newspapers. With all that choice, what a president chooses to read is now a more interesting and revealing question than ever.

Sometimes a president's reading directly affects his policy, as when Jimmy Carter read Christopher Lasch's *The Culture of Narcissism*. Sometimes it doesn't, as when Franklin Roosevelt went to bed with *The Punch and Judy Murders*. In any case, a president's reading selections affect how the public views him. Some reading for diversion is fine, but if that's all the reading he does, then he signals a lack of seriousness. As Amie Parnes wrote in *Politico*, presidents want to convey "a sense of gravitas. The president can't really be seen reading that year's beach novel, like *The Da Vinci Code*."[1]

To judge from their reading, the postwar presidents have for the most part been a remarkably serious group. Presiding over the most powerful country on earth in what has arguably been the most perilous epoch in human history, they have taken their responsibility to heart by reading widely, especially in history and in biography. However, some have read more widely, and more seriously, than others. And the great readers have not always been the ones you might expect.

Truman and Ike: Reading under the Radar

Harry Truman was the last president without a college education, but he was hardly unread. In fact, he was quite the autodidact and a regular reader throughout his life.[2] Some presidents have pretended that they read more than they did. Some—most notably George W. Bush—read a great deal, contrary to their reputations. But with Harry Truman there was no doubt. He was a reader from an early age, with a tremendous ability to retain what he had read years or even decades beforehand.[3]

Truman's love of reading came from his parents. His father saved money to purchase a set of Shakespeare, which Harry read, as well as Plutarch's *Lives* and the Bible (twice through).[4] He was never bored because, as he put it, "we had a houseful of books." He loved reading but didn't boast about it—it "was just something you did."[5]

History and biography, the staples of modern presidential reading, were Truman's favorites. "The only thing new in the world is the history you don't know," he said.[6] His business partner Eddie Jacobson lamented that their clothing business failed because of Truman's distraction with biographies of Andrew Jackson.[7] Truman also developed a taste for good literature, especially for the works of his fellow Missourian, Mark Twain. He once lavished twenty-five dollars—a large amount at the time—on a twenty-five-volume set of Dickens. "I have been reading David Copperfield and have really found out that I couldn't appreciate Dickens before," he wrote.[8] Detective stories were an occasional indulgence. The creator of *Perry Mason*, Erle Stanley Gardner, used to send President Truman signed copies of his books, a service he performed for Franklin Roosevelt before him. Truman also shared his love of reading with his wife. He'd often sit and read with Bess, who enjoyed mysteries as well.[9]

Truman's daughter, Margaret, recalled that both of her parents constantly read and that her father always had a book with him.[10] She marveled at his powers of concentration: "He has always been able to read a book or a memorandum with the radio or the phonograph playing and my mother and me conducting a first-class family argument." If the world were about to come to an end, Margaret said, "he could not look up until he got to the bottom of the page he was reading."[11]

Truman shared a basic conviction with the Founding generation. "Readers of good books, particularly books of biography and history, are preparing themselves for leadership," he said. "Not all readers become leaders. But all leaders must be readers."[12] Truman's reading shaped one of his most historic decisions. His support for establishing the state of Israel, despite the strong opposition of his own State Department, had roots in his boyhood reading. In addition to his multiple readings of the Bible, the young Truman had devoured the multi-volume history *Great Men and Famous Women*, edited by Charles Horne.[13] One of the heroes of this work was Cyrus the Great, the Persian ruler who allowed the exiled Israelites to return to Jerusalem and rebuild their holy temple. When Eddie Jacobson introduced his old friend at New York's Jewish Theological Seminary as "the man who helped create the State of Israel," Truman corrected him, "What do you mean, helped create? I am Cyrus, I am Cyrus!"[14]

Truman's reading seems to have contributed to the rehabilitation of his historical reputation as well. Though decidedly deeply unpopular when he left office,[15] the work of David McCullough and other friendly biographers accomplished a remarkable turnaround, making Truman one of the most admired presidents. These revisionist biographers were particularly impressed by Truman's assiduous reading.

In contrast to the academically humble Truman, Dwight Eisenhower—a graduate of West Point and the president of Columbia University—had a reputation for not being much of a reader. As president, he relied on staff-generated press summaries or single-page summaries of lengthy reports. These were necessary but insufficient, as Ike often appeared ignorant about ongoing developments.[16]

The truth, however, reveals itself more complicated. Just as historians have revised their view of Eisenhower the president, they have also discovered that he was a more serious reader than was previously believed. Even though he didn't read much as president, he was, for example, an avid reader in his youth. As a child, Ike's mother locked his books in a closet to prevent him from reading too much—not a problem many mothers have today.[17] He was particularly enamored with the adventure works of Jack London.[18]

Eisenhower also received the equivalent of a graduate education from his military mentor, General Fox Conner. The two met in 1919, and Conner brought the young officer with him to Panama. Conner encouraged his protégé to read a wide variety of books, focusing on military history, but also including Shakespeare, Plato, and Nietzsche. Ike proved a willing pupil, continually reading whatever Conner offered and coming back for more. The general placed a heavy emphasis on Carl von Clausewitz's classic *On War* and made Eisenhower read the book three times. Ike remembered the lessons as president and would refer to Clausewitz in meetings with his national security team.[19]

In later years Eisenhower used his influence to encourage reading. In a famous speech at Dartmouth College in 1953, he warned the students not to join "the book burners," telling them not to "be afraid to go in your library and read every book...."[20] His own library had over a thousand volumes, including *A History of Western Art* by John Ives Sewall, Bruce Catton's *Mr. Lincoln's Army* and *A Stillness at Appomattox*, multiple copies of the Bible, and of course, a selection of Western novels.[21]

This is not to suggest that Ike was some kind of intellectual. In fact, he intentionally assumed an anti-intellectual air. Ike dismissed an intellectual as someone "who takes more words than are necessary to tell more than he knows."[22] In addition, his TV-watching habit alone was enough to scare away the intelligentsia. Perhaps Eisenhower ought to have read more in order to keep up with what was going on around him. For example, it wasn't until 1962, when he read Richard Nixon's *Six Crises*, that he learned Nixon was upset about the uncertainty of whether he would be Ike's running mate again in 1956.[23] As Harry Truman might have told him, reading can teach you things you did not already know.

JFK Inc.:
Consciously Promoting Presidential Reading

John F. Kennedy and his team understood the benefits of outreach to intellectuals and to authors. Before the administration even began, Kennedy asked Richard Neustadt, the author of *Presidential Power*, for a tutorial on transitions—a gesture for which presidential historians have continually praised him.[24] This intellectual outreach continued after the inauguration. In a memorandum of February 1961, Arthur Schlesinger Jr. encouraged Kennedy to present himself as a champion of the values of "artistic and cultural achievement," in part through "stories about the books you and the first lady have been reading...."[25]

The effort to portray Kennedy as a reader had some foundation, to be sure. At the same time, the White House was eager to capitalize on the national embrace of intellectuals in the wake of the Soviets' 1957 launch of the *Sputnik* satellite and the beginning of the space race. Kennedy and his team recognized an opportunity to break new ground by actively associating the Harvard-educated senator with America's growing intellectual elite. This was a bold new step, but the need for technical expertise to address America's economic and foreign policy challenges, coupled with an increasingly educated populace, gave the Kennedy strategy a promising opening. Intellectuals suddenly had more appeal than they did in the 1930s when Congressman Dewey Short of Missouri denounced Franklin Roosevelt's "brain trust" as "theoretical, intellectual, professorial nincompoops who could not be elected dog catcher."[26]

This was possible due to a middlebrow cultural explosion in the years following World War II, complete with highbrow movies and orchestras emerging even outside the country's large urban centers. As Franklin Foer writes in the *New Republic*, "Even television, which Newton Minow famously described as a 'vast wasteland,' featured Leonard Bernstein on CBS on Saturday nights, explaining how to properly appreciate a sonata."[27] The Kennedy team saw the value in bringing intellectuals like Schlesinger and John Kenneth Galbraith into the administration, but also in portraying the handsome young Kennedy as a high-minded man of culture himself.

The American people responded to these efforts. When Kennedy revealed a liking for the novels of Ian Fleming, it helped turn superspy James Bond into a publishing sensation.[28] Or at least this was the story. Kennedy liked the books, but only to a degree, and not to the degree portrayed in the media. *Newsweek* reporter and Kennedy pal Ben Bradlee—and the future editor of the *Washington Post*—notes that Kennedy "seemed to enjoy the cool and the sex and the brutality" of the Bond books and films. Beyond that, Kennedy's interest was overblown.[29] Schlesinger even admits that pushing Kennedy's link to Fleming—his "supposed addiction to James Bond"—was a "publicity gag." As gags go, it proved very successful, for both Kennedy and Fleming.[30]

Highlighting and even exaggerating Kennedy's reading not only helped him with middlebrow Americans, but also aided him among the intellectuals themselves. Suitably impressed by the new president's outreach to intellectuals, they wrote fulsomely about Kennedy's interest in the life of the mind. Norman Podhoretz, a liberal at the time, wrote in his first memoir, *Making It*, that thanks to the Kennedy administration, "from having carried a faint aura of disreputability, the title 'intellectual' all at once became an honorific...."[31]

Even after his death, Kennedy's team relentlessly pressed stories about his reading. Schlesinger described a bookish morning routine: "Dressing in the morning, he would prop open a book on his bureau and read while he put on his shirt and tied his necktie." The president preferred history and biography, Schlesinger said, but he rarely read novels.[32]

Jackie Kennedy told Theodore White in their post-assassination interview that "Jack had more to do with myth, magic, legend, saga, and story than with political theory or political science.... [Y]ou must think of him as this little boy, sick so much of the time, reading in bed, reading history, reading the *Knights of the Round Table*, reading Marlborough."[33] The young widow's efforts at myth-building are perhaps a bit strained. She obviously wasn't there to observe little Jack's sickbed reading, although she had clearly heard stories about it, but she wanted to promote the image of Kennedy as a great reader.

Archibald Cox recalled taking a flight with Kennedy and sheepishly reading a Perry Mason story while Kennedy read a volume of Proust. Ken Gormley, who recounts this story in a biography of Cox, also cites on the same page an "anonymous assistant" saying that Kennedy "could never sit still for five minutes."[35] It seems typical that the on-the-record story would promote the myth, while the unnamed source would mention the well-known reality of Kennedy's restlessness. Along these lines, a host of biographers have noted Kennedy's impatience and inability to sit still, even while on vacation.[36]

> Bruce Jay Friedman solved the mystery of George Plimpton's indescribable accent. When asked directly where exactly that accent came from, Plimpton acknowledged that it was "an affectation."[34]

The image-makers nevertheless have succeeded in establishing Kennedy's reputation as a reader. What he read, however, is less certain. What remains beyond doubt is that Kennedy was certainly *conversant* with intellectual trends. This familiarity can be partially accredited to Schlesinger's tireless tutorials. Kennedy had come under Schlesinger's spell in his teens when he found himself engrossed by the Pulitzer Prize–winning *The Age of Jackson*.

Kennedy's intellectual reputation was also bolstered by his Pulitzer Prize–winning book, *Profiles in Courage*, an admiring study of eight senators who had made tough decisions when the times called. Here again, there is more to the story than meets the eye. It did not take long for rumors to percolate that Ted Sorensen, not Kennedy, wrote the book, a charge that originated with the columnist Drew Pearson in 1957. The rumors spread so rampantly that the first question the prospective defense secretary Robert McNamara asked Kennedy, to his face, was whether Kennedy had indeed written the book. Kennedy assured him that he had, and McNamara, impressed by the book, took the job.[37]

The most definitive analysis of *Profiles'* provenance comes from Herbert Parmet. He looked at the initial drafts themselves and concluded, "The research, tentative drafts and organization were left to the collective labors of others, and the literary craftsmanship was clearly the work of Ted Sorensen."[38] Garry Wills looked into this question as well, and, typically, came up with a catchier way of expressing his findings: Kennedy did not so much "author" the book as "authorize" it.[39]

Wills saw *Profiles* as part of a larger plan. He had a Boorstinian view of the creation of the Kennedy image by the president's father, Joe. According to Wills, the patriarch made a world in which "his family [would] outshine any star in the fan magazines, any heroic astronaut on the cover of *Life*, any popular professor on the Harvard campus." In the world Joe Kennedy and his wealth had created, "you were whatever you could make people think you were. In that sense, John Kennedy was the writer of *Profiles in Courage*."[40]

Still, the consensus of historians is that Kennedy did not write *Profiles*. He certainly was not the author in the conventional sense. His historical acolyte Michael O'Brien tries to soften the truth, but he acknowledges that Kennedy was "the author only in a limited sense."[41] Kennedy critic James Piereson writes that "Sorensen actually wrote the bulk of the manuscript based on Kennedy's oral comments and rough notes, supplemented by Sorensen's own research."[42] James McGregor Burns, another historian friendly to JFK, determined that Kennedy received "more help on the book than you or I could get if we were doing one." Wills added acrimoniously, "The rules for Kennedys are different, that's all."[43]

Those rules also earned Kennedy credit for reading a book he never read. Such was the case in the most famous incident of Kennedy's reading, Michael Harrington's *The Other America*. In 2003, the *New York Times'* Michiko Kakutani, reflecting the conventional wisdom on this subject, noted that Harrington's book "is widely credited with helping catalyze the Kennedy-Johnson war on poverty in the 1960's and the creation of Great Society programs."[44] A searing chronicle of persistent poverty in the United States, *The Other America* was indeed influential in inspiring the War on Poverty. But Kennedy was moved not by the book itself but by Dwight Macdonald's thirteen-thousand-word *New Yorker* essay on Harrington's book, one of the longest pieces ever to run in the magazine. In fact, *The Other America* had not made much splash until Macdonald's article. Walter Heller, the chairman of Kennedy's council of economic advisors, gave the president Macdonald's article, and most aides believed he read the review rather than the book. Nicholas Lemann, who looked into the question for the *Atlantic,* determined that Macdonald's review, "dry, witty, and elegantly written, would have been much more to Kennedy's taste than the book, which is earnest and impassioned."[45]

After reading the review, Kennedy asked his staff to look into the problem of poverty. The War on Poverty followed but was not necessarily caused by Harrington's book or even by Macdonald's essay. It's true that Kennedy's staff came up with a plan for an "attack on poverty," which Heller discussed with the president a few days before the fateful trip to Dallas in November of 1963. On the other hand, there is little to no proof that Kennedy made a war on poverty his last wish or that he would have energetically pursued a legislative plan to wage it. Lyndon Johnson, a newspaper junkie and skilled legislator, seized the idea and exploited it politically. After a briefing from Heller, Johnson responded, "That's my kind of program. It's a people program."[46] Johnson was also apparently influenced by the British economist Barbara Ward's *The Rich Nations and the Poor Nations*—a rare instance of Johnson's actions being shaped by his book reading.

In the *Daily Beast*'s ranking of the twenty best-read presidents, Kennedy places fourteenth: "Any man that asked Robert Frost to read at his inauguration and Arthur Schlesinger Jr. to join his Cabinet must have a passion for literature...."[47] Not necessarily, but such a man would know that he could develop a reputation as a man with "a passion for literature." Still, the Kennedy team proved both bold and prescient in creating the image of the intellectual hero. It was not an obvious call, but it was a successful one, and the Kennedy mystique lives on.

After Kennedy:
Less Promotion, If Not Less Reading

Despite the success of Kennedy's intellectual branding campaign, his successors did not always imitate it. Kennedy put a lot of effort into showing himself as a reader, but reading is hard to fake. The truth is generally apparent to the American people; Kennedy was successful because he convinced the intellectual elites that he was reading their books and that they mattered.

None of the next three presidents was known as a reader, although Nixon, like Truman, was a reader without enjoying a reputation for reading. Nixon was defensive about his reading and about his reputation. The *New York Times*' Nicholas Kristof has described him as "a self-loathing intellectual," and he was indeed ambivalent about his intellectual side.[48] In his farewell address to his staff, Nixon noted that "I am not educated, but I do read books." It is not clear why the graduate of Whittier College and Duke Law School considered himself not educated, but he did like to read. As a child, he was often seen reading, and he particularly liked *National Geographic*. He read Tolstoy as a college student, at the urging of the Whittier English professor Albert Upton, and Nixon even referred to himself as a "Tolstoyan." From an early stage, however, Nixon seemed to read with a purpose in mind. In 1952, for example, he reviewed Whittaker Chambers's masterpiece *Witness* for the *Saturday Review of Literature*, which fits in with his 1950s reputation as a staunch anticommunist.[49]

In the years he spent in New York, between his failed gubernatorial bid in California and his successful run for the presidency in 1968, Nixon began in earnest to read for pleasure. He had the leisure that he had never enjoyed before in his adult life, and he used it to become a more cultured man, not only by reading but by attending the theater as well.[50]

As president, Nixon mostly read political biography or history.[51] Occasionally his reading was determined by what was going on around him. He bought a volume of Winston Churchill's World War II series *Triumph and Tragedy* because, he wrote in his memoir, "after the recent Soviet Summit I wanted to reread his analysis of the

Yalta conference."[52] His reading even affected the shape of the administration in his second term. He told his top staff members that re-reading Robert Blake's biography of Disraeli drove home Disraeli's description of William Gladstone's cabinet as "exhausted volcanoes." Nixon told the group that they were his "first team," but that "today we start fresh for the next four years." The staff members and cabinet secretaries who then had to write letters of resignation may not have appreciated the historical origins of Nixon's epiphany,[53] and Nixon himself later regretted the move.

Of course, Nixon never finished that second term. While he was still vice president but when Nixon's downfall loomed as a real possibility, Gerald Ford told Robert Novak that he had read *The Twilight of the Presidency*, written by Lyndon Johnson's old press secretary, George Reedy. The book criticized the pre-Watergate Johnson presidency for being too regal and remote. (Arthur Schlesinger made a similar argument in 1973 in *The Imperial Presidency*.) Reedy's book, which the *New York Times* reporter Marjorie Hunter had given to Ford, struck a chord. He complained to Novak about a rising sense of presidential infallibility and, with the book in hand, said, "Anybody that's hired over there [at the White House] ought to read this book, because what it describes is 'avoidable.'" Novak found this "remarkable": "While other presidents prepared to enter the oval office intent on maximizing their power, Ford was concerned with minimizing his."[54]

Some of Ford's reading suggestions came from the political philosopher Robert Goldwin. He led the Ford administration's outreach to intellectuals such as Irving Kristol, Thomas Sowell, and James Q. Wilson. He gave the president excerpts from their writings and invited said intellectuals to periodic White House dinners. Ford's chief of staff, Donald Rumsfeld, recalled after Goldwin died in 2010, "Bob Goldwin was the Ford administration's one-man think tank" and "intellectual compass."[55]

Yet Ford's reading was not confined to policy or political philosophy. At some point he discovered that there was no Bible on Air Force One, and he specifically requested that a Bible be placed in the Air Force One stateroom whenever he was aboard.[56] The lack of a Bible on the president's plane had been felt on November 22, 1963. Lyndon Johnson was sworn in on Air Force One using a book wrongly assumed to be a Bible. It was actually a missal, the liturgical prayer book of the Catholic Church, an error that was not discovered and made public for over three years.[57] Following Ford's request, keeping a Bible onboard has remained an Air Force One tradition.

Jimmy Carter:
Speed-Reading on the Road to Malaise

Jimmy Carter would have appreciated Ford's insight. Carter, a devout Southern Baptist, was well-versed in the Bible. In retirement he even wrote *NIV Lessons from Life Bible: Personal Reflections with Jimmy Carter*, one of about two dozen books he has written since leaving office, making him the most prolific author in presidential history. And he has found readers as far afield as Pakistan—Osama Bin Laden read Carter's *Palestine: Peace not Apartheid* in his Abbottabad hideout.[58]

One recurring theme in Carter's works is the importance of books throughout his life. In 2001's *An Hour Before Daylight*, he contrasted the reading habits of his parents: "Daddy mostly limited his reading to the daily and weekly newspapers and farm journals," while "my mother read constantly and encouraged us children to do the same." This encouragement led to the children's taking "a magazine or book to read while eating our meals, and this became a lifetime habit for my own family and me."[59]

Reading was undeniably linked to faith in Carter's childhood memories. In *An Hour Before Daylight*, he recalls being praised in chapel for "reading *War and Peace* when I was in the fifth grade."[60] In his book *Christmas in Plains*, Carter notes that his "most common request to Santa Claus was for two or three books, and I would prepare my choices very carefully." Carter spent a lot of time poring over the Sears, Roebuck catalog's book section, confident that "[a]bove all my other requests, this was the one that was most certain to be honored, because Mama was always encouraging me to read as much as possible."[61]

Carter was not an antisocial bookworm, however. He wrote in yet another memoir, *Sharing Good Times*, "When I look back over the past eighty years for times of greatest pleasure and enjoyment, it is possible to remember only a few such experiences that didn't involve other people." The only exception was reading, although he added that "much of the satisfaction of these quietest of times is the later sharing of ideas and discoveries with others."[62]

As president, Carter continued to read and carried on with this "sharing of ideas and discoveries with others." His *White House Diaries* are replete with references to books he had read, sometimes with titles, but often with just a number of books that he had read in a particular period. One of the ways that he was able to read so much was because he took speed-reading classes with his daughter, Amy, the only president to do so while in office. (John F. Kennedy was reported to have taken speed-reading classes while in the Senate, but he took only a few lessons before dropping out.)[63]

Carter's reading proved eclectic. It was certainly more varied than the history and biography that have preoccupied most modern presidents and suggested someone trying to put his finger on the pulse of the times. On October 29 and 30, 1977, he recorded that he "read four books over the weekend and had plenty of time to watch movies." He described one of those books, Saul Bellow's novel *Herzog*, in somewhat blasé fashion, as "[o]ne of the better novels I've read in several years."[64] In February 1978, he reported reading John McPhee's latest book about Alaska (*Coming into the Country*) and *Watership Down*, which he described as "about a group of rabbits, kind of an allegory similar to Tolkien's books and Alice in Wonderland."[65]

Carter's attempt to keep up with the *Zeitgeist* of the 1970s eventually backfired spectacularly. In the spring of 1979, his advisor Pat Caddell began working on a massive memorandum that was informed by Christopher Lasch's surprise nonfiction hit, *The Culture of Narcissism*.[66] The book contained a complicated argument and a depressing message: it mentioned both "malaise" and America's "crisis of confidence" on its first page. But it had a catchy title that seemed to apply to the grim conditions of the late 1970s. Caddell admired the book and advised Carter to address the country's focus on "personal gratification."[67]

Caddell finished the memo on April 23, 1979. The first part alone numbered seventy-five pages—staggeringly long for a memo to the president—and was grandly titled "Of Crisis and Opportunity." The inside joke at the White House was that a better title would have been "Apocalypse Now."[68]

Carter may have been a reader but he was also a politician. Caddell's dour prescription for a narcissistic nation sounded too stark, too gloomy to sell to the American public. Carter discussed the memo with Caddell but remained unconvinced. He pledged to speed-read a number of books, including Lasch's, as well as de Tocqueville's *Democracy in America*. Then he wanted to let things develop, a passive approach in troubling times.[69]

The energy crisis intensified during the spring and summer, giving Caddell his opportunity to press his Lasch-inspired version. On May 30, Caddell organized a White House dinner with Charles Peters, Jesse Jackson, Daniel Bell, and Bill Moyers, as well as Lasch, who impressed Caddell in person. Then, in early July, Carter postponed a planned energy speech and instead invited 130 experts to Camp David for an ideas summit of sorts. Then, on July 15, he gave the most famous—and disastrous—speech of his presidency, titled "Energy and the Crisis of Confidence."[70]

Sixty-five million Americans watched Carter's attempt to unite the country behind the common goal of energy independence. The speech initially received good reviews, but after Carter fired four cabinet secretaries and his rival Ted Kennedy put down the speech, the political situation turned dark. By September, his approval had dropped to a devastatingly low 19 percent. The address became known as the "malaise" speech, even though the word appears nowhere in the text, and it came to symbolize Carter's presidency.[71]

Reagan:
Reading More than You Thought

Jimmy Carter, whose presidency was colored by his gloomy reading, was followed by one of the sunniest men ever to occupy the White House, Ronald Reagan. His opponents habitually dismissed him as an intellectual lightweight—Clark Clifford famously called him "an amiable dunce." As was often the case with Reagan, the reputation and the reality did not match up.

Reagan read a great deal in his youth, in part to cope with a difficult childhood punctuated by poverty and by a dipsomaniac father. Jon Meacham tries to turn that reading against Reagan, suggesting that he remained influenced as an adult by "the fantastical novels of Edgar Rice Burroughs—including one in which a special space shield protects Earth from invading Martians." This explains, Meacham maintains, Reagan's interest in a missile defense shield.[72] This need by liberal analysts to denigrate Reagan's reading depicts a kind of defense mechanism in order to deal with the cognitive dissonance of Reagan reading more than his reputation suggested.

Reagan was a heavy reader in the years before he became president. His wife, Nancy, remembers him carrying a "small library" of books with him when he travelled in the 1950s.[73] Douglas Brinkley writes in the introduction to *The Reagan Diaries* that he "enjoyed reading books of all sorts—if the writing was inspiring."[74] He also liked the Bible, affirming that "[a]ll the complex questions that we face at home and abroad have their answers in that single book."[75]

Reagan continued to read despite the crush of duties as president. The shelves of his California ranch house were filled with books, including Westerns as well as works of conservative nonfiction. According to Steven Hayward, "The Reagan aide who told Carl Bernstein that 'it's true that he's got more horses than books' clearly never saw these bookshelves."[76] Others, however, viewed those shelves differently. They demonstrated Reagan's "down to earth tastes and lack of intellectual curiosity about things outside his normal ken of the West and the outdoors," says Ken Walsh.[77]

Reagan could have drawn attention to his reading had he wanted to. At one point, his spokesman Marlin Fitzwater suggested that he could let the media know Reagan was reading some recent nonfiction. Fitzwater thought this might play out better in the press than the typical stories of Reagan reading Louis L'Amour Westerns. In other words, Fitzwater wanted to take a page out of the Kennedy-Schlesinger playbook. But Reagan declined—"No, Marlin, I don't think we need to do that."[78]

Even so, word that Reagan liked a particular book could have powerful effects. The president helped transform the obscure insurance salesman Tom Clancy into a publishing phenomenon. After Reagan called Clancy's Cold War techno-thriller *The Hunt for Red October* "a perfect yarn" in 1985, the book skyrocketed up the best-seller list.[79] Even the author admitted, "President Reagan made *The Hunt for Red October* a best-seller." Clancy added modestly, "What happened to me was pure dumb luck—I'm not the new Hemingway." Hemingway or not, Reagan helped Clancy become quite wealthy, as he would go on to sign a three-million-dollar contract for three more novels and is still publishing best-sellers, albeit co-authored ones, today.

Ultimately, Reagan revealed himself a "closet bookworm," in the words of his long-time aide Martin Anderson.[80] For all we know, Reagan may have read more than Kennedy. In fact, this seems somewhat likely. But for whatever reason, Reagan did not want a spotlight on his reading. Modesty may have played a part, but he also may have been making a political calculation that being rugged rather than bookish would better suit the American people.

The one aspect of his reading that Reagan didn't mind sharing was his familiarity with conservative authors. He was immersed in conservative writing, including Whittaker Chambers's *Witness*, Milton Friedman's *Capitalism and Freedom*, and George Gilder's *Wealth and Poverty*. Gilder was the author Reagan cited more than any other. Reagan also read conservative magazines regularly, including *National Review, Human Events*, and the *American Spectator*. Reagan even discovered his future ambassador to the United Nations, Jeane Kirkpatrick, by reading her famous article "Dictatorship and Double Standards" in *Commentary* magazine.[81]

Reagan went even further than Ford in cultivating relations with conservative intellectuals. By promoting the works of conservative authors from the presidential podium, Reagan gave the conservative movement a legitimacy it had never had previously. Only three decades after the New York intellectual Lionel Trilling famously dismissed conservatism as "irritable mental gestures which seek to resemble ideas," conservative ideas were being studied—and amplified—by the most powerful man in the world.

George H. W. Bush proved less motivated by conservative ideology than Reagan. At the start of the 1988 Presidential campaign, Bush proclaimed, "I am a practical man.... I am not a mystic, and I do not yearn to lead a crusade."[82] Bush also called for a kinder, gentler nation in his 1988 Republican convention speech, an implicit knock on his conservative predecessor. This dig prompted Nancy Reagan to turn to a seatmate and ask pointedly, "Kinder than who?"[83]

Garry Wills reports that when asking Bush about his reading, Bush replied, "Now I don't have time." He did, however, claim to have read the classics in school, including *Catcher in the Rye*. As Wills somewhat gleefully pointed out, the 1951 novel came out well after Bush had not only finished prep school, but also his naval service and college as well. Perhaps, Wills tartly suggested, Bush was actually recalling that his sons had read the book at school instead.[84]

In a 1995 interview, Bush claimed to have read *War and Peace* twice, as well as "a book about discrimination called *Gentleman's Agreement*." "These books I think helped shape my life," he said, although the "I think" makes it sound as if he wasn't sure. Muddying the waters even further, he added, "To be honest with you, not one book stands out as the defining book for me."[85]

Bush even joked about his reputation as a non-reader. He described his plans for a 1991 vacation as including "a good deal of golf, ... a good deal of tennis, a good deal of horseshoes, a good deal of fishing, a good deal of running—and some reading. I have to throw that in there for the intellectuals out there."[86] The statement is revealing on many levels. First, the variety of his outdoor hobbies was astounding for anyone, let alone a president who protested how little time he had for reading. Second, there is the contrast between the amount of time he wanted to devote to his outdoor activities—"a good deal" for each—and the amount of time he would devote to reading—"some" and almost as an afterthought. This corresponds to the recollection of his Secret Service protectors, who thought him too hyperactive to ever sit down and read a book.[87] Finally, the comment about how he had to mention reading "for the intellectuals out there" suggests Bush was aware of his reputation as a non-reader among the smart set, and, while defensive about it, was having a little fun with them as well.

Bush was clearly no bookworm, but it's too much to dismiss him as a non-reader. In his epistolary memoir, *All the Best*, Bush mentions books he is reading on numerous occasions. In 1944, he wrote to his parents that he "finished the 4 books you gave me Mum and loved them all."[88] He added that he was also "trying to read a few on Russia, because I have become pretty much interested in that end of our diplomatic relations. Then, too, I know so little about it all that a couple of books wouldn't hurt anyway." Here again, he was self-deprecating about his reading and level of knowledge; he was also reading pragmatically, with a specific goal in mind—in this case, learning about Russia.

Bush's reading was almost always pragmatic. While serving as the U.S. envoy to China, he noted in another letter, "On the Chinese side, I have read Pearl Buck's *Good Earth*. I read the story of Empress Tzu Hsi, *The Dowager Empress*. Barnett's book *After Mao*. Teddy White's book *Thunder Out of China*."[89] Here again, with the comment "On the Chinese side," he indicates that there was purpose to his reading. As one of the first U.S. representatives in China following a long period sans diplomatic relations, it made sense that he was making a special effort to learn more about a country quite alien to American citizens and government officials alike.

Even as president, when he had "no time," he did find the time to read David McCullough's great biography of Truman. During his unsuccessful 1992 reelection effort, he told his friend and political ally the former New Hampshire governor Hugh Gregg that he had "[r]ead McCullough's new book on Truman, and read how Harry put it in perspective." He added that "Clinton-Gore have gone into orbit. They have been hyper critical of me. I have been relatively silent."[90] Given how the 1992 election turned out for him, perhaps he should have been less silent, both about his reading and about criticism of him.

Like many presidents, Bush enjoyed meeting with authors, but these meetings were more likely to be on athletic courts than in dinner salons or in policy sessions. The late author George Plimpton used to tell a story about playing tennis with

President Bush on the Camp David courts. During the match, the red telephone that accompanied the president in those pre-cell phone days began to ring, and both Plimpton and the president stopped playing while Bush went to answer the phone. Plimpton watched Bush on the phone anxiously, concerned about what world calamity might have taken place while they were playing. After a few moments, Bush passed the phone to Plimpton and said, "It's for you, George."[91]

Bush read far less than Nixon, but like Nixon, he read with a specific purpose in mind: learning about Russia, understanding China, or trying to get perspective from a predecessor who had also sought reelection. As I have written elsewhere, "Bush did not derive his worldview from books but from his understanding of Washington, from the people he knew, from the process of governing."[92]

Clinton:
Wearing Reading on His Sleeve

Clinton's approach could not have been more different from that of Bush. He had less Washington experience than his predecessor and read far more. Clinton's reading was enormously varied, and he often invited authors to the White House and asked them to recommend more books. He referred to books in a way few presidents ever have, not just mentioning their titles or even one-sentence summaries of their arguments, but whole paragraphs about their significance. Books heavily influenced Clinton's decisions on policy and personnel.

My Life, Clinton's 992-page autobiography, would have been considerably shorter if it did not include so much information on the books he read. In the prologue, he tells us that after law school he read *How to Get Control of Your Time and Your Life* by Alan Lakein. Even though he lamented that he could no longer find the book, it taught him lessons on prioritization that he maintained throughout his career.[93]

Reading, along with a few other famous habits, was ingrained during Clinton's childhood. His mother fed him prodigious amounts of food as she played cards, but she also read to him from the Sally, Dick, and Jane readers as well as from the *World*

Book encyclopedia. Clinton grew up in modest circumstances, and the encyclopedia volumes "were often the only books besides the Bible in working people's houses." Clinton jokes that his mother's ministrations "probably explain why I now read a lot, love card games [and] battle my weight...."[94]

That he read a lot is an understatement. The books he read—and how he came to read them—is a constant theme of Clinton's autobiography. He read an autographed copy of Senator William Fulbright's *The Arrogance of Power*, which shaped his views on Vietnam. As a Rhodes scholar at Oxford he "read hundreds of books." A Soviet guard tried to confiscate the books he was bringing into Russia, only to find that Clinton was carrying "Tolstoy, Dostoevsky, and Turgenev" instead of "dirty books." Professor Marvin Chirelstein of Yale Law School caught Clinton reading Gabriel Garcia Marquez's *One Hundred Years of Solitude* in class. Clinton brashly responded by holding "up the book and [telling] him it was the greatest novel written in any language since William Faulkner died." He took Ernest Becker's *The Denial of Death* on his honeymoon since "[i]t seemed like a good time to keep exploring the meaning of life." Before selecting his running mate in 1992, he had read Al Gore's book *Earth in the Balance*. He "[l]earned a lot" and "agreed with [Gore's] argument." As president, he was so frightened by the bioterror scenario in Richard Preston's *The Cobra Event* that he "urged several cabinet members and Speaker [Newt] Gingrich to read it."[95]

The many books mentioned in *My Life* demonstrate a number of Clintonian traits. One is that Clinton wants to "make sure that others know what he's reading (and *that* he's reading)," writes Samuel Jacobs in the *Daily Beast*.[96] He also wanted the authors he was reading to know that he was reading them. One trick he employed was leaving books he was reading on his desk so that visitors, and particularly reporters, would see them and report on them. He did this with Yale professor Stephen Carter's *The Culture of Disbelief*, garnering multiple media mentions for the book—and the fact that he was reading it—including one in *Time*, which still meant something then.[97] The president's encounter with Carter's book yielded the insight (shared at a White

House interfaith prayer breakfast) that "we have to be guided by a few basic principles and an absolute conviction that we can re-create a common good for America."[98]

"If you wanted to know how Bill Clinton thought when he was president," begins an interview published in *Foreign Policy* after he left office, "you ignored the scripted set-piece speeches and instead went to listen to him talk off the cuff at an evening fundraiser." In these off-the-cuff remarks, "he would ruminate extemporaneously on race, religion, science, and the nature of the human soul. His mind would roam widely and yet pull together disparate themes into a coherent narrative as no other politician of his generation." In the process, he would spout out book titles by the dozen. In the *Foreign Policy* interview alone, he mentioned thirteen authors and nine books.[99]

Clinton's reading was also a window on his policy. Reading Robert Kaplan's *Balkan Ghosts*, for example, which describes the intensity of that region's long-standing ethnic hatreds, left him wary of intervening in the bloody struggle for control of Bosnian territory that had once been part of Yugoslavia. Senior national security officials fretted about a single book's power to put off American action in Bosnia and remained angry about the incident for years. *Salon*'s Laura Rozen wrote in 2001, "some can't hear the name Robert Kaplan without blaming him for the delay in U.S. intervention." Kaplan was shocked by his influence: "The idea that any policymaker would read it, I didn't even consider. I saw it purely as an entertaining journalistic travel book about my experiences in the 1980s."[100]

There was a commercial advantage to being on Clinton's reading list. When word got out that the president was reading Walter Mosley's detective story *White Butterfly*, its sales jumped, though not as much, Mosely mused, as he might have expected. For a really robust presidential sales boosts, authors would have to wait for Barack Obama.[101]

Mosley was not an outlier, though. Clinton devoured mysteries, sometimes as many as three or four a week. He even told C-SPAN's Brian Lamb, "I love mysteries. I'm an addict; that's one of my little cheap thrills outlet. I'm always reading mysteries." (Alas, it turned out that mysteries were not his only cheap thrill.)[102]

It was difficult to pin Clinton down about his reading. While other presidents may have had one or two favorite books, Clinton had a list of twenty-one. There were some highbrow works, like those of Max Weber, Marcus Aurelius, and Reinhold Niebuhr; some politically correct picks, such as Maya Angelou's *I Know Why the Caged Bird Sings*; and at least one uxorious choice, Hillary Rodham Clinton's *Living History*. An air of studied elitism surrounds this list, as if one were trying to impress fellow students in a college seminar. As Elizabeth Renzetti wrote about Clinton's affection for Weber, "[R]emember Bill Clinton saying that Max Weber was his summer reading? No wonder college girls threw themselves at him."[103]

Speaking of college girls, books of course played a role in the most sordid episode of the Clinton presidency, his West Wing dalliance with the intern Monica Lewinsky. The lovebirds bought each other several books as gifts. Clinton gave Monica Walt Whitman's *Leaves of Grass*, while she gave him Nicholson Baker's semi-smutty *Vox*, Nicholas Sparks's maudlin *The Notebook*, and *Oy Vey! The Things They Say*, a Jewish joke book.[104] While the affair was playing out in public, Clinton attended a performance of E. L. Doctorow's *Ragtime* at the National Theater. When asked to speak for a few minutes after the show, he recalled having read the novel, of course, and being moved by it. He might have been talking about himself when he said, "Yes, this is the story of America, and it reminds us that we have a good system and the best ideals, but we always fall a little short."[105]

Misunderestimating Bush's Reading

Clinton read widely and made sure everyone knew it. George W. Bush, in contrast, was a reader and very few people knew it—until it was too late to change the public perception of him. During the campaign of 2000, he was regularly derided as incurious and unread. In his 2000 book *Bull Run*, Daniel Gross described Bush as "A graduate of Yale who doesn't read books...."[106] Similarly, *Slate*'s Steve Chapman somehow determined that "W's aversion to serious reading is undisputed."[107] Neither of these statements would have passed muster in any kind of serious fact-checking process beyond that of liberal presumption. As Bush's aide and fellow bibliophile Karl Rove puts it, "There is a myth perpetuated by Bush critics that he would rather burn a book than read one."[108]

Chapman and Gross notwithstanding, Bush read a great many books and had been a reader for a long time. Rove wrote in 2008, "In the 35 years I've known George W. Bush, he's always had a book nearby."[110] At Yale, Bush notes in his memoir, his "passion was history."[111] Walt Harrington, a self-described liberal journalist who detailed his surprising two-and-a-half decade relationship with Bush in *The American Scholar*, writes that back in 1986 he found "books by John Fowles, F. Scott Fitzgerald, James Joyce, and Gore Vidal lying about [in Bush's house in Midland, Texas], as well as biographies of Willa Cather and Queen Victoria." According to Laura Bush,

---

Peter Robinson Interviewing George Bush on Books:

Peter Robinson: What have you got on your book side table these days?

George W. Bush: I am reading a history of Joe DiMaggio's hit streak.

Robinson: Really?

Bush: Yeah, it's good. I have got on my—we don't have book stands anymore, we've got iPads. Please.

Robinson: Ok, I'm a little behind on that stuff.

Bush: Yeah. Anyway, the great debate. The compromise Henry Clay forged right before the Civil War. I'm looking forward to reading a book that was given to me by a fine book critic about the Alamo. I believe you just gave that to me.

Robinson: I did just give you that.

Bush: I'm still reading quite a bit and enjoying it a lot.[109]

---

by this same period, Bush had already picked up the regular habit of reading before going to sleep at night.[112]

Before becoming president, Bush's reading was mainly behind the scenes. Once he became president, it was harder for journalists to ignore the fact that he was a reader. Harrington reports that the president read 186 books between 2006 and 2008, mainly history and biography. By way of comparison, the *Washington Post* reported that the typical American claimed to read four books annually and that 27 percent of Americans had read no books in the preceding year.[113] In further contrast to the typical American, Bush "reads instead of watching TV,"[114] says Rove. "[Y]ou can sit there and be absorbed by TV, let the news of the moment consume you. You can just do nothing," Bush observes. "I choose to read as a form of relaxation."[115]

Bush's reading was weighted heavily toward nonfiction. In 2006 alone, he read ninety-five books, fifty-eight of which were nonfiction. In a conversation with Bush in 2011, Harrington "tick[ed] off a partial list of people Bush has read books about in recent years in addition to Washington, Truman, and Acheson: Abraham Lincoln, Andrew Carnegie, Mark Twain, Huey Long, Lyndon Johnson, Theodore Roosevelt, Andrew Mellon, Dietrich Bonhoeffer, Ulysses S. Grant, John Quincy Adams, Genghis Khan." Bush read fourteen biographies of Lincoln alone while in the White House.[116] This was in addition to his annual reading of the entire Bible, along with a daily devotional.[117]

To his credit, Bush read both liberal and conservative authors without appearing to discriminate. Clinton and Obama, by contrast, read almost exclusively liberal authors, while Reagan favored conservatives. The author of *Salt: A World History*, Mark Kurlansky first reacted to hearing that Bush read his book with a dismissive "Oh, he reads books?" On further reflection, however, Kurlansky was grudgingly impressed that the president read the work of a professed "virulent Bush opponent." "What I find fascinating," Kurlansky said, "and it's probably a positive thing about the White House, is they don't seem to do any research about the writers when they pick the books."[118]

In his memoir *Decision Points*, "Bush cites book after book that influenced his thinking in the White House," Harrington observes. Among them are Eliot Cohen's *Supreme Command*, which "argued that a president must hold his generals accountable for results," and H. R. McMaster's *Dereliction of Duty*, which found "that the Vietnam War military leadership had not done enough to correct the flawed strategy adopted by President Johnson and Defense Secretary Robert McNamara." Bush told Harrington that his decision to bail out the banks in 2008 was shaped by his reading on the Great Depression: "I had read enough history about the Depression to know the consequences.... I didn't want history to record that there was a moment when George W. Bush could have done something to prevent the depression and chose not to."[119] A fascinating book reference in *Decision Points* that Harrington doesn't mention is to a novel, Aldous Huxley's *Brave New World*. That book, Bush says, shaped his compromise that limited government funding for embryonic stem-cell research.[120] On a less policy-oriented note, Bush told the New York Yankees coach Don Zimmer at the 2001 World Series that the only book he had had time to read since the 9/11 terrorist attack was Zimmer's *Zim: A Baseball Life*.[121]

Bush's reading helped determine his second-term agenda. In 2004, he was taken with *The Case for Democracy* by the Israeli politician and former Soviet dissident Natan Sharansky. Bush read the book in galleys at the suggestion of his former Texas Rangers partner Tom Bernstein. He responded by meeting with Sharansky and instructing many of his top staffers to read the book. He took up Sharansky's theme in his second inaugural address, announcing America's intention "to seek and support the growth of democratic movements and institutions in every nation and culture, with the ultimate goal of ending tyranny in our world."[123] Sharansky was impressed by the president's reaction to his book: "Not only did he read it," he told the *Washington Post*, "he felt it."[124]

Those who met him were impressed with Bush's reading. In addition to Harrington and Rove, Yale's John Lewis Gaddis wrote of being surprised to find that Bush "reads more history and talks with more historians than any of his predecessors

The Full List of Bill Clinton Book Favorites:

- *I Know Why the Caged Bird Sings*, Maya Angelou
- *Meditations*, Marcus Aurelius
- *The Denial of Death*, Ernest Becker
- *Parting the Waters: America in the King Years, 1954–1963*, Taylor Branch
- *Living History*, Hillary Rodham Clinton
- *Lincoln*, David Herbert Donald
- *The Four Quartets*, T. S. Eliot
- *Invisible Man*, Ralph Ellison
- *The Way of the World: From the Dawn of Civilizations to the Eve of the Twenty-First Century*, David Fromkin
- *One Hundred Years of Solitude*, Gabriel Garcia Marquez
- *The Cure at Troy: A Version of Sophocles' "Philoctetes,"* Seamus Heaney
- *King Leopold's Ghost: A Story of Greed, Terror, and Heroism in Colonial Africa*, Adam Hochschild
- *The Imitation of Christ*, Thomas à Kempis
- *Homage to Catalonia*, George Orwell
- *The Evolution of Civilizations: An Introduction to Historical Analysis*, Carroll Quigley
- *Moral Man and Immoral Society: A Study in Ethics and Politics*, Reinhold Niebuhr
- *The Confessions of Nat Turner*, William Styron
- *Politics as a Vocation*, Max Weber
- *You Can't Go Home Again*, Thomas Wolfe
- *Nonzero: The Logic of Human Destiny*, Robert Wright
- *The Collected Poems of W. B. Yeats*, William Butler Yeats[122]

since at least John F. Kennedy." As we have seen, Bush probably read more history than Kennedy, although, thanks to Schlesinger, Kennedy certainly talked to his share of historians. Gaddis also found that Bush "has surprised me more than once with comments on my own books soon after they've appeared, and I'm hardly the only historian who has had this experience." Amusingly, Gaddis confessed to "improvising excuses to him, in Oval Office seminars, as to why I hadn't read the latest book on Lincoln, or on—as Bush refers to him—the "first George W."[125] Michael Medved recalled an Oval Office meeting in which Bush spoke "knowledgeably and passionately about Lincoln's reliance in even the darkest days of the Civil War on unwavering support from Union soldiers and Christian clergy, and expressed the hope that he could sustain a similar connection with the same forces in our society."[126]

The people who don't know him are the ones who insist that Bush is an intellectual lightweight. The *New York Times* book critic Michiko Kakutani pronounced that Bush "raced through books" and that he "favored prescriptive books."[127] The *Washington Post*'s Richard Cohen, despite admitting that Bush's reading list was "prodigious," found confirmation in it of "the intellectually insulated man." The list "is long, but it is narrow."[128] The *New York Times*' Nicholas Kristof even claimed that Bush "adopted anti-intellectualism as administration policy," adding that he had never interviewed anyone "who appeared so uninterested in ideas."[129]

Bush understood how his critics viewed him. He read and liked Juan Williams's book *Enough*, a critique of the way black leaders failed to address the real problems black Americans face. But he told a White House colleague of mine that he preferred to keep quiet about his interest in the book so as to not spoil its influence on policy debates.[130]

To be fair, Bush was not blameless in acquiring a reputation for not reading. In 1978, he ran for Congress in West Texas against Kent Hance, the conservative Democratic incumbent. Degrees from Yale and Harvard might help a politician in some parts of the country, but not where Bush was running. After he lost, he vowed "never to get out-countried again.[131] "He plays up being a good ol' boy from Midland, Texas," says Rove, "but he was a history major at Yale and graduated from Harvard Business

School."[132] Playing down the Ivy League credentials helped him get elected governor of Texas and president of the United States—two times each—but the cost was being treated like a bumpkin by the media.

Part of Bush's cowboy persona was by no means entirely affected. Even when discussing the books he reads, he proves more low key than Clinton. His brief comments about books make him seem less professorial than Clinton as well. In a 2012 interview with the Hoover Institution's Peter Robinson, Bush gave short, almost monosyllabic answers to questions about his reading. A book about Joe DiMaggio's hitting streak? "Yeah, it's good." To a question about his reading in general, he answered cryptically, "I'm still reading quite a bit and enjoying it a lot." He interrupted the discussion to tease Robinson for assuming he reads printed books—"we don't have book stands anymore, we've got iPads. Please."[133]

The interaction was classic Bush. He was reading a lot, and inundating himself in some serious books, but the manner in which he talked, with the iPad braggadocio and the uncomplicated analysis, gave an impression of unseriousness. This image stuck. Even after his presidency, and after much has been written about his love of books, comedians still joke about the unread Bush. As Jimmy Fallon joked about the opening of Bush's presidential library, it will contain "items from the former president's life, including pictures and memorabilia, or as Bush put it, 'best of all, no books.'"

Despite considerable evidence of the influence of books on the presidents, many observers prove skeptical of presidential reading. The late Gore Vidal sneered, "Today public figures can no longer write their own speeches or books; and there is some evidence that they can't read them either."[134] It's true that in Washington, books are often more discussed than read. Yet if people read only a portion of a book or simply absorb its argument, it can still shape policy. As Emily Parker put it in the *New York Times*, "in today's Washington, books do matter—even if they often have the most influence when presented in abbreviated form."[135]

It's remarkable, then, that the presidents themselves have usually *not* taken that approach. Not only are most modern American presidents readers, but they tend to read a lot and to read thoughtfully. Reading is only one of a vast array of choices in the all-you-can-eat buffet of modern culture. A person who reads makes a conscious decision to turn off the TV or log off the Internet and open a book (or switch on an e-reader, as the case may be). Reading makes presidents more serious in an era where leadership often debases itself. If there's anything presidential left about the presidency, we may have the president's reading to thank.

CHAPTER 11

OBAMA, FULL-FLEDGED PRODUCT OF AMERICAN POP CULTURE

A day in the life of the young Barack Obama reveals a person shaped by popular culture more thoroughly than any other president in our history. Barack Obama's after-school routine in Hawaii as described in his memoir *Dreams from My Father* proves so saturated by pop culture that it must be reproduced in full in order to be believed:

> I might stop off at a newsstand run by a blind man who would let me know what new comics had come in. Gramps would be at home to let me into the apartment, and as he lay down for his afternoon nap, I would watch cartoons and sitcom reruns. Homework would be done in time for dinner, which we ate in front of the television. There I would stay for the rest of the evening, negotiating with Gramps over which programs to watch, sharing the latest snack food he'd discovered at the supermarket. At ten o'clock, I went to my room (Johnny Carson came on at that time, and there was no negotiating around that), and I would go to sleep to the sounds of Top 40 music on the radio.[1]

From comics to cartoons to sitcoms to prime time to Johnny Carson to Top 40 radio, Barack Obama's formative years were spent soaking up American popular culture.

By his own account, his and his grandfather's entire afternoon and evening centered on television. For all the talk of Obama as an intellectual, Obama had the stereotypical pop-culture childhood, and then some.

This should not be a surprise. Obama spent most of his youth with his grandparents, Madelyn ("Toot" in the memoir) and Stanley ("Gramps") Dunham, both of whom were immersed in popular culture. Obama's biographer David Maraniss reports that Madelyn named her daughter Stanley after a character played by Bette Davis in the 1942 movie *This is Our Life*. Madelyn's brother Charles Payne recalled she was quite enamored of the idea of a woman with the name Stanley, considering it "the height of sophistication!"[2] Before moving in with his grandparents, Barack considered visits to their pop culture–infused household an "idyll in paradise," as Maraniss puts it, with "ice cream, the cartoons, the days at the beach."[3]

Obama's nonstop television viewing was a point of contention in the one brief interaction he ever had with his father. Barack Obama Sr.'s visit to Hawaii in 1971 was uncomfortable for everyone. He had abandoned his young wife and child for the better part of a decade. Her parents had understandably never approved of their daughter's union with Barack Sr. Stanley, who had left her son with her parents and was living in Jakarta, returned to Hawaii for her estranged husband's visit.[4]

Against the backdrop of a fight among the four adults, Obama "turned on the television to watch a cartoon special—*How the Grinch Stole Christmas*." His father turned away from the adults and said, "Barry, you have watched enough television tonight. Go into your room and study now, and let the adults talk." His grandmother kindly suggested that Obama retire to his room and watch the show there, but his father objected, "No, Madelyn, that's not what I mean. He has been watching that machine constantly, and now it is time for him to study." After his father left for the evening, his grandmother allowed him to watch the end of his show, but the damage was done. The father who had not wanted his son to continue "watching that machine" had made a lasting and unhappy impression. The young TV watcher felt that "something had cracked open between all of us." He could not have known that this visit would be the last time he would ever see his father, but he did start "to count the days until my father would leave and things would return to normal."[5]

By "normal," he meant in part a return to uninterrupted television. While Obama was living in Indonesia from 1967 to 1971, his step-father, Lolo Soetero, found a new job. The family's improved economic circumstances resulted in the arrival of all the pop-culture entertainment staples: "a television and hi fi replaced the crocodiles and Tata, the ape." At this point, Obama relates, an important change in his thinking occurred. "On the imported television shows that had started running in the evening, I began to notice that Cosby never got the girl on *I Spy*, that the black man on *Mission: Impossible* spent all his time underground." In con trast to Jimmy Carter's fond memories of picking books from the Sears, Roebuck catalog, Obama "noticed that there was nobody like me in the Sears, Roebuck Christmas catalog that Toot and Gramps sent us, and that Santa was a white man."[6]

> —›·›·›·•·‹·‹·‹—
>
> But it's not all sports all the time for Obama. He likes *Homeland, Mad Men, Boardwalk Empire, Entourage,* and *The Wire* (which he calls "one of the best shows of all time"). If *The Wire*'s characters were broken down as a March Madness bracket, he says, Omar (a gay, Robin Hood-esque killer) would be "the No. 1 seed."

The young Obama also liked *Star Trek*. Years later, while posing for an Oval Office picture with Nichelle Nichols, the African American actress who played Lieutenant Uhura of the starship *Enterprise*, he confirmed a report that he had developed a crush on her in his youth. She verified that Obama "was definitely a Trekker," adding, "How wonderful is that?!"[7] Obama lost some of that Trekker street cred in March 2013 when he referred to the "Jedi mind meld," confusing *Star Trek*'s "Vulcan mind meld" with *Star Wars*' "Jedi mind trick." That the error received so much attention spoke not only to the obsessiveness of fans in both camps, but also to the high expectations Americans had regarding Obama's apparent pop-culture mastery.[8]

Obama's youthful observations about race and his TV-star crushes were the first indications that American culture had much to teach him about the broader world. During those junior-high years with his grandparents, he believed that "whatever it was I was after, whatever it was that I needed, would have to come from some other source. TV, movies, the radio; those were the places to start."[9]

His fondness for television continued into college, though he now had fewer leisure hours to pour into it. At Occidental College, Obama would watch Lakers games with his buddies.[10] And he would get together nightly with basketball friends to watch Johnny Carson's opening monologue on *The Tonight Show*.[11] This nearly unbroken commitment to Carson is reminiscent of his grandfather's non-negotiable nightly appointment with *The Tonight Show*.

Of course, if Obama had remained a couch potato, he would never have become our forty-fourth president. For one thing, he had some athletic inclinations, playing on his high school basketball team. And he soon developed a degree of disillusionment with pop culture, writing dismissively in one of his two memoirs about "the narrower path to happiness to be found in television and the movies...." Once he left Hawaii, he even started encouraging people to switch off the TV, chiding his sister Maya "for spending one evening watching TV instead of reading the novels I'd bought for her."[12]

Still, the influence of all that youthful television-watching is difficult to extinguish. In a book on the inner workings of Obama's presidential reelection campaign, *Politico*'s Glenn Thrush reports that although Obama's biographers "have been more enamored with his complexity," Obama himself "seeks shallower waters, especially in times of crisis." When the going gets tough in the White House, Thrush says, the president plays sports and watches ESPN.[13] Indeed, while Obama's administration was beset by scandals regarding improper IRS investigations and the death of U.S. officials in Benghazi, the *New York Times*' Peter Baker reported that Obama "talked longingly of 'going Bulworth,' a reference to a little-remembered 1998 Warren Beatty movie ['Bulworth'] about a senator who risked it all to say what he really thought."[14]

Thrush, it seems, was right that movies and TV served as Obama's version of "comfort food."

Vanity Fair's Michael Lewis reports that Obama continues to watch TV regularly, spending the hours from ten o'clock at night to one in the morning with the television and his iPad.[15] No wonder, then, that he knows what's happening on *Real Housewives* and *Jersey Shore*, shows he says he doesn't like and doesn't watch. Given this well-known presidential propensity for TV-watching well into the night, the *Weekly Standard*'s Mark Hemingway even asked if Obama was watching TV instead of following the terror attack that killed U.S. Ambassador Chris Stevens in Benghazi.[16]

Although he has a wide variety of TV interests, Obama's favorite programming is sports. His advisor Valerie Jarrett complained in 2009 that the president's interests are "Sports, sports, and more sports." On the "campaign trail, as soon as we would get on the bus, the first thing he would do is turn the channel to sports channels."[17] ESPN seems to be the default channel on most of the TVs in the West Wing of the White House.[18]

Obama caught the sports bug early, watching hours and hours of basketball on TV with his Hawaiian prep school chum Joe Hanson. David Maraniss even claims that if "there was a rhythm of hipness to the way he walked," it came from "emulating the professional basketball icons he saw on television, Tiny Archibald and the Iceman, Earl the Pearl and Dr. J."[19]

Obama's TV watching and his day job get in the way of his reading. The presidency is so taxing, he says, that "you have very little chance to really read. I basically floss my teeth and watch *SportsCenter*."[20] Obama himself appears annually on ESPN to share his NCAA basketball tournament brackets, and he especially likes to watch sports in what *Politico*'s Amie Parnes calls "the ultimate man-cave—Air Force One."[21]

Obama takes his sports seriously and does not want to be interrupted by conversation during games. It was made clear to guests at his annual Super Bowl party that they were there to watch the game with the president, not to schmooze with him.

Pennsylvania congressman Mike Doyle recalls that Obama "was sitting up front, he was watching the game, and he didn't move."[22] The CEO of Verizon, Ivan Seidenberg, complained that he received a mere fifteen seconds with the president at the 2010 White House Super Bowl party. After that brief and impersonal greeting, the president made his way to the front of the room and spent the rest of the game with his friends, immersed in the action rather than his guests.[23] The long-time Obama aide Michael Strautmanis recalls "sitting in a hotel lobby with him when he was running for the Senate and watching 'SportsCenter' in silence." Strautmanis explained, "When he's watching the game, he's watching the game.... We're not talking about work or politics."[24]

But it's not all sports all the time for Obama. He likes *Homeland*, *Mad Men*, *Boardwalk Empire*, *Entourage*, and *The Wire* (which he calls "one of the best shows of all time"). If *The Wire*'s characters were broken down as a March Madness bracket, he says, Omar (a gay, Robin Hood-esque killer) would be "the No. 1 seed."[25] "That's not an endorsement," he adds. "He's not my favorite person, but he's a fascinating character." Another of his favorites is the 1960s advertising retrospective *Mad Men*, which "explains my grandparents, their tastes."[26] His TV habits distinguish Obama from previous presidents, but not from today's TV-loving public.

During the 2008 campaign, HBO's *Entourage* revealed itself a particular Obama favorite. One of the characters, the fast-talking and foul-mouthed Ari, was reportedly based on Ari Emanuel, the brother of Obama's first chief of staff, Rahm Emanuel. Obama "would talk about 'Entourage' all the time," according to his press secretary, Robert Gibbs. The candidate would even try to arrange his schedule so he could watch the show—a reminder of the White House ushers' complaint that TV dictated Eisenhower's schedule. Gibbs recalled that "we would have these Sunday night calls at the same time as 'Entourage.'" "Just be late," he would tell his boss, "and we can just watch 'Entourage' and still get on and do the call." Gibbs reports that "it worked.... We got to see 'Entourage.'" Obama's devotion to cable TV fare has earned him the moniker "the HBO president."[27]

Hollywood loves this presidential enthusiasm for television. The star of Showtime's *Homeland*, the British actor Damian Lewis, was thrilled to learn about Obama's interest in the show. "Not only has Obama been watching it," he gushed, "but his aides have been calling up going, 'We need to see it.' … So he's been getting entire state departments, top of the U.S. government, asking to see it because their boss watches it and they feel they need to know what their boss has been watching."[28] Government bureaucrats, it seems, think what the president is watching on TV is a window into what he is thinking.

Word of Obama's interest came to the creators of *Homeland*, Alex Gansa and Howard Gordon, "anecdotally" through a friend of the series' star Claire Danes, who heard it from a friend of hers who dated an Obama speechwriter. They were skeptical, but then the story got into the press, and eventually they couldn't remember where they had heard it first:

Obama's preferred shows are dark and edgy—decidedly not family fare—so he usually watches them alone. The First Lady seems to have no interest in his gritty favorites. Her tastes and her daughters' run to *Modern Family*. At a fundraiser with *Modern Family*'s Jesse Tyler Ferguson in 2011, the president assured everyone that "Michelle and the girls love them some *Modern Family*.… They love that show."[29]

Modern Family's co-creator Steve Levitan loves them back. He told NBC's Warren Littlefield that the darkest years were when "Bush [was] in the White House and [Jeff] Zucker in the NBC chair."[30] When Ann Romney revealed that she liked his show, Levitan thumbed his nose at her in a tweet: "We'll offer her the role of officiant at Mitch & Cam's wedding. As soon as it's legal."[31] The Obama girls also like *iCarly*, and Mrs. Obama even agreed to guest star on the show, becoming the first First Lady to appear on a sitcom since Nancy Reagan plugged her "Just Say No" campaign in *Diff'rent Strokes* in 1983.[32]

Gordon: [W]e were dismissing it, but then the *Rolling Stone* article came out.

Gansa: I think it was *Elle* at first.

Gordon: And then it was *Oprah*.

The Hollywood Reporter included "multiple shoutouts from President Obama" among the top accolades garnered by the show, along with a Golden Globe and a Peabody. As Gansa gratefully noted, Obama "stumped for us. He should be on the payroll, he's been amazing."[33] According to Lewis, Obama even said that "While Michelle and the two girls go play tennis on Saturday afternoons, I go in the Oval Office, pretend I'm going to work, and then I switch on *Homeland*."[34]

Obama's TV habits have won the approval of television critics. *Entertainment Weekly*'s Ken Tucker congratulates him for "[d]emonstrating excellent taste in drama."[35] And *Politico*'s Parnes writes that Obama's knowledge of television allows him "to show off his pop-culture cool."[36] The public relations downside, however, depicts how Obama's personal picks are mostly "niche" shows on expensive cable channels. None of his favorites is on network TV, in stark contrast to the days of Eisenhower and Reagan. The scandalous truth is that Obama likes to watch the shows of the 1 percent rather than the 99 percent. His preferences also reflect the recent stratification of TV programming. The days when *I Love Lucy* or *All in the Family* captured a third or even a half of the national television audience are gone. Name any of today's most successful shows, and most Americans will never have seen it. TV has become a niche medium, micro-targeting specific demographic groups with narrowly tailored shows, with a corresponding advertising or pay-subscription strategy. Apart from certain sporting events, the president can no longer watch what everyone else is watching—no one can. Instead, Obama has developed a persona that appeals to elite opinion makers as cool or hip or sophisticated, cultivating an image with television as Kennedy did with books. The American people may not have been reading the books that Kennedy was supposedly reading, but they appreciated that he was reading them.

Like the TV shows he prefers, Obama's movie choices tend to the dark side. *The Godfather* and *One Flew Over the Cuckoo's Nest* number among his all-time favorites. Among new films, he likes the gritty and the edgy.[37] Early in his White House tenure, he watched *Slumdog Millionaire* and *The Wrestler*—definitely edgy even if not classic.[38]

Obama has been relatively quiet about his use of the White House theater. Its most frequent users seem to be his daughters. In 2009, he told a group of schoolchildren that the Obama family had recently watched *Where the Wild Things Are*, but he seemed more enthusiastic about the original book by Maurice Sendak than about the film version. "When I was really small," he told the children, "I used to love the book that they just made a movie of called 'Where the Wild Things Are.'" About the movie, he was more restrained, saying "I thought it was really interesting.... I think it's worth seeing."[39]

Obama kept up with his shows even in the midst of the tight 2012 reelection campaign. Jetting across the country on Air Force One, he was never far from a TV. *SportsCenter* constantly played, and the president made sure not to miss *Homeland* or *Boardwalk Empire*.[40] He even attacked his opponents with TV talk. He belittled the Republican National Convention as "a re-run," adding, "We've seen it before. You might as well have watched it on a black-and-white TV."[41] For the hippest president in history, there could hardly be a worse insult. And on a 2013 trip to Israel, he even showed himself up-to-date on Israeli television, making a joke about the hit show *Eretz Hanehederet*.

It is apparently still possible, however, to watch too much television. Tending to his popular reputation, Obama did not want to appear to have crossed the line. On *Late Night with Jimmy Fallon* in April 2012, he maintained, perhaps somewhat disingenuously, "I don't get a chance to watch a lot of TV." By the standard of his school days in Hawaii, that might be true. Obama may understand that the American people don't want their president to watch TV all the time. They assume that he has a lot of work to do. There's also the intellectual snobbery of the cultural elites toward television—the "vast wasteland" problem. Since Obama is at pains to cultivate his image as an intellectual, he doesn't want people to think he spends too much time with the idiot box. Better to say that he doesn't "get a chance to watch a lot of TV."[42]

A little hypocrisy here is good for the nation. The president has to set an example for America's youth—especially with his wife working so diligently to reduce childhood obesity. And there is no doubt that American children watch "a lot" of TV. According to the Nielsen Company, children from age six to eleven average twenty-eight hours a week in front of the television.[43] Those are twenty-eight hours that they are not preparing the United States to be a more successful and economically competitive nation. That's why Obama told kids to focus on real homework rather than *Real Housewives*. In a July 2012 speech to the National Urban League, he departed from his prepared text to tell the youths, "America says, 'we will give you opportunity, but you've got to earn your success.'" "You're competing against young people in Beijing and Bangalore," he continued, and "they're not hangin' out. They're not gettin' over. They're not playin' video games. They're not watching 'Real Housewives.'" This wasn't his first dig at reality television. He told Jay Leno in 2011, "I am probably a little biased against reality TV, partly because there's this program on C-SPAN called 'Congress.'"[44]

Excessive television-watching is not the only activity of Obama's youth that children would do well to avoid. In any case, the president who once received dreams from his father can now pass on advice from his father—shut off "that machine" and go study.

Obama as Reader: Breaking Free from the Couch

After high school, Obama broke free from the couch. He had already started reading in high school, working through works by James Baldwin, Ralph Ellison, Langston Hughes, W. E. B. Du Bois, Richard Wright, and other black authors. He particularly enjoyed *The Autobiography of Malcolm X*, with its protagonist's "repeated self-creation." Although he rejected Malcolm's anti-white rhetoric, the book did provide a model and an example for an anonymous young man looking to make a name for himself. Curiously enough, while young Obama showed no embarrassment about watching copious amounts of TV with his grandfather, he preferred to keep his literary pursuits private, closing his door and telling his grandparents that he was doing his homework.[45]

Obama became a real reader in college, as well as highly political. In his memoir, he writes that a radical friend "Marcus" criticized him for reading Joseph Conrad's *Heart of Darkness*: "Man, stop waving that thing around.... I'm telling you, man, this stuff will poison your mind." Obama agreed with him: "Actually, he's right. The way Conrad sees it, Africa's the cesspool of the world, black folks are savages, and any contact with them breeds infection." Obama had adopted what would later be called the "politically correct" view of the world.[46]

After transferring to Columbia, Obama began reading even more. "I had tons of books. I read everything. I think that was the period when I grew as much as I have ever grown intellectually." His sister and mother "made fun of [him] for being so monk-like,"[47] and his roommate, Sohale Siddiqi, agreed, complaining that Obama was becoming "a bore."[48]

> **One particularly embarrassing finding was that the absence from the healthcare policy debate of Kathleen Sebelius, the secretary of health and human services, was "a topic that another former senior administration aide now calls the Lord Voldemort of policy questions, the issue that must not be named."**

His high school interest in African-American literature persisted through college. Mir Mahboob Mahmood, a friend in New York City, noted that Obama "carried and at every opportunity read and reread a fraying copy of Ralph Ellison's *Invisible Man*." With his girlfriend, Genevieve Cook (the real person, not the composite girlfriend in the memoir), he read black female authors, including Maya Angelou, Toni Cade Bambara, Toni Morrison, and Ntozake Shange.[49]

The reading continued while he worked as a community organizer in Chicago. Now the reading became even more political, and he tended to African-American literature, history, philosophy, and radicalism.[50] Johnnie Owens, his assistant in Chicago, was impressed with Obama's books: "[Y]ou'd go by his house and his bookshelf…. Clearly the books he had, they weren't just there for display." He read Robert Caro's *The Power Broker*—one of the best books ever written about urban politics—and radical activist Saul Alinsky's *Reveille for Radicals*.[51]

All this reading helped prepare him for Harvard Law School, where he became the first black president of the law review. It was this position that led to a publishing contract for *Dreams from My Father*, the memoir that established his reputation as an intellectual and launched his career. The authenticity of parts of his account has been called into question, but *Dreams* is an impressive literary achievement. It is unlikely that he would have made it to the presidency without it.

Obama's choice of books showed that he recognized the symbolic power of reading. He knew, for example, that his grandparents would somehow be uncomfortable with his heavy reading of African American literature at Punahou. At the same time, Genevieve was not only comfortable with it but found it appealing.

When Obama ran for the Senate, he read Caro's famous account of Lyndon Johnson's career there, *Master of the Senate*. Ever mindful of appearances, however, he kept that reading to himself during election season to avoid appearing presumptuous. After his victory, however, he went out of his way to let people know that he was reading Caro's book.[52]

Obama has remained self-conscious about his reading as the political spotlight on him has intensified. His reading as a presidential candidate and as president has attracted enormous attention. He seems acutely aware of this attention, and he matches his reading to the political exigencies of the moment.

Richard Nixon did the same thing, perhaps, when he re-read Churchill's *Triumph and Tragedy* after a summit meeting with the Soviets. Obama, however, has made his topical reading far more public. He read Doris Kearns Goodwin's *Team of Rivals* in 2008—a few years after George W. Bush did. He also let it be known that the book had an effect on his thinking, telling Joe Klein, "I don't want to have people who just agree with me. I want people who are continually pushing me out of my comfort

The heightened attention to the influence of the president's reading on his policy led several Jewish guests to give Jewish-themed books to the non-Jewish president. In the spring of 2012, the Israeli prime minister, Benjamin Netanyahu, gave Obama a copy of the Book of Esther, part of the Hebrew Bible. It tells the story of a scheme by an advisor to the Persian king to wipe out the Jews, narrowly averted by the intercession of the Jewish Queen Esther and her uncle-stepfather Mordecai. Referring to the Iranian nuclear threat to Israel, Netanyahu told Obama, "Then, too, they wanted to wipe us out."[53]

Not long afterward, the Jewish journalist Jeffrey Goldberg presented Obama with a new translation of the Passover Hagaddah. The reasoning behind the gift remains obscure. Netanyahu's gift, the Book of Esther, is at least part of the Christian canon. It is unclear what use Obama would make of a book outlining the structure of the Passover Seder, even though the White House does host an annual Seder for select Jewish staffers and supporters.[54]

This series of Jewish gifts continued when the embattled Jewish journalist Peter Beinart brought two copies of his get-tough-on-Israel book, *The Crisis of Zionism*, to his meeting with Obama, one for the president, the other for his national security aide Ben Rhodes. Obama responded by telling Beinart, who had been severely criticized in the Jewish community for writing the book, to "hang in there."[55] It seems a little odd that Jewish guests give Jewish books to Obama. Imagine what the reaction from the Jewish community would be if a Christian gave a Jewish politician a breviary or a new translation of the letters of St. Paul.

zone."[56] The prevailing narrative in Washington was that his selection of his onetime rival Hillary Clinton as secretary of state was the fruit of his thoughtful reading of Goodwin's book.[57] *Team of Rivals* became obligatory reading for job-seekers in the new administration, and sales of the three-year-old title jumped.[58]

Hiring his rivals might have worked for Lincoln, but the strategy was less effective for Obama. In July 2012, *Vanity Fair*'s Todd Purdum wrote a tough critique of the Obama cabinet, cruelly titled "Team of Mascots." "[W]hat the president has created is something that doesn't look Lincoln-esque at all," he wrote. Purdum asked an anonymous Obama aide if the team-of-rivals approach to cabinet appointments had lived up to the president's expectations. "No! God, no!" was the response. One particularly embarrassing finding was that the absence from the health care policy debate of Kathleen Sebelius, the secretary of health and human services, was "a topic that another former senior administration aide now calls the Lord Voldemort of policy questions, the issue that must not be named."[59]

Obama's reading for public effect continued through his first term. Soon after the inauguration, word got out that he was reading a book about Franklin Roosevelt's famous "Hundred Days," which had established expectations of frenzied activity by which a new administration might be judged. When he was pressing for his health-care law, he announced, "We've been talking about health care for nearly a century. I'm reading a biography of Teddy Roosevelt right now. He was talking about it. Teddy Roosevelt." The biography was Edmund Morris's *The Rise of Theodore Roosevelt*, which both George W. Bush and Ronald Reagan had read as well.[60] Obama told co-owner of Washington's Politics and Prose bookstore, Barbara Meade, that he read both that book and its sequel and "just loved it." She concluded from this that he was "obviously a tremendous reader."[61]

The selection of the president's vacation reading has turned into an annual ritual in the Obama White House, one that is played out before the adoring media. In August, he goes to Martha's Vineyard with his family (and much of the East Coast elite). While there, Obama makes a pilgrimage to the Bunch of Grapes bookstore. His selection of titles is inevitably reported in the press, where it is dissected, analyzed, and defended or criticized by his advocates and detractors, respectively. Books that have received this summer vacation treatment included Daniel Woodrell's *The Bayou Trilogy* and Ward Just's *Rodin's Debutante* in 2011, and Jonathan Franzen's *Freedom* in 2010.

Freedom, in particular, caught a wave. At the time of his visit to the bookstore, this title was still embargoed, and Obama's ability to procure the work from the store set off a wave of helpful publicity. The Sunday *New York Times* of September 5, 2010, mentioned Obama's purchase of Franzen's book in three separate sections—"Styles," the late "Week in Review," and the "Book Review." The book soon climbed up the bestseller lists.[62] Franzen liked the publicity, to be sure, but he had a question: "[W]hen I heard he was reading 'Freedom' I thought, 'Why are you reading a novel? There are important things to be doing!'" In addition to wondering, somewhat jokingly, about Obama's time management, he also added to the mountains of praise that have been heaped upon Obama the reader, explaining, "One of the reasons I love Barack Obama as much as I do is that we finally have a real reader in the White House."[63]

Franzen was not the only author with good reason to love Obama. The correlation between Obama's blessing and a spike in sales helped a number of books, including Morris's Roosevelt biography, Kent Haruf's *Plainsong*, and Richard Price's *Lush Life*. Sales of Joseph O'Neill's *Netherland* jumped by 40 percent. The presidential book bump is nothing new, but it has been more frequent and more pronounced under Democratic presidents than under Republicans—part of the mystique of bookish Democratic presidents established under Kennedy.

Obama took the book bump to a new level. His ability to drive book sales approached that of Oprah Winfrey, whose monthly book club episodes created many a bestseller, including Franzen's *The Corrections* in 2001.[64] Typically, Franzen also criticized Oprah after receiving this blessing, saying that "She's picked some good books, but she's picked enough schmaltzy, one dimensional ones that I cringe...."[65]

The presidential book bump indicates that presidents themselves have become actors on the cultural stage. By endorsing a book—implicitly or explicitly—a president serves as a pop-culture validator for the author. In return, the president—unless he's George W. Bush—gets validated himself by the commentariat, most of whom hope that someday the president will read—and give a sales boost—to their own books.

Expectations of an Obama book bump have occasionally been extravagant. In 2011, when he picked some more difficult, and frankly, more obscure books, the *Washington Post*'s Melissa Bell wondered if he had gone into a "book bump slump." Bell even compared chart movements of books that Obama had read at different times in his presidency, theorizing that the slump was the result of lower approval ratings or difficult economic circumstances. A more likely reason, and a lesson for presidents and publishers, is that presidents can affect sales when they pick books that Americans find more accessible. A biography of Lincoln, like *Team of Rivals*, is more likely to shoot up the charts after a presidential blessing than a challenging or unknown novel. This does not mean that presidents should not read challenging books if that is their interest. It does, however, mean that presidents should not expect that their reading of such books improve their rapport with the American people.[66]

Despite all of the excitement about Obama's reading, his actual literary consumption may be more limited than some people think. For example, the *New York Times*' Peter Baker reported in early October 2010 that Obama was "seeking guidance in presidential biographies," including Taylor Branch's *The Clinton Tapes*.[67] On December 25, more than two-and-a-half months later (and more, if you think about the lead time for pieces in the *New York Times*

> —➤➤➤·●·◄◄◄—
>
> **The correlation between Obama's blessing and a spike in sales helped a number of books, including Morris's Roosevelt biography, Kent Haruf's *Plainsong*, and Richard Price's *Lush Life*. Sales of Joseph O'Neill's *Netherland* jumped by 40 percent. The presidential book bump is nothing new, but it has been more frequent and more pronounced under Democratic presidents than under Republicans— part of the mystique of bookish Democratic presidents established under Kennedy.**

Magazine), the *Washington Post* also reported that Obama was reading Branch's book. This double-reporting across a lengthy period suggests that the very busy president was, understandably, taking a long time to get through the book's 720 pages.[68] The delay also suggested that Obama's reading was not as regular or as assiduous as enthusiasts claimed.

A slightly embarrassing incident, characterized as a "mini scandal," took place in August of 2009, when Obama's staff told the press that he was reading Thomas Friedman's *Hot, Flat, and Crowded*. The problem was that Obama was also reported to have been reading that very same book in September 2008. When asked about this discrepancy, Friedman gave Obama cover in the *Daily Beast*: "Given the pressure of a campaign, I doubt that the President got to read anything cover to cover. And for most of his presidency, the Great Recession has really swamped debate and discussion about climate and energy. So, I was very pleased to hear that he is diving into it again...."[69] It is hard to imagine Friedman taking such a charitable view if George W. Bush had been caught in the same kind of literary double accounting. Consider the irony: poor President Bush was insulted by authors he read—recall Kurlansky's "Oh, he reads books?"—while Obama is defended by the authors he hasn't read.

Whatever the pace or volume of Obama's reading, almost no evidence proves that he reads, let alone is influenced by, conservative authors. One of the very few occasions of Obama's engaging conservative political philosophy was in September 2005 during his senatorial tenure. Obama had a chat with the *New York Times* columnist David Brooks. At some point the conversation turned to Edmund Burke. "I don't want to sound like I'm bragging," Brooks wrote, "but usually when I talk to senators, while they may know a policy area better than me, they generally don't know political philosophy better than me. I got the sense he knew *both* better than me."[70] On another occasion, shortly before his inauguration, he met with several conservative journalists, including Brooks, Charles Krauthammer, William Kristol, Larry Kudlow, Rich Lowry, Peggy Noonan, Michael Barone, and Paul Gigot, at the home of George Will.[71] Other than these two instances and the praise he received for giving conservatives a fair shake at the *Harvard Law Review*, one looks in vain for examples of

Obama's engaging conservative ideas. He shares this parochialism with his similarly lionized Democratic predecessors. For the most part, liberal presidents, even smart and well-read ones, don't read conservative authors. Obama is no exception.

The idea that Obama is an intellectual is nevertheless simply assumed. After his election, the *New York Times'* Nicholas Kristof called him "an open, out-of-the-closet, practicing intellectual."[72] The *New Yorker*, backed by its legendary fact-checking operation, called him a "certified intellectual," thereby making the designation at least semi-official.[73] When he faced a reelection contest against the Republican Mitt Romney—who, for good or for ill, had more Harvard degrees than Obama—the *New Republic*'s Walter Kirn called Obama "singularly literate." Romney, in contrast, was deemed "exceptionally numerate," based on his experience reading balance books.[74]

Harvard professor James Kloppenberg has written an entire book dedicated to the proposition that Obama is an intellectual. In *Reading Obama: Dreams, Hopes, and the American Political Tradition*, Kloppenberg discerns a philosophy in Obama's words and writings, identifying him as a stealth intellectual of the pragmatist school. Obama is not just any pragmatist, but a specific kind, one who has achieved a "congruence between antifoundationalism, historicism, experimentalism, and democracy in his way of thinking."[75] If presented with this theory, Kloppenberg told the *New York Times*, Obama "would have had to deny every word" because of the suspicion with which populists view intellectuals.[76] This was all heady stuff for the child who grew up watching cartoons, sitcom reruns, and prime-time TV from the moment he came home until he went to bed.

Celebrity: How All That TV Paid Off

As president, Obama has put all of his knowledge of and experience with pop culture to work. His great insight has been that by being part of pop culture—being a celebrity himself—a president can influence how pop culture portrays him. As *Politico*'s Parnes puts it, "when you're the president, you don't just watch TV—you are TV."[77] This approach can backfire—recall Gerald Ford's fate with *Saturday Night Live*—but Obama has worked pop culture with astonishing deftness.

Kennedy was glamorous and Reagan was a movie star, but Obama has worked more aggressively than any other president to establish his preferred image through a variety of media—not only books, television, and movies, but new media such as Twitter, Reddit, and Google+.[78] Embracing the celebrity culture, he became a rock star himself. Though it was impossible to sustain that level of coolness once he became president—"Now he's playing golf with John Boehner, which is about the most uncool thing there is," observes Elayne Rapping[79]—he managed to become what *Entertainment Weekly*'s Hillary Busis calls a "cool dad," kind of like *Modern Family*'s Phil Dunphy.[80] When his wife appeared by video feed in front of an adoring crowd at the 2013 Academy Awards, the *Huffington Post*'s Howard Fineman called it a "glitteringly dramatic example of how the Obama administration has conquered the world of celebrity and social communication."[81]

Obama himself sensed the diminution in his cool quotient after he entered the White House. "I'm sort of old news," he told supporters during his reelection campaign. Regarding 2008, he said, "I was young and vibrant and new.... And let's face it, it was cool to support me back then." While extracting prodigious amounts of campaign cash from his audience, he acknowledged that the Obama brand "is not going to feel exactly the same.... It's not going to be as fresh and new and trendy."[82] Nevertheless, Obama remained a celebrity and kept his cool.

If you're running for president, it's good to be loved by Hollywood. There's a lot of money there, and Obama got a lot of it in both of his campaigns. George Clooney earned the title "Mr. Obama's biggest bankroller," and Eva Longoria co-chaired his 2012 campaign. Hollywood has long been a liberal stronghold, of course—78 percent of Hollywood dollars in the 2008 campaign went to Democrats—but Obama seemed to take things to a new level.[83] At a Hollywood fundraiser in February 2012, he exhorted the faithful: "I'm going to need you. You're going to carry this thing like you did in 2008."[84]

America's celebrities did more than open their wallets to Obama. They went on the hustings for him. Bruce Springsteen, a veteran of John Kerry's 2004 campaign, made appearances for Obama in 2008 and 2012. Springsteen's endorsement carried more weight than most because of his universal appeal. The executive producer of *Face the Nation*, Mary Hager, says she has never met a politician who disliked the Boss "who's willing to go on the record." Americans expect Springsteen "to embody our values, understand our struggles and illuminate our future," writes Chris Richards in the *Washington Post*. Obama himself joked in 2008, "The reason I'm running for president is because I can't be Bruce Springsteen."[85]

Celebrity campaigning for Obama became an art form. The comedienne Sarah Silverman made "The Great Schlep" southward in 2008 to encourage Jewish grandparents in Florida to vote for Obama—"the goodest person we've ever had as a presidential choice."[86] The super-documentarian Davis Guggenheim (*An Inconvenient Truth*, *Waiting for Superman*) produced the seventeen-minute campaign film for the 2012 Democratic National Convention, with Tom Hanks (star of just about everything) narrating.[87] George Clooney narrated another campaign video. Natalie Portman, Scarlett Johansson, Kerry Washington, Obama aide and actor Kal Penn, and a host of other celebrities brought their star power to the convention. In those hyper-partisan precincts, "everything the Democrats do is good. And everything Republicans do is evil. It doesn't bother me," joked the comedian Craig Ferguson, "I live in Hollywood. It is like that here every day."[88] During the fall, Morgan Freeman lent his "voice of God" to one of the rare upbeat Obama ads.

Obama's own celebrity is important not only because of what his fellow stars do *for* him, but also because of what the media do not do *to* him. As a candidate and as president, he has received unusual deference from the TV comedians who eviscerated some of his predecessors. Comedians of course poke fun at him, but gently and infrequently. The comedian Will Durst complained that in 2008 "you couldn't tell jokes about Obama" because "the halo was too bright." Don Steinberg wrote in the *Wall Street Journal* that since the Center for Media and Public Affairs began tracking late-night humor in 1988, 2008 was the "first time that any presidential candidate wasn't the year's No. 1 or No. 2 joke-getter." To the extent that jokes about Obama did make it on the air, they were softballs like Jon Stewart's line about Obama's deviating from a Middle East itinerary for "a side trip to Bethlehem to visit the manger he was born in."[89]

There are, of course, potential pitfalls for a celebrity president. The speed of a celebrity's rise is often exceeded by the speed of his fall. In 2008 John McCain tried to turn Obama's celebrity against him with an ad linking him to Britney Spears and Paris Hilton. He failed. In 2012, the Republican super PAC American Crossroads put together a montage of images of Obama with celebrities, including clips of his singing an Al Green song, dismissing Kanye West as a "jackass," and dancing with Ellen DeGeneres. The video ends with the question, "After four years of a celebrity president, is your life any better?" As Emily Miller wrote in the *Washington Times*, Republicans were trying to make the case that if "he's seen hanging out too often at Mr. Clooncy's house, voters might realize he's out of touch with real Americans' problems."[90] But the Republican jujitsu effort failed. The Al Green clip went viral, provoking fulsome praise of Obama's singing. The political analyst and ex-songwriter Mark McKinnon called Obama's Al Green moment a "home run," adding, "History will judge his presidency, but it's probably not a stretch to say he may be the best crooner to occupy the Oval Office."[91]

On rare occasions, the celebrity strategy backfires. In her book *The Obamas*, Jodi Kantor reported that the actor Johnny Depp and the director Tim Burton threw an extravagant "Alice in Wonderland" costume party at the White House, but the White House communications apparatus covered it up so that the president would not appear uncaring during a period of economic difficulties.[92] The White House press corps cooperated, at least until Kantor's book came out a few years later. Even then, interest in the story was short-lived.

A more serious problem arose when the first lady invited the rapper Common to conduct a rap workshop at a White House event for schoolchildren. This silly idea began to look sinister when it was revealed that Common rapped about killing policemen and burning former president George W. Bush. *White House Dossier*'s Keith Koffler called the invitation "a gross error" and suggested that either "Common wasn't vetted properly" or worse, "he was vetted just fine, and nobody thought there was much wrong with all this."[93] Under pressure, the White House rescinded the invitation. The failure to see the pitfalls in bringing in a noxious entertainer to address kids suggested that this White House was too close to pop culture and popular music. It may be appealing for a president to work with celebrities, but they also bring potential perils that presidents and their teams need to keep in mind. Despite the occasional misstep, however, the benefits of Obama's celebrity outreach—the fundraising, the in-kind contributions, and the reflected glamour of popular stars—have outweighed the disadvantages.

Obama and the News

Based in large part on Obama's understanding of pop culture, his team has aggressively managed—perhaps micromanaged—its relations with the news media. "The White House is very careful who[m] it picks for which message," says Jonathan Wald, a producer at CNN.[94] This care reflects the administration's awareness that for all the talk about the growth of alternative media like Twitter, YouTube, and Facebook, television is still how most Americans get most of their news, along with their impressions of their political leaders.

Despite his insistence that "I don't watch network news or cable news,"[95] Obama is quite aware of what is said about him on TV and who is saying it. At the press conference at which he released his birth certificate to the media, he complained that they were paying too much attention to the "birther" issue and not enough to national security: "I was just back there listening to Chuck [Todd]—he was saying, it's amazing that he's not going to be talking about national security. I would not have the networks breaking in if I was talking about that, Chuck, and you know it."[96]

Obama's flip-flop on same-sex marriage was an example of news coverage driving presidential policy. Vice President Joe Biden angered the White House by getting ahead of the president on the issue in a *Meet the Press* interview, in which he revealed that his own change of heart was in part the work of a sitcom ("I think *Will & Grace* probably did more to educate the American public than almost anything anybody has done so far").[97] Later that week, Obama watched his press secretary, Jay Carney, struggle with questions about the discrepancy between the president's and the vice president's positions. He then consulted with a number of advisors, telling them, "We've got to save Jay!"[98] The White House soon reversed its position.

Obama also looks to specific reporters to sell specific messages. The White House arranged for the president to announce his new position on marriage in an interview with ABC's Robin Roberts. Instead of making announcing a major reversal of policy in a press conference or an Oval Office address, Obama turned to a daytime television interview on the second-ranking network with a reporter who does not typically focus on politics. Although the move was "controversial," as the *Washington Post*'s Paul Farhi put it, there was a method to the strategy.[99] According to *Politico*'s Dylan Byers, the choice of Roberts, who is black and a Christian, might have softened the blow of Obama's policy shift in those particular communities, both of which were disinclined to back same-sex marriage. She was also a friend of the Obama family.[100]

While the White House has favored reporters, like Robin Roberts, it has also punished those less friendly. The *Post*'s Farhi wrote an article about its tough tactics with stubborn reporters and noted that CBS's Sharyl Attkisson was "cussed" at by White House aide Eric Schultz for her reporting on the Department of Justice's "Fast

In September 2012, *Late Night* host David Letterman asked if he knew the size of the national debt. Somewhat unbelievably, Obama responded, "I don't remember what the number was precisely...." It is hard to imagine that the president of the United States did not know the size of the burgeoning U.S. debt. More likely, he knew the answer but did not want to admit to the large number—$16,000,000,000,000 and counting—in a soft venue that was supposed to be portraying him in a favorable light.

and Furious" gun-running scandal. Many, if not most, mainstream reporters avoided writing about the scandal when it first emerged, and so the White House pushed back hard on the reporters who took a different tack. This behavior was not limited to Attkisson, although most reporters refused to speak on the record, figuring, probably correctly, that it could damage their already prickly relations with White House communicators. Still, Farhi noted that another half-dozen anonymous reporters "described censorious e-mails or phone calls from Carney or his staff members that they characterized as heavy-handed." As veteran White House reporter Julie Mason observed, the approach of the Obama press team was to "shoot first and ask questions later."[101] And Watergate legend Bob Woodward got into a kerfuffle with senior White House aide Gene Sperling, who warned Woodward, in the midst of a friendly email exchange, that Woodward would "regret" criticizing the White House over the 2013 sequester battle.

These moves were indicative of a hard-edged approach to the press. Kantor even noted that for the position of press secretary, a job the president is closely involved in filling, Obama selected Robert Gibbs, "who had devoted the past five years of his life to the president but did not seem to care much for reporters."[102]

Attkisson, Woodward, and the others were just individual reporters. The Obama team has also directed its ire toward an entire network, Fox News, thereby communicating to other networks that tough coverage would invite a retaliatory response. The White House even designated a communications staffer, Anita Dunn, to lead the campaign against Fox News. "What I think is fair to say about Fox—and certainly it's the way we view it—is that it really is more a wing of the Republican Party," she charged.[103] The president himself piled on. He told *Rolling Stone*, laughing, that Fox had "a point of view that I think is ultimately destructive for the long-term growth of a country that has a vibrant middle class and is competitive in the world." He did, however, concede that "as an economic enterprise, it's been wildly successful."[104]

There is significant evidence that Obama is personally involved in the White House media strategy. At a minimum, he pays close attention to what is going on in TV news, even if he may not be watching news programming. As *Politico*'s Parnes discovered, the White House presses the line that "when it comes to the real news, and not the fake kind, Obama takes a pass—rarely ever tuning in to twenty-four-hour cable chatter or to replays of his own performances." At the same time, he pays close attention in a number of ways. First, as Valerie Jarrett disclosed, "We usually tell him how we think he did" on TV. In addition, Gibbs recalled that even if he does not watch live, "Sometimes we'll show him like a YouTube clip or something off a website itself, and he gets a kick out of that."[105]

New technologies certainly help Obama keep his eye on things. He uses what the *Washington Post*'s Scott Wilson calls his "indispensable iPad" to keep up with newspapers, blogs, and magazines.[106] Similarly, the *New York Times*' Amy Chozick called him "a voracious consumer of news, reading newspapers and magazines on his iPad and in print and dipping into blogs and Twitter." While voracious, he is not passive. "He regularly gives aides detailed descriptions of articles that he liked, and he can be thin-skinned about those that he does not." Obama understands, says Chozick, that the media helped "make him a national star not long after he had been an anonymous state legislator," and he "developed a detailed critique of modern news coverage that he regularly expresses to those around him." He complains about press "coverage that focuses on political winners and losers rather than substance." The press, he believes, strives for a "'false balance,' in which two opposing sides are given equal weight regardless of the facts." As a result of this supposed "false balance," Obama feels that the White House must put its finger on the scale to influence mainstream media coverage of him and his activities.[107]

Obama aggressively circumvents the mainstream media when necessary. In the 2012 campaign, he favored "niche online outlets that did not have access, or did not exist, during previous administrations, including personal finance Web sites like The Consumerist and Fool.com, and African American Web sites like Jack & Jill Politics, The Root and the Grio."[108] He also likes to grant interviews to "soft" news sources that cover entertainment or sports. These are venues in which Obama has little fear of being hit with controversial questions. He granted ESPN's Bill Simmons a podcast interview in which he talked at great length and in impressive depth about professional basketball.[109] On rare occasions these interviews can trip him up, such as the time in 2010 when baseball announcer and former pitcher Rob Dibble asked Obama to name his "favorite White Sox players growing up?" Obama swung and missed at the pitch, saying, "You know … uh … I thought that … you know … the truth is, that a lot of the Cubs I liked too." As if this admission was not bad enough to Cubs-hating White Sox fans, he added that "When I moved to Chicago, I was living close to what was then Cominskey Park [sic] and went to a couple of games and just fell in love with it." This answer compounded the problem, as all baseball fans know that the White Sox used to play at "Comiskey" park. Obviously uncomfortable with the direction of the interview, Obama moved onto the more familiar ground of class warfare, criticizing highfalutin Cubs fans "sipping their wine" at Wrigley Field. *Chicago Tribune* columnist John Kass wrote that the awkward incident recalled for him when "CBS' Katie Couric sweetly asked Sarah Palin what she liked to read. Palin drew a blank and reporters never let her live it down."[110]

Occasionally a soft interviewer asks an uncomfortable substantive question. In September 2012, *Late Night* host David Letterman asked if he knew the size of the national debt. Somewhat unbelievably, Obama responded, "I don't remember what the number was precisely…."[111] It is hard to imagine that the president of the United States did not know the size of the burgeoning U.S. debt. More likely, he knew the answer but did not want to admit to the large number—$16,000,000,000,000 and counting—in a soft venue that was supposed to be portraying him in a favorable light. The Letterman curveball was an exception, and for the most part Obama was secure in knowing that most of the questions on popular entertainment shows would be about his preferences in the areas of sports or pop culture.

As long as he stayed away from baseball or the debt, the soft interviews worked well. Accordingly, the pace of celebrity-style turns increased as the 2012 election neared. He "slow jammed" the news on *Late Night with Jimmy Fallon*, and talked about the issue of college loans to Fallon's youthful audience.[112] Fallon called Obama the "Preezy of the United Steezy," which did not appear to faze the commander in chief. In the summer of 2012, he went on a New Mexico radio station to tell the DJs that he likes green chilis over red, enjoys working out to Carly Rae Jepsen's "Call Me Maybe," and that his superpower of choice would be the ability to speak any language.[113] He was also a popular guest on *Oprah* and *The View*, appearing five times on the latter, including at a time when he was apparently unable to meet with world leaders in this country for the United Nations General Assembly.[114] *The View*, of course, was the venue in which he denied knowledge of Snooki, even though she was probably well-known to watchers of that program. According to Sam Stein, Obama had given twenty-six of these "soft" interviews by mid-September of the presidential election year of 2012, with more of these interviews flooding in by the day.[115]

The soft media approach left an opening for critics. Even though it may have protected him from tough questions, Obama's practice of "giving exclusives to unconventional outlets while shunning harder news reporters," as *Talking Points Memo*'s Benjy Sarlin described it, opened the president to mockery from his Republican opponents and murmurs of dissatisfaction from the neglected White House press corps.[116] But Obama proved so successful at purveying an aura of cool that even some of his toughest critics had to concede his skill at manipulating the media. On TV with Piers Morgan, the conservative critic Jonah Goldberg joked that Obama had an advantage when making the play for soft media because "*Rolling Stone* would burst into flames before" they would put Mitt Romney on its cover. Goldberg, whose writing regularly combines politics and pop culture, felt that Obama did face the vulnerability that "You can only be cool for so long in American life." At the same time, Goldberg acknowledged that Obama's cool had not yet subsided, and that "all in all, it's better to have a cool president than a not cool president."[117] The Obama team recognized this as well, and its campaign spokeswoman Stephanie Cutter brushed aside criticism of Obama's media appearances, telling CNN that soft media outlets such as *People* or *Entertainment Tonight* were "equally important" as the hard news outlets.[118]

Cutter's defense rang false after Obama's disastrous October 3, 2012, debate against Mitt Romney, in which the president seemed unprepared for Romney's hard-hitting critique of his record. The soft media appeared to have softened Obama, who was unable to cope with non-obsequious questioning. As one observer tweeted during the debate, "Hey Obama, this is what happens when the hardest question the MSM asks you for the past 5 years is 'What's your favorite color?' #debate."

Obama hit a rough patch in the spring of 2013 when a number of things went wrong for him. Bob Woodward called out the White House for their tough-on-reporters strategy after the White House aide Gene Sperling threatened him for his tough questioning, and Ruth Marcus of the *Washington Post* questioned the White House's strategy of negotiating budget proposals through blog posts ("Really, a blog post?" she asked).[119] NPR's Alan Greenblatt asked whether Obama was overexposed on the pop-culture front.[120] There was a sense of Obama's pop culture strategy in danger of "jumping the shark."

Usually though, Obama used this soft media strategy because it worked for him. He sold himself as a pop-culture president when the pop culture had evolved to the point where no one source—no Walter Cronkite, no *New York Times*, no *I Love Lucy*—either dictated or reflected the nation's tastes. In this new environment, the president could pick and choose his outlets, micro-targeting voters inclined to support him, and avoiding pesky political reporters in venues in which he might be unpopular. This was no Rose Garden strategy—the president was not cloistered in the White House, appearing only to promote one image a day. It was instead an approach for the multi-channeled twenty-first century, in which consumers follow their interests, and no one media source handles all comers.

Back in 1962, Daniel Boorstin foresaw the ways in which emerging technologies would shape American politics. Boorstin wrote that "Our national politics has become a competition for images or between images, rather than between ideals." The regnant technology of the time was television, of course, and Boorstin added, "The domination of campaigning by television simply dramatizes" the point. But Boorstin's point was not limited to the technology of television, and it applied to the broadcasting of images by whatever media were available. He wrote, "An effective President must be every year more concerned with projecting images of himself."[121] Boorstin transcribed *The Image* a half-century before Obama. But clearly the Hawaiian-born son of a Kenyan who spent much of his childhood in Indonesia and the rest of it far from the U.S. mainland, learned what he needed to know from constant TV watching. He understood Boorstin's central lesson as well as his warning. In his quest for the presidency, and in his pursuit to retain it, Obama was a relentless master of "projecting images of himself" to wherever receptive voters might be watching.

CONCLUSION

The American presidency is based on provisions of a written Constitution that have hardly changed since Washington held the office. Yet Washington would hardly recognize the role the presidency plays in American life today. While the presidency was changing over the last two and a quarter centuries into the powerful office it has become, popular culture and the media by which it is transmitted underwent a radical transformation as well.

As the late Irving Kristol observed, in centuries past, "The uneducated had their entertainments and diversions—singing, dancing, cockfighting, drinking, fornication, and an occasional festivity at the church." The revolution in the means of communication changed what was once "popular culture" into "mass culture." "Whereas 'popular culture' was the culture of a class (the uneducated)," said Kristol, "'mass culture' is a culture shared to a greater or lesser degree, by everyone. We all watch the same TV shows, read the same advertisements, see the same movies."[1]

In America's democracy, these tremendous changes in the popular culture were bound to affect the nation's most prominent political institution, the presidency. I have identified some of the more important and interesting ways that popular culture has shaped the presidency. In addition, I have told the story of how our presidents have tried to understand and adjust to the vertiginous pace of change in the manners and customs, the entertainments and diversions, the modes of thought and systems of belief of the people they govern and to whom they must answer every four years. Some presidents, we have seen, have been more astute judges of popular culture than others.

The Founders sought wisdom and virtue in reading. Presidents in the early nineteenth century tried to appeal to the common man through popular theater. Abraham Lincoln and Theodore Roosevelt turned to reading for self-improvement—rising out of childhood poverty in Lincoln's case, and changing the image he projected to the world in Roosevelt's.

But the arrival of broadcast technology gave presidents, starting with Franklin Roosevelt, unprecedented power to craft their own public image by appearing directly before the people, unconstrained by distance or time. Television magnified this power, as presidents took advantage of the shared experience of a universal medium to relate to average Americans. More recently, presidents have turned to the pop-music culture, which they once ignored, trying to appropriate the hipness—a concept that pop culture itself created—of rock stars and rappers, as well as movie and TV stars.

At the same time, as the celebrity culture of the mass media has intruded more and more on the presidency, the press has paid increasing attention, with the eager cooperation of the White House, to the presidents' reading as well. Perhaps the American people seek reassurance that their leaders, although thoroughly enmeshed in the celebrity culture, are somehow people of more substance than other celebrities.

Through it all, popular culture and the democratic process are inextricably connected. Leaders must prove that they are "of the people" by displaying their conversance with popular culture while maintaining an appearance of intellectual achievement. These goals can be mutually contradictory, and presidents must walk a careful line between flaunting their intellectual worth and relating to the populace. Indeed, every administration in the age of mass media has tried to project a carefully filtered image of the president's engagement with popular culture. The White House's accounts of what the president is reading or watching or how he is entertaining himself might not always be entirely candid.

A number of presidents, in fact, have been deliberately inauthentic about their cultural appetites. Bill Clinton advertised his highbrow reading but not his "little cheap thrills outlet" of mystery reading; George H. W. Bush claimed that *Catcher in the Rye* was meaningful to him in school even though the book wasn't published until he was an adult. Perhaps the most audacious cultural *poseur* was John F. Kennedy, with his claim to have written *Profiles in Courage* and his highly publicized mingling with intellectuals.

On the other hand, presidents have occasionally concealed or downplayed their cultural activities. Ronald Reagan refused to let his communications team advertise his reading. Sometimes these attempts have gone too far. George W. Bush's attempt "never to be out-cowboyed again" made it hard for him to convey seriousness once he became president.

Presidents have many motives, therefore, for reading what they read and watching what they watch. They may simply wish to be entertained, as Eisenhower was by watching or reading Westerns. And there is the need to connect with fellow citizens by keeping abreast of their interests, as asceticism can be dangerous. The cultural critic Camille Paglia maintains, "Not having a TV is tantamount to saying, 'I know nothing of the time or country in which I live.'"[2] Presidents can ill afford to betray such disengagement.

At the same time, awareness of cultural developments differs from pursuing every base or degrading cultural phenomenon. Reading informs presidents on policy and provides philosophical perspective. There was a time when presidents read more enlightening material, ingesting information that was helpful to them and to the country in the performance of their duties.

When faced with the panoply of choices, there are a number of different approaches presidents can take. They can try to be aware of as many new cultural developments as possible. This keeps them in touch but is time-consuming and can be unedifying. Two recent presidents exemplify this contrast. George W. Bush dismissively declared that he did not watch TV and strove to have his head on the pillow by ten o'clock each night. Barack Obama stays up from ten o'clock to one o'clock watching TV and playing on his iPad. Obama certainly seems more in tune with popular culture than Bush, but opinion may differ on which approach is better for the president or the presidency.

Ideology influences the cultural choices and preoccupations of the presidents. Bush disdained television in part because it had so little regard for him and for things he valued. Obama and Clinton proved pop-culture heroes, and the entertainment world tended to share their political point of view. This bifurcation is a relatively new phenomenon, but it has hardened to the point where it seems unlikely to change in the foreseeable future. Conservatives now see the entertainment industry as an enemy, much as the entertainment industry itself sees Republicans as an enemy.

The "pervasiveness of American popular culture," says Michael Hogan, "of blue jeans and basketball, of jazz music and rock-and-roll, of Hollywood movies and television, represented one of the most important cultural developments of the [twentieth] century."[3] Spreading Americanism is certainly an achievement, but of what sort? As Laura Ingraham complained after visiting a mall on a weekend, "Is this what our forefathers fought for? What my parents struggled for? Is this the American culture the Greatest Generation had in mind when they stormed the beaches at Normandy? So we could aspire to be like the Kardashians or land a role on *The Real Housewives of Miami*?"[4]

This complaint brings us back to Irving Kristol, who explains the bitterness of pop culture's critics: "[P]opular taste now has a coercive power such as civilization has never before witnessed," he observed. "By its sheer massive presence, 'mass culture' tends to crowd culture of any other kind to the margins of society."[5]

This mass culture affects and influences all of our citizens, up to and including the president. It shapes us, our worldviews, and in the president's case, his policies. It is inescapable, and presidents, like the rest of us, must find ways to deal with it.

RULES FOR PRESIDENTS ENGAGING POP CULTURE

While I don't presume to have all the answers, this book does offer some lessons for those who would be instructed. Here are some principles distilled from the experience of presidents as they grappled with America's boisterous, all-consuming, unpredictable popular culture.

1. *Boorstin's Law*: Our national politics has become a competition for images or between images. Presidents must therefore understand popular culture, even if they don't endorse it.

2. *Mark Knoller's Vacation Tally Law*: You must convey that you are hardworking and compassionate. Despite all the time they spend on mass media, Americans don't want presidents watching copious amounts of TV and movies or reading airport fiction. The public wants a president who is plugged in, but not a couch potato.

3. *"Where's the Beef?" Law*: Understanding the top shows, bestsellers, and blockbusters is valuable, but it doesn't mean you must comment on it. Pop culture references are best used humorously—especially against opponents.

4. *The Corner of the Desk Rule*: What you do read and watch should be communicated subtly. It will gain momentum and attention on its

own. You are not running Oprah's book club, so keep the fiction to a minimum.

5. *The Law of HBO and Showtime*: Know what critics and the opinion elite watch. They are not the same shows that the rest of the populace watches, so adjust your message carefully.

6. *Murphy (Brown)'s Law*: If you criticize artists or celebrities, you empower them to criticize you.

First Corollary: If you are going to praise or criticize a show, use the language of artists, not politics (as Obama did when rebuking Matt Damon).

Second Corollary: Be indirect, not ham-fisted. If you don't like the message of the Dark Knight, praise Catwoman.

1. *The Omar Rule*: Comment on *snapshots* of culture or specific scenes or characters, not entire shows or works. Otherwise, you own it all (good and bad) and invite misunderstandings.

2. *The Twitter Rule*: There is value—and earned media—to be gained from being the first to endorse a new technology or new form of cultural expression.

3. *Minow's Law*: Better to use a new technology to communicate your presidential message than to comment on the new technology. (Understanding the opportunity of television helped JFK in his debates, but it didn't change the fact that TV was a "vast wasteland.")

4. *The Five-Hundred-Channel Opportunity*: The five-hundred-channel world is an opportunity to micro-target your message for niche audiences. Use it well. Use it often.

5. *The Law of Celebrity*: Politicians who live by the rules of celebrity die by the rules of celebrity. You can't be a Kardashian president without the cameras, criticism, and up-and-down cycles of popularity.

6. *The Phil Dunphy Law*: American culture moves fast. A president can be cool for only so long. Define the standards by which you will be judged and then work on delivering.

7. *The Left Coast Law*: Republicans—especially conservatives—will *never* get the benefit of the doubt on intellectual or artistic matters from Hollywood or from New York.

Corollary: Genuine praise will *not* be graciously received.

1. *The Left Coast Is Not America Law*: Democrats make their worst mistakes when they think they will *always* get the benefit of the doubt from the entertainment and news media. Hollywood, especially, does not understand the burdens of governing or compromise.

First Corollary: They will turn on you eventually.

Second Corollary: But courting and feting them will keep the damage to a minimum.

1. *Ford's Law*: Comedians are more dangerous than producers or reporters.
2. *Dana Carvey's Law*: If you are going to use humor or laugh at yourself, do it early. Otherwise, you are just endorsing the joke, not killing it.
3. *You Never Get a Second Chance to Make a First Impression Law*: Know and understand the comedic archetypes. Politicians—especially Republicans—fit into a narrow band of categories:
   a. Stupid (George W. Bush, Sarah Palin, Joe Biden)
   b. Cruel or Machiavellian (Dick Cheney, Newt Gingrich)
   c. Randy or Slick (Bill Clinton, John Edwards)
   d. Old (Bob Dole, John McCain)
   e. Greedy, Rich, Disconnected (George H. W. Bush, Mitt Romney)
   f. Flip-Floppers (all of them—but once you get the label it colors all other jokes. Just ask John Kerry.)

Corollary: You can use these presentations of your opponents once they are endorsed by comedians.

1. *The Prime Directive*: Popular culture can help you get elected. Occasionally it can help you communicate. But reading is still king. History and biography are what will help you lead and govern successfully.

2. *"The Simpsons" Rule*: Don't pick a fight with someone who distributes photons by the megapixel.

3. *Harry Truman's Law*: Try reading. It can teach you things you did not already know.

4. *Truman's Second Law*: You can't be Harry and vice president at the same time.

5. *The Washington Read Rule*: Don't assume that presidents you think are readers are, and don't assume that presidents you think aren't readers aren't.

6. *Clancy's Law*: Presidents can have an effect on sales, but the effect is bigger when they pick books that Americans are inclined to read.

ACKNOWLEDGMENTS

Writing a book is an intense process that requires a great deal of help every step of the way. The first thank-you goes to my brother Dan Troy, who heard me give a speech on this topic and recommended that I turn the speech into a book proposal. Thanks also to Scott Yonover, Jonah Goldberg, Jay Lefkowitz, Vin Cannato, Ben Wildavsky, Bob Goldberg, Adam Keiper, and Jeremy Katz for helping me on the increasingly important agent search, and to Gene Brissie for agreeing to serve as said agent.

Alex Novak, associate publisher of Regnery History, and Marji Ross, president and publisher of Regnery Publishing, agreed to take on the book, and crack editor Tom Spence has always been ready to handle queries from a nervous second-time author. If you are reading this book, it is in large part due to the efforts of Alberto Rojas, Erin Haft, Hannah Sternberg, Mark Bloomfield, and their teams, who publicized the book and made sure copies went where they needed to go.

Once I had a book contract in hand, I had to figure out how to find the time to write the book and what I wanted to say. For the first part, I am grateful to Hudson Institute CEO Ken Weinstein, who was supportive of the project throughout the entire process. John Walters and Kate Smyth helped figure out how best to have Hudson back my work. For the writing part, thanks are due to weekly participants at the Hudson scholars' luncheon, especially those who helped provide direction for the book at an early stage in the process: Abe Shulsky, Doug Feith, Hanns Kuttner, John Weicher, Jack David, Chris DeMuth, Chiko Punn, Max Singer, Scooter Libby,

Eric Brown, Tim Kane, and Chris Sands. Chris Sands gets a special shout-out for his library privileges and all-around help in tracking down books

Once I started writing, the number one thank you has to go to Matt Robinson, for his editorial wisdom and infectious optimism about the project throughout.

Stanley Kurtz read many of the chapters as they were written and provided excellent directional assistance.

Kathryn Lopez and Seth Leibsohn deserve recognition for their strong encouragement at an early and unpromising point in the process.

Researching a book such as this is a tough job, and I was lucky to have help from indispensable researchers Peter Grabowski and Jason Bedrick, as well as Hudson interns (listed alphabetically) Sam Englander, Michael Friedman, Henrik Hoem, Izzy Kates, Matthew Kritz, Shmuale Mark, Chad Roahrig, Margot Schumann, Matt Shiraki, Hadassah (Dassy-doodle) Solomson, Jessica Stertzer, and Julie Xie.

Once the manuscript was done, Gil Troy, Dan Troy, John McConnell, Jamie Bologna, and Matt Robinson read the entire draft manuscript and made many important catches and suggestions. Their (mostly) positive feedback was both encouraging and indispensable to improving the product you have in your hands.

Helpful title suggestions came from Alan Rechtschaffen, Matt Gerson, Jonah Goldberg, Sam Garfield, Michael Ungar, and Matt Rees.

David Tell, Daniel McKivergan, and Peri Farbstein on the Hudson communications staff are a huge help to all Hudson scholars, as were Grace Terzian, Jamie Bologna, Phil Ross, and Ioannis Saratsis when they were at Hudson.

Garrett Graf and my college buddy Cathy Merrill have given me a great venue at *Washingtonian* to work through parts of this book, and I look forward to continuing my association with them and their always interesting magazine. John Podhoretz at *Commentary*, Yuval Levin at *National Affairs,* Kathryn Lopez and Rich Lowry at National Review Online, Brian Anderson at *City Journal*, Carlos Lozada at the *Washington Post*'s Outlook section, David Mark, Allison Silver, and then Bill Nichols at *Politico*, Phil Terzian at the *Weekly Standard*, and Adam Keiper at the *New Atlantis* have made me feel welcome at their prestigious publications, and I look forward to writing for them (and others) more regularly now that this book is on the shelf.

Finally, family is what gets one through this process. Thanks go first to my adorable kids—Ezra, Ruthie, Rina, and Noey. I look forward to them reading and enjoying this book, perhaps during the George P. Bush or Chelsea Clinton administration. My in-laws, Drs. Vita and Ray Pliskow, destroy the stereotype of the annoying in-laws, and I am grateful to them for their unfailing support. My parents, Dov and Elaine Troy, to whom this book is dedicated, gave me every opportunity to succeed in this great country, and I am eternally grateful to them.

The biggest thank-you goes to my wife, Kami Troy, for her perseverance throughout the process. Most authors thank their spouses for unyielding support in ways that make readers such as this one somewhat skeptical. In contrast, my mostly loving wife said: "You sure are a lot more fun when you are not writing a book." Here's to my (hopefully) becoming fun again.

NOTES

Introduction

1. Lynn Sweet, "Obama and Snooki: Now the president knows who she is," *Chicago Sun-Times*, July 29, 2010, http://blogs.suntimes.com/sweet/2010/07/obama_and_snooki_now_the_presi.html.

2. Philip Rucker and Karen Tumulty, "On trail, Romney on and off message," *Washington Post*, September 15, 2012. A1, A4.

3. Trevor Colbourn, *The Lamp of Experience: Whig History and the Intellectual Origins of the American Revolution* (Indianapolis: Liberty Fund, 1998), xviii-xix.

4. Tevi Troy, "Republican Reading," National Review Online, November 18, 2010, http://www.nationalreview.com/articles/253488/republican-reading-tevi-troy. (Note: information on Cantor's reading was provided by his Communications office.)

5. Carrie Budoff Brown and Jonathan Allen, "The Humbling of the House GOP," *Politico*, December 23, 2011, http://dyn.politico.com/printstory.cfm?uuid=06624466-62C5-4E93-B196-B7EAB128A133. (Note: For those readers requiring a translation, the message reads: Everyone should see what $40 means to folks: groceries, day care, gas, and copayments on your health insurance. Please continue to spread this message. I will discuss this very subject at a speech tomorrow at 12:15 PM, Eastern Time. President Barack Obama.)

6. David Janssens, *Between Athens and Jerusalem: Philosophy, Prophecy, and Politics in Leo Strauss's Early Thought* (Albany: State University of New York Press, 2008).

7. Gil Troy, *Morning in America: How Ronald Reagan Invented the 1980s* (Princeton: Princeton University Press, 2005), 261.

8. Kevin Mattson, *What the Heck Are You Up To, Mr. President?* (New York: Bloomsbury USA, 2009).

9. Robert Darnton, *George Washington's False Teeth* (New York: W. W. Norton, 2003), 99.

10. Ibid.

11. "Nielsen Ratings," *Wikipedia*, July 24, 2012, http://en.wikipedia.org/wiki/Nielsen_ratings.

Chapter 1

1. Jefferson quoted in Robert Darnton, *George Washington's False Teeth* (New York: W. W. Norton, 2003), 100.

2. Forrest McDonald, "Founding Father's Library: A Bibliographical Essay," *Literature of Liberty: A Review of Contemporary Liberal Thought* 1, no. 1 (January/March 1978).

3. Darnton, *George Washington's False Teeth*, 100.

4. Christopher Geist, "The Emergence of Popular Culture in Colonial America," *CW Journal* (Spring 2008), http://www.history.org/foundation/journal/spring08/pop.cfm.

5. Forrest McDonald, "Founding Father's Library."

6. Anthony Brandt, "Do We Care If Johnny Can Read?" *American Heritage* 31, no. 5 (August/September 1980), http://www.americanheritage.com/content/do-we-care-if-johnny-can-read?page=show.

7. Jack Lynch, "Every Man Able to Read: Literacy in Early America," *CW Journal* (Winter 2011), http://www.history.org/foundation/journal/winter11/literacy.cfm.

8. Forrest McDonald, "Founding Father's Library."

9. Paul F. Boller Jr., *Presidential Diversions: Presidents at Play from George Washington to George W. Bush* (New York: Houghton Mifflin, 2007), 9.

10. Ibid.

11. "George Washington's 221-year overdue library book: A timeline," *The Week*, May 21, 2010, http://theweek.com/article/index/203282/george-washingtons-221-year-overdue-library-book-a-timeline.

12. Darnton, *George Washington's False Teeth*, 98.

13. Catherine Allgor, *A Perfect Union: Dolley Madison and the Creation of the American Nation* (New York: Henry Holt, 2006), 185.

14. *History of George Washington: Bicentennial Celebration* (Washington, D.C.: United States George Washington Bicentennial, 1932), 3:280.

15. Bernard Bailyn, *The Ideological Origins of the American Revolution* (Cambridge: Harvard University Press, 1967), 24–26.

16. Carl J. Richard, *The Founders and the Classics: Greece, Rome, and the American Enlightenment* (Harvard: Cambridge University Press, 1994), 63.

17. Gordon Wood, *The Creation of the American Republic* (Chapel Hill: University of North Carolina Press, 1969), 49–50.

18. Alan Wallace, "Shelf life: Read like a Founder," *Pittsburgh Tribune-Review*, June 26, 2011, http://www.pittsburghlive.com/x/pittsburghtrib/opinion/apageofbooks/s_743776.html#.

19. Thomas Jefferson, "Letter to Doctor Walter Jones," *The Works of Thomas Jefferson*, federal edition 11 (New York and London, G. P. Putnam's Sons, 1904–5), http://oll.libertyfund.org/title/807/88123, accessed on April 1, 2011.

20. Myron Magnet, "When George Washington Became Great," *City Journal* 22, no. 1 (Winter 2012): 104.

21. Geist, "The Emergence of Popular Culture in Colonial America."

22. Bernard Bailyn, *Faces of Revolution: Personalities and Themes in the Struggle for American Independence* (New York: Alfred A. Knopf, 1990), 67.

23. Geist, "The Emergence Of Popular Culture In Colonial America."

24. "List of best-selling books," *Wikipedia,* http://en.wikipedia.org/wiki/List_of_best-selling_books#Between_10_million_and_20_million_copies.

25. Adams quoted in Boller, *Presidential Diversions*, 20.

26. Letter from Thomas Jefferson to John Adams, June 10, 1815, Lester J. Cappon, ed., *The Adams-Jefferson Letters* (Chapel Hill: University of North Carolina Press, 1959), http://www.monticello.org/site/jefferson/i-cannot-live-without-books-quotation.

27. Bill Bryson, *At Home: A Short History of Private Life* (New York: Doubleday, 2011), 296.

28. Peter Brimelow, "Why they call it Harvard College," *Forbes*, March 9, 1998, http://www.forbes.com/forbes/1998/0309/6105050a.html.

29. Bryson, *At Home*, 305.

30. Joseph J. Ellis, *Passionate Sage: The Character and Legacy of John Adams* (New York: Norton, 2001), 88.

31. Trevor Colbourn, *The Lamp of Experience: Whig History and the Intellectual Origins of the American Revolution*, (Indianapolis: Liberty Fund, 1965), 15.

32. Joseph J. Ellis, *Passionate Sage: the Character and Legacy of John Adams* (New York: Norton, 2001), 88.

33. Ibid., 88–89.

34. Darnton, *George Washington's False Teeth* (New York: W. W. Norton, 2003), 96–97.

35. Forrest McDonald, foreword to *Cato: A Tragedy and Selected Essays*, by Joseph Addison (Indianapolis: Liberty Fund, 2004).

36. Colbourn, *The Lamp of Experience: Whig History and the Intellectual Origins of the American Revolution*, 16–19.

37. Stephen Greenblatt, *The Swerve: How the World Became Modern* (New York: W. W. Norton, 2011).

38. Ibid, 262.

39. Michael Meyerson, *Liberty's Blueprint: How Madison and Hamilton Wrote the Federalist Papers, Defined the Constitution, and Made Democracy Safe for the World* (New York: Basic Books, 2009), 52; Richard Brookhiser, *James Madison* (New York: Perseus Books, 2011), 47.

40. Jonathan Sacks, *The Home We Build Together: Recreating Society* (London: Continuum, 2007), 111.

41. Adams quoted in John Ferling, *John Adams: A Life* (New York, Oxford University Press, 1992), 153.

42. David Hackett Fischer, *Paul Revere's Ride* (New York: Oxford University Press, 1995), 164; Mellem Chamberlain interview, John Pancake, *1777: The Year of the Hangman* (University of Alabama Press: 1977).

43. Donald Lutz, "The 'Top 40' Authors cited by the Founding Generation," Liberty Fund, http://oll.libertyfund.org/index.php?Itemid=259&id=438&option=com_content&task=view.

44. James Ceaser, *Reconstructing America* (New Haven: Yale University Press, 1997), 28. Jefferson related the story of Franklin and Raynal in a letter to Robert Walsh of December 4, 1818, available at http://oll.libertyfund.org/?option=com_staticxt&staticfile=show.php%3Ftitle=808&chapter=88380&layout=html&Itemid=27#lf0054-12_footnote_nt_015.

45. Jay Winik, *The Great Upheaval: America and the Birth of the Modern World, 1788–1800* (New York: HarperCollins, 2007).

46. Matthew Robinson, *Mobocracy: How the Media's Obsession with Polling Twists the News, Alters Elections, and Undermines Democracy* (New York: Prima, 2002), 219.

47. Jefferson quoted in Anthony Brandt, "Do We Care If Johnny Can Read?" *American Heritage* 31, no. 5 (August/September 1980), http://www.americanheritage.com/content/do-we-care-if-johnny-can-read?page=show.

48. Thomas Jefferson, letter to Colonel Charles Yancey, January 6, 1816. Paul L. Ford, ed., *The Writings of Thomas Jefferson*, 10.

Chapter 2

1. "President Grover Cleveland's Son Was Broadway Star," *Broadway Magazine*, January 20, 2009, http://www.broadway.tv/blog/broadway-magazine/president-grover-cleveland%E2%80%99s-son-was-broadway-star/.

2. Eric Metaxas, *Amazing Grace: William Wilberforce and the Heroic Campaign to End Slavery* (San Francisco: Harper San Francisco, 2007), 14.

3. Heather S. Nathans, *Early American Theatre from the Revolution to Thomas Jefferson*, (Cambridge: Cambridge University Press, 2003), 14.

4. Metaxas, *Amazing Grace*, 14.

5. Nathans, *Early American Theatre from the Revolution to Thomas Jefferson*, 37.

6. John J. Miller, "On Life, Liberty and Other Quotable Matters," *Wall Street Journal*, July 2, 2011.

7. Dr. Joe Wolverton II, "The Founding Fathers & the Classics," *New American* 20, no. 19 (September 20, 2004): 35–39, http://21stcenturycicero.wordpress.com/tyrrany/the-founding-fathers-the-classics/.

8. Carl J. Richard, *The Founders and the Classics: Greece, Rome, and the American Enlightenment* (Harvard: Cambridge University Press, 1994), 63.

9. Ibid.

10. Forrest McDonald, foreword to *Addison's Cato: A Tragedy and Selected Essay*, by Joseph Addison (Indianapolis: Liberty Fund, 2004).

11. Paul F. Boller Jr., *Presidential Diversions: Presidents at Play from George Washington to George W. Bush* (New York: Houghton Mifflin, 2007), 122, 125.

12. McDonald, foreword to *Addison's Cato*.

13. Christopher Geist, "The Emergence Of Popular Culture In Colonial America," *CW Journal* (Spring 2008), http://www.history.org/foundation/journal/spring08/pop.cfm.

14. Boller, *Presidential Diversions*, 8.

15. Thomas A. Bogar, *American Presidents Attend the Theatre: The Playgoing Experiences of Each Chief Executive* (Jefferson, NC: McFarland, 2006), 41.

16. Ibid., 19.

17. Ibid., 50.

18. Ibid., 52

19. Theodore Rosengarten and Eli N. Evans, *A Portion of the People: Three Hundred Years of Southern Jewish Life* (Columbia: University of South Carolina Press, 2002), 84.

20. Jacob Rader Marcus, *United States Jewry, 1776–1985*, vol. 1, *The Shephardic Period* (Detroit: Wayne State University Press, 1989), 451.

21. I ran this theory about the Harby's *Alberti* being the first work of fiction by a Jewish author by Rabbi David Dalin, Professor Jonathan Sarna, and Professor Heather Nathans. Dalin is a historian of Jews and the presidency, Sarna is the preeminent historian of Jews in

America, and Nathans is an expert on nineteenth-century American theater and Jews and the theater. Each confirmed my theory, and I am grateful to them for their assistance.

22. David G. Dalin, "House of Learning," *Weekly Standard*, February 27, 2012, http://www.weeklystandard.com/articles/houses-learning_630025.html#.

23. "From Haven to Home," Library of Congress, Washington, D.C. [exhibition marking 350 years of Jewish life in America], September 2004–February 2006, http://www.loc.gov/exhibits/haventohome/haven-haven.html.

24. Marcus, *United States Jewry, 1776–1985*, 1:451.

25. Ibid., 1:494.

26. Rosengarten and Evans, *A Portion of the People*, 84.

27. Bogar, *American Presidents Attend the Theatre*, 74–75.

28. Ibid., 68.

29. Ibid., 60.

30. Jimmy Carter, *White House Diary* (New York: Farrar, Straus, and Giroux, 2010), 213.

31. Heather Nathans, "Spheres of Action: Theatre, Politics, and Culture in Lincoln's America," lecture in "Lincoln and Shakespeare: On Freedom's Stage," Ford's Theater, Washington, D.C., April 13, 2009.

32. Ibid.

33. Rosengarten and Evans, *A Portion of the People*, 84.

34. Gerald Bordman and Thomas S. Hischak, *The Oxford Companion to American Theatre* (Oxford: Oxford University Press, 2004), 118.

35. "Essay: 19th Century American Theater," University of Washington Digital Archive, http://content.lib.washington.edu/19thcenturyactorsweb/essay.html.

36. Nathans, "Spheres of Action."

37. Ibid.

38. Edward P. Crapol, *John Tyler: The Accidental President* (Chapel Hill: University of North Carolina Press, 2006), 30, 37.

39. Ibid., 4.

40. Ibid., 244. The original line is both from and by Othello (Act V, Scene ii): "Like the base Indian, threw away a pearl Richer than all the tribes."

41. Nathans, "Spheres of Action."

42. "How to Behave At a Theatre," *Punchinello* 1, no. 1 (New York, April 9, 1870), http://www.lhsmn.org/research/theatre_etiquette.pdf. Courtesy of The Living History Society of Minnesota, Inc.

43. Thomas B. Horton, "Book on American manners outraged ancestors," Moultrie News, March 14, 2011, 43. http://www.moultrienews.com/article/20110309/MN24/303099988/0/MN&slId=22.

44. Bogar, *American Presidents Attend the Theatre*, 50.

45. Ibid., 52.

46. Ibid., 54.

47. Ibid., 55–56.

48. Andrea Mitchell, *Talking Back: To Presidents, Dictators, and Assorted Scoundrels* (New York: Penguin, 2006), 330.

49. Bogar, *American Presidents Attend the Theatre*, 55–56. It is a good thing that these days the president has his own box at the Kennedy Center, which prevents the occurrence of this kind of embarrassing mishap.

50. Paul C. Nagel, *John Quincy Adams: A Public Life, A Private Life* (Cambridge: Harvard University Press, 1997), 342–43.

51. Bogar, *American Presidents Attend the Theatre*, 61.

52. Ibid., 62.

53. John Adams, Letter to Abigail Adams, undated, 1780. Frank Shuffelton, ed., *The Letters of John and Abigail Adams* (New York: Penguin, 2004), 264.

54. Boller, *Presidential Diversions*, 51.

55. Nagel, *John Quincy Adams*, 331.

56. Boller, *Presidential Diversions*, 52.

57. John Quincy Adams, "Letter VI," *Letters of John Quincy Adams to his Son on the Teachings of the Bible* (Auburn: James L. Alden, 1850), 77.

58. Nagel, *John Quincy Adams*, 344.

59. Ibid., 374.

60. Boller, *Presidential Diversions*, 61.

61. Paul Johnson, *A History of the American People* (New York: HarperCollins, 1998), 337–38.

62. Ibid., 353.

63. Boller, *Presidential Diversions*, 61.

64. Nagel, *John Quincy Adams*, 343.

65. Boller, *Presidential Diversions*, 62.

66. Bogar, *American Presidents Attend the Theatre*, 75.

67. Ibid., 77–78.

68. Joseph Shattan, "One Term Wonder," *American Spectator*, October 1996, 32.

69. Boller, *Presidential Diversions*, 82.

Chapter 3

1. Benjamin Franklin, "The Autobiography of Benjamin Franklin," Archiving Early America, http://www.earlyamerica.com/lives/franklin/chapt1/.

2. Alexis de Tocqueville, *Democracy in America* (Stilwell, KS: Digireads.com, 2007), 345.

3. Douglas L. Wilson, "His Hour Upon the Stage," *American Scholar* (Winter 2012), http://theamericanscholar.org/his-hour-upon-the-stage/.

4. Mary Church Terrell, *Harriet Beecher Stowe: An Appreciation* (Washington, D.C.: Murray Bros. Press, 1911). Accessed at the University of Virginia's "Uncle Tom's Cabin and American Culture Archive," created by Professor Stephen Railton, at http://utc.iath.virginia.edu/.

5. Anthony Brandt, "Do We Care If Johnny Can Read?" *American Heritage* 31 (August/September 1980), http://www.americanheritage.com/content/do-we-care-if-johnny-can-read?page=show.

6. Lord Charnwood, *Abraham Lincoln* (New York:Cosimo Classics, 2009), 11. This work was originally published in 1917.

7. David Herbert Donald, *Lincoln* (New York: Touchstone, 1996), 30.

8. Doris Kearns Goodwin, *Team of Rivals: The Political Genius of Abraham Lincoln* (New York: Simon & Schuster, 2005), 51–52.

9. Carl Schurz, "Abraham Lincoln: An Essay by Carl Schurz," *Introduction to the Writings of Abraham Lincoln: Volume One*, edited by Arthur Brooks Lapsley (Project Gutenberg, 2004), 9, http://www.gutenberg.org/ebooks/3253.

10. Joseph H. Choate, "Abraham Lincoln," address delivered before the Edinburgh Philosophical Institution, November 13, 1900, *Introduction to the Writings of Abraham Lincoln*, vol. 1.

11. Douglas L. Wilson, *Honor's Voice: The Transformation of Abraham Lincoln* (New York: Knopf, 1998), 105.

12. Robert Bray, "What Abraham Lincoln Read—An Evaluative and Annotated List," *Journal of the Abraham Lincoln Association* 28, no. 2 (Summer 2007): 28–81, http://hdl.handle.net/2027/spo.2629860.0028.204.

13. Ibid.

14. Goodwin, *Team of Rivals*, 52.

15. Charnwood, *Abraham Lincoln*, 10.

16. I have heard that Kristol made the comment, and that it may have been directed toward the late Jack Kemp, but I have not found the comment written down anywhere.

17. Charnwood, *Abraham Lincoln*, 11; Choate, "Abraham Lincoln," 58.

18. Charnwood, *Abraham Lincoln*, 11.

19. Choate, "Abraham Lincoln," 58.

20. Ibid.

21. Goodwin, *Team of Rivals*, 52.

22. Ibid.; Donald, *Lincoln*, 31; Fred Kaplan, *Lincoln: The Biography of a Writer* (New York: HarperCollins, 2008), 18; Schurz, "Abraham Lincoln: An Essay by Carl Schurz," 9; Daniel Kilham Dodge, *Abraham Lincoln: The Evolution of his Literary Style* (Champaign and Urbana: University of Illinois Press, 1900), 6.

23. Choate, "Abraham Lincoln," 58.

24. Ibid.

25. Dodge, *Abraham Lincoln: The Evolution of his Literary Style*, 8.

26. Donald, *Lincoln*, 30–31.

27. Kaplan, *Lincoln: The Biography of a Writer*, 25.

28. Donald, *Lincoln*, 32.

29. Schurz, "Abraham Lincoln: An Essay by Carl Schurz," 19.

30. Malcolm Gladwell, *Outliers: The Story of Success* (New York: Little, Brown, 2008).

31. Choate, "Abraham Lincoln," 61.

32. Donald, *Lincoln*, 99.

33. Dodge, *Abraham Lincoln: The Evolution of his Literary Style*, 8.

34. Kaplan, *Lincoln: The Biography of a Writer*, 21.

35. Schurz, "Abraham Lincoln: An Essay by Carl Schurz."

36. John William DeForest, "The Great American Novel," *Nation*, (January 9, 1868). Accessed at the University of Virginia's "Uncle Tom's Cabin and American Culture Archive," created by Professor Stephen Railton, at http://utc.iath.virginia.edu/.

37. David S. Reynolds, *Mightier Than the Sword: Uncle Tom's Cabin and the Battle for America* (New York: Norton, 2011), 11.

38. Terrell, *Harriet Beecher Stowe*.

39. David McCullough, "The Unexpected Mrs. Stowe," *American Heritage* 24 (August 1973), http://www.americanheritage.com/content/unexpected-mrs-stowe?page=show.

40. Ron Christie, *Acting White: The Curious History of a Racial Slur* (New York: St. Martin's Press, 2010), 12.

41. McCullough, "The Unexpected Mrs. Stowe."

42. Nathans, "Spheres of Action."

43. Reynolds, *Mightier Than the Sword*, 13.

44. Letter, Millard Fillmore to Mrs. S. M. Greeley, April 8, 1852. Shapell Manuscript Collection, http://www.shapell.org/manuscript.aspx?171575. The full text of the letter reads as follows:

My Dear Madam

Accept my thanks for a copy of Uncle Tom's Cabin which you were so kind as to send me on leaving Washington. I have only found time to glance at it and see that it is a work of fiction on the "vexed" Subject of Slavery. Mrs. F. however has read some chapters and is much pleased with its Style and interested in its story. This question of Slavery may well command the pens and sympathies of the fair sex, as it does the deep and anxious reflection of every Statesman in the country. It presents a problem which time only can solve. Who can penetrate the dark future and say whether this ever disturbing subject may not send this Union asunder. Whether the war of races may not result in the final overthrow and extermination of the weaker, or whether by wise and brilliant counsels the bonds of the slave may not be gradually relaxed and as they drop off, the blackman find a home in his native Africa, and bear with him to that benighted region the blessings of Christianity and civilization. I confess that I can not look without apprehension to the future, but I hope for the best, and am ever

Sincerely your friend
MILLARD FILLMORE

45. Richard Scarry, *Millard Fillmore* (Jefferson, NC: MacFarland, 2001), 226.

46. Edward P. Crapol, *John Tyler: The Accidental President* (Chapel Hill: University of North Carolina Press, 2006), 241–43.

47. Frederick Douglass, "The Key to Uncle Tom's Cabin," *Frederick Douglass' Paper* (Rochester, 1853). Accessed at the University of Virginia's "Uncle Tom's Cabin and American Culture Archive," created by Professor Stephen Railton, at http://utc.iath.virginia.edu/.

48. Sand quoted in McCullough, "The Unexpected Mrs. Stowe."

49. Charnwood, *Abraham Lincoln*, 51.

50. Scott Farris, *Almost President: The Men Who Lost the Race But Changed the Nation* (Guilford: Lyons Press, 2012), 67.

51. Reynolds, *Mightier Than the Sword*, 149, 162.

52. Michael Knox Beran, "Lincoln, Macbeth, and the Moral Imagination," *HUMANITAS* 11, no. 2 (1998).

53. Daniel J. Boorstin, *The Americans: The Democratic Experience* (NewYork: Random House, 1973), 171.

54. Edward Channing, *The United States of America, 1765–1865* (New York: Macmillan, 1896), 242.

55. Reynolds, *Mightier Than the Sword*, 166.

56. Joan D. Hedrick, *Harriet Beecher Stowe: A Life* (New York, Oxford University Press, 1994), 305.

57. Reynolds, *Mightier Than the Sword*, 9–10.

58. Dodge, *Abraham Lincoln: The Evolution of his Literary Style*, 54.

59. Theodore Roosevelt, "Abraham Lincoln," *Introduction to The Writings of Abraham Lincoln: Vol. One.*

60. Choate, "Abraham Lincoln," 63.

61. Dodge, *Abraham Lincoln: The Evolution of his Literary Style*, 5.

62. Harry V. Jaffa, *Crisis of the House Divided: An Interpretation of the Issues in the Lincoln-Douglas Debates*, 50th anniversary edition (Chicago: University of Chicago Press, 2009), 188.

63. Richard Norton Smith, "How Abraham Lincoln Shaped American Politics, Popular Culture Post Assassination," interview with Hari Sreenivasan, PBS *Newshour*, February 20, 2012, http://www.pbs.org/newshour/bb/politics/jan-june12/lincoln_02-20.html?print.

64. Walt Harrington "Dubya and Me," *American Scholar* (Autumn 2011), http://theamericanscholar.org/dubya-and-me/.

65. Jaffa, *Crisis of the House Divided*, 190.

66. Bogar, *American Presidents Attend the Theatre*, 89.

67. Ibid., 92.

68. Kaplan, *Lincoln: The Biography of a Writer*, 347.

69. Goodwin, *Team of Rivals*, 51.

70. Michael Burlingame, ed., *At Lincoln's Side: John Hay's Civil War Correspondence and Selected Writings* (Carbondale: Southern Illinois University Press, 2000), 137.

71. Bogar, *American Presidents Attend the Theatre*.

72. Kaplan, *Lincoln: The Biography of a Writer*, 347.

73. Letter, Abraham Lincoln to James Hackett, quoted in Douglas L. Wilson, "His Hour Upon the Stage."

74. Donald, *Lincoln*, 459, 548; Bogar, *American Presidents Attend the Theatre*.

75. Donald, *Lincoln*, 588.

76. Ibid., 594.

77.   Abraham Lincoln, "Daily Routines and Schedule," *Lehrman Institute*, http://www.mrlincolnswhitehouse.org/inside.asp?ID=518&subjectID=5.

78.   James Swanson, *Bloody Crimes: The Chase for Jefferson Davis and the Death Pageant for Lincoln's Corpse* (New York: William Morrow, 2010), 96, 114.

Chapter 4

1.   Andrew Wheen, *Dot-Dash to Dot.Com: How Modern Telecommunications Evolved from the Telegraph to the Internet* (New York: Springer Praxis Books, 2010), 92.

2.   "Talking Across the Ocean," blog, Theodore Roosevelt Center at Dickinson State University, http://www.theodorerooseveltcenter.org/Blog/2012/January/18-Talking-Across-the-Ocean.aspx.

3.   John Milton Cooper Jr., *The Warrior and the Priest—Woodrow Wilson and Theodore Roosevelt* (Cambridge: The Belknap Press of Harvard University Press, 1983), 5.

4.   Edmund Morris, *Colonel Roosevelt* (New York: Random House, 2010), 4.

5.   Theodore Roosevelt, *An Autobiography* (New York: Charles Scribner's Sons, 1913), 14–21.

6.   Ibid., 332.

7.   Edmund Morris, *The Rise of Theodore Roosevelt* (New York: Random House, 1979).

8.   Ibid., 64.

9.   Candice Millard, *The River of Doubt: Theodore Roosevelt's Darkest Journey*, (New York: Doubleday, 2005), 311–12. Roosevelt's need to read is reminiscent of the episode of the *Odd Couple* in which Oscar Madison is visiting a monastery where no outside reading material is allowed. Desperate, he takes the toothpaste from the bathroom so he can read the ingredients. Felix initially mocks him for it, but then asks Oscar if he can borrow the tube when he is done. "The Odd Monks," *Odd Couple*, TV show, season 3, episode 52, October 13, 1972.

10.   Lewis Gould, *Theodore Roosevelt* (New York: Oxford University Press, 2012), 6.

11.   Cooper, *The Warrior and the Priest*, 32.

12.   Ibid.

13.   Millard, *The River of Doubt*, 24.

14.   Paul F. Boller Jr., *Presidential Diversions: Presidents at Play from George Washington to George W. Bush* (New York: Houghton Mifflin, 2007), 178.

15.   Roosevelt, *An Autobiography*, 169.

16.   Ibid., 186–87.

17.   Morris, *The Rise of Theodore Roosevelt*, 434.

18. Philip A. Crowl, "Alfred Thayer Mahan: The Naval Historian," *Makers of Modern Strategy: From Machiavelli to the Nuclear Age*, edited by Peter Paret (Princeton: Princeton University Press, 1986), 450.

19. Morris, *The Rise of Theodore Roosevelt*, 434.

20. Scott Miller, *The President and the Assassin: McKinley, Terror, and Empire at the Dawn of the American Century* (New York: Random House, 2011), 53.

21. Cooper Jr., *The Warrior and the Priest*, 73.

22. Morris, *The Rise of Theodore Roosevelt*, 434.

23. Richard W. Turk, *The Ambiguous Relationship: Theodore Roosevelt and Alfred Thayer Mahan* (Westport: Greenwood Press, 1987).

24. Roosevelt, *An Autobiography*, 333.

25. Edmund Morris, *Theodore Rex* (New York: Random House, 2002), 108.

26. Morris, *Colonel Roosevelt*, 35.

27. Roosevelt, *An Autobiography*, 334.

28. Ibid., 334–35.

29. Boller, *Presidential Diversions*, 168.

30. Miller, *The President and the Assassin*, 92–93.

31. Ibid., 15. The magazine dropped "Monthly" from its title in 2007.

32. Cullen Murphy, "A History of the *Atlantic Monthly*," The Atlantic Monthly Group, 1994, http://www.theatlantic.com/past/docs/about/atlhistf.htm.

33. Miller, *The President and the Assassin*, 316.

34. "Table 102. High school graduates compared with population 17 years of age, by sex and control of school: Selected years, 1869–70 to 2004–05," National Center for Education Statistics, http://nces.ed.gov/programs/digest/d04/tables/dt04_102.asp.

35. Cooper, *The Warrior and the Priest*, 5.

36. Roosevelt, *An Autobiography*, 336.

37. Ibid., 318

38. Cooper, *The Warrior and the Priest*, 31.

39. "Roosevelt's Bar Fight," National Park Service, http://www.nps.gov/thro/historyculture/roosevelts-bar-fight.htm.

40. Roosevelt, *An Autobiography*, 78.

41. Ibid., 332.

42. Morris, *Theodore Rex*, 243–44.

43. Charles Murray, *Coming Apart: The State of White America* (New York: Crown Forum, 2012), 141.

44. Morris, *The Rise of Theodore Roosevelt*, 32.

45. Edna Nahshon, ed., *From the Ghetto to the Melting Pot: Israel Zangwill's Jewish Plays* (Detroit: Wayne State University Press, 2005), 242–43.

46. Ibid., 243.

47. Werner Sollors, *Beyond Ethnicity: Consent and Descent in American Culture* (New York: Oxford University Press, 1987), 66.

48. Nahshon, ed., *From the Ghetto to the Melting Pot*, 213–14.

49. Ibid., 241. Judah P. Benjamin was Secretary of the Treasury in the Confederate States of America.

50. Thomas A. Bogar, *American Presidents Attend the Theatre* (Jefferson, NC: McFarland, 2006), 195.

51. Jonathan Sacks, *The Home We Build Together: Recreating Society* (London: Continuum, 2007), 25.

52. Dewey Grantham, ed., *Theodore Roosevelt* (Saddle River: Prentice Hall, 1971), 166.

53. Chris Bachelder, "The Jungle at 100: Why the reputation of Upton Sinclair's good book has gone bad," *Mother Jones*, January/February 2006, http://motherjones.com/media/2006/01/jungle-100.

54. Theodore Roosevelt, "The Man with the Muck-rake," delivered April 14, 1906, http://www.americanrhetoric.com/speeches/teddyrooseveltmuckrake.htm.

55. H. W. Brands, *T.R.: The Last Romantic* (New York: Basic Books, 1998), 550.

56. Miller, *The President and the Assassin*, 20.

57. Ibid.

58. Scott Farris, *Almost President: The Men Who Lost the Race But Changed the Nation* (Guilford: Lyons Press, 2012), 11.

59. "U.S. Presidential Audio Recordings," Michigan State University's Vincent Voice Library, http://www.lib.msu.edu/cs/branches/vvl/presidents/index.htm; "Mr. Edison's Music Makers," Rutherford B. Hayes Presidential Studies Center, http://www.rbhayes.org/hayes/tempexhibits/display.asp?id=533&arc=y&subj=tempexhibits.

60. Karen C. Lund, "The First Presidential 'Picture Man': Theodore Roosevelt and His Times on Film," *U.S. Library of Congress Information Bulletin* 58, no. 9 (September 1999), http://www.loc.gov/loc/lcib/9909/tr.html.

61. Allan Metcalf, *Presidential Voices: Speaking Styles from George Washington to George W. Bush* (New York: Houghton Mifflin, 2004), 52. Taft used this phonographic technique as well.

62. Peter Collier, *The Roosevelts: An American Saga* (New York: Simon & Schuster, 1994), 134–35.

63. Daniel J. Boorstin, *The Americans: The Democratic Experience* (New York: Random House, 1973), 137.

64. Jon Stewart, *Earth (The Audiobook)* (New York: Hachette Audio, 2010), disk 2, track 16.

Chapter 5

1. Daniel J. Boorstin, *The Genius of American Politics*, (Chicago: University of Chicago Press, 1953), 165.

2. John Milton Cooper Jr., *Warrior and the Priest* (United States of America: Harvard University Press, 1983), 131.

3. John Milton Cooper Jr., *Woodrow Wilson: A Biography* (New York: Random House, 2009), 123.

4. H. W. Brands, *Woodrow Wilson* (New York: Henry Holt, 2003), ii.

5. Cooper, *Woodrow Wilson*, 26.

6. Ibid.

7. Ibid., 38.

8. William Barksdale Maynard, *Woodrow Wilson: Princeton to the Presidency* (New Haven: Yale University Press, 2008), 24.

9. Cooper, *Warrior and the Priest*, 242.

10. Ibid., 55.

11. Ibid., 256.

12. Ibid., 279.

13. Maynard, *Woodrow Wilson: Princeton to the Presidency*, 333.

14. Wilson letter quoted in Carolyn Wells and Joseph Berg Esenwein, *The Technique of the Mystery Story* (Springfield: The Home Correspondence School Publishers, 1913), 17.

15. Edmund Wilson, "Why Do People Read Detective Stories?" *New Yorker*, October 14, 1944, http://www.newyorker.com/archive/1944/10/14/1944_10_14_078_TNY_CARDS_000016796#ixzz1tq6tUVxD.

16. Cooper, *Woodrow Wilson*, 44.

17. Thomas A. Bogar, *American Presidents Attend the Theatre* (Jefferson, NC: McFarland, 2006), 221.

18. Ibid., 221–22.

19. "President Woodrow Wilson Gets His Broadway: President Wilson Loved Theater," *Broadway Magazine*, January 19, 2009.

20. Alan Schroeder, *Celebrity-in-Chief: How Show Business Took Over the White House* (Boulder: Westview, 2004), 183.

21. Bogar, *American Presidents Attend the Theatre*, 27, 237, 390.

22. Ibid., 235.

23. Ibid., 232.

24. Jim Newton, *Eisenhower: The White House Years* (New York: Doubleday, 2011), 15.

25. David S. Reynolds, *Mightier Than the Sword: Uncle Tom's Cabin and the Battle for America* (New York: Norton, 2011), 211, 213.

26. Ibid., 216, 225.

27. Philip C. DiMare, *Movies in American History: An Encyclopedia* (Santa Barbara: ABC-CLIO, 2011), 44. Note: Since the line "history written by lightning" was likely never uttered by Wilson, it is difficult to find a consensus on how the never-uttered line was configured.

28. John Milton Cooper, *Reconsidering Woodrow Wilson: Progressivism, Internationalism, War, and Peace* (Washington, D.C.: Woodrow Wilson Center Press, 2008), 12, 55.

29. DiMare, *Movies in American History*, 44.

30. Paul Johnson, *A History of the American People* (New York: HarperCollins, 1997), 337–38.

31. Nathaniel Hawthorne, "Preface," *The Life of Franklin Pierce* (Eldritch Press, August 27, 1852), http://www.eldritchpress.org/nh/fppf.html.

32. Boller, *Presidential Diversions*, 131.

33. Charles Bracelen Flood, *Grant's Final Victory: Ulysses S. Grant's Heroic Last Year* (Cambridge: Da Capo Press, 2011), 91–93.

34. Ibid., 8.

35. Ibid., 147.

36. Ulysses S. Grant, *Personal Memoirs of Ulysses S. Grant* (New York: Cosimo, 2007), 1; Saul Bellow, *The Adventures of Augie March* (New York: Penguin Books, 1996), 3.

37. Newton, *Eisenhower: The White House Years*, 51.

38. Victor Davis Hanson, *Ripples of Battle: How Wars of the Past Still Determine How We Fight, How We Live, and How We Think* (New York: Doubleday, 2003), 139.

39. Schroeder, *Celebrity-in-Chief*, 115–16.; John R. Coyne Jr., "Reassessing the Coolidge Legacy," *National Interest* (March–April 2013), http://nationalinterest.org/bookreview/reassessing-the-coolidge-legacy-8150?page=1.

40. George W. Bush, *Decision Points* (New York: Simon and Schuster, 2010), 4.

41. William Mead and Paul Dickson, *Baseball: The Presidents' Game* (Washington, D.C.: Farragut, 1993), 68.

42. John Sayle Watterson, *The Games Presidents Play: Sports And the Presidency* (Baltimore: Johns Hopkins University Press, 2006), 110; Wayne Stewart, *Babe Ruth: A Biography* (Westport, CT: Greenwood Press, 2006), 58.

43. Stewart, *Babe Ruth: A Biography*, 19.

44. Kal Wagenheim, *Babe Ruth: His Life and Legend* (New York: e-reads, 1990), 152. Eliot was the long-standing and well-respected president of Harvard.

45. Mead and Dickson, *Baseball*, 68.

46. Watterson, *The Games Presidents Play*, 135.

Chapter 6

1. Tom Shroder, "For Washington Nationals Radio Team Dave Jageler and Charlie Slowes, Baseball's in the Air," *Washington Post Magazine* (July 5, 2012): 12–13.

2. W. Barksdale Maynard, *Woodrow Wilson: Princeton to the Presidency* (New Haven and London: Yale University Press, 2008), 336–37.

3. "June 14, 1922: Harding becomes first president to be heard on the radio," History, http://www.history.com/this-day-in-history/harding-becomes-first-president-to-be-heard-on-the-radio.

4. Daniel J. Boorstin, *The Americans: The Democratic Experience* (New York: Random House, 1973), 154.

5. "A Million Persons Will Hear Coolidge's Voice When He Addresses Congress This Afternoon," *New York Times*, December 6, 1923, A1.

6. Giuliana Muscio, *Hollywood's New Deal* (Philadelphia: Temple University Press, 1997), 19.

7. Boorstin, *The Americans*, 471.

8. Arthur F. Fleser, *A Rhetorical Study of the Speaking of Calvin Coolidge* (Lewiston: Edwin Mellen Press, 1990), 87.

9. Allan Metcalf, *Presidential Voices: Speaking Styles from George Washington to George W. Bush* (Boston: Houghton Mifflin, 2004), 275.

10. Muscio, *Hollywood's New Deal*, 19.

11. Scott Farris, *Almost President: The Men Who Lost the Race But Changed the Nation* (Guilford: Lyons Press, 2012), 129.

12. Ibid., 11.

13. Betty Houchin Winfield, *FDR and the News Media* (New York: Columbia University Press, 1994), 17.

14. William Safire, "On Language: Happy Warrior," *New York Times Magazine*, June 13, 2004, http://www.nytimes.com/2004/06/13/magazine/the-way-we-live-now-6-13-04-on-language-happy-warrior.html?pagewanted=all&src=pm.

15. Christopher H. Sterling and John Michael Kittross, *Stay Tuned: A History of American Broadcasting*, 3rd ed. (Mahwah: Lawrence Erlbaum Associates, 2002), 862.

16. Robert J. Brown, *Manipulating the Ether: The Power of Broadcast Radio in Thirties America* (Jefferson, NC: McFarland, 1998), 28.

17. "The Nomination," *Time*, July 9, 1928, http://cgi.cnn.com/ALLPOLITICS/1996/analysis/back.time/9607/08/.

18. Anthony Rudel, *Hello, Everybody! The Dawn of American Radio* (Orlando: Harcourt Books, 2008), 292.

19. In context to current-day occupiers, the bonus marchers had real grievances and were legitimately penurious.

20. Jim Newton, *Eisenhower: The White House Years* (New York: Doubleday, 2011), 34.

21. Winfield, *FDR and the News Media*, 105.

22. David M. Ryfe, "Franklin Roosevelt and the Fireside Chats," *Journal of Communication* 49 (1999): 90–91.

23. Winfield, *FDR and the News Media*, 107.

24. Ryfe, "Franklin Roosevelt and the Fireside Chats," 82.

25. Ibid., 89–90.

26. Ezra Klein, "The Unpersuaded: Who Listens To A President?," *New Yorker*, March 19, 2012.

27. David Suisman and Susan Strasser, *Sound in the Age of Mechanical Reproduction* (Philadelphia: University of Pennsylvania Press, 2009), 21.

28. Winfield, *FDR and the News Media*, 103.

29. Brown, *Manipulating the Ether*, 36–37.

30. Ibid., 29.

31. Winfield, *FDR and the News Media*, 104.

32. Ibid.

33. Richard Aldous, *Reagan and Thatcher: The Difficult Relationship* (New York: Norton, 2012), 32.

34. Donald Rumsfeld, *Known and Unknown: A Memoir* (New York: Sentinel, 2011), 46.

35. Ryfe, "Franklin Roosevelt and the Fireside Chats," 89–90.

36. Alan Schroeder, *Celebrity-in-Chief* (Boulder: Westview Press, 2004), 126.

37. Geoffrey C. Ward and Ken Burns, *Baseball: An Illustrated History* (New York: Knopf, 1996), 210; Alan Howard Levy, *Joe McCarthy: Architect of the Yankee Dynasty* (Jefferson, NC: McFarland, 2005), 178.

38. Schroeder, *Celebrity-in-Chief*, 117.

39. Ibid., 119.

40. Bruce Lenthall, *Radio's America: The Great Depression and the Rise of Modern Mass Culture* (Chicago: Chicago University Press, 2007), 87.

41. "FDR and His Book Collection," *The Franklin D. Roosevelt Presidential Library and Museum*, July 11, 2008, http://www.fdrlibrary.marist.edu/pressmedia/pdfs/oheightfour.pdf.

42. Paul F. Boller Jr., *Presidential Diversions: Presidents at Play from George Washington to George W. Bush* (New York: Houghton Mifflin, 2007), 231–32.

Chapter 7

1.   Paul F. Boller Jr., *Presidential Diversions: Presidents at Play from George Washington to George W. Bush* (New York: Houghton Mifflin, 2007), 89–90, 132, 148.

2.   Daniel J. Boorstin, *The Image: A Guide to Pseudo-Events* (New York: Vintage, 1987), 174.

3.   William Hillman, "Mr. President: Music and Art in the President's Life," *Milwaukee Journal*, May 10, 1952, 6, http://news.google.com/newspapers?nid=1499&dat=19520510&id=3sMqAAAAIBAJ&sjid=YH4EAAAAIBAJ&pg=7114,4333618.

4.   David McCullough, *Truman* (New York: Simon & Schuster, 1992), 52.

5.   Hillman, "Mr. President," 6.

6.   McCullough, *Truman*.

7.   Ibid., 419.

8.   Lucien E. Marins, "Bacall on Truman's Piano," *Iconic Photos* (blog), July 3, 2012, http://iconicphotos.wordpress.com/2009/04/25/bacall-on-trumans-piano/.

9.   Paul Deutschman, "Outsize Governor," *Life*, (September 15, 1947), 62.

10. Harold Foote Gosnell, *Truman's Crises: a Political Biography of Harry S. Truman* (Westfield: Greenwood Press, 1980), 213.

11. Harry S. Truman, *Off the Record: The Private Papers of Harry S. Truman*, edited by Robert H. Ferrell (Columbia: University of Missouri Press, 1997), 204.

12. Paul Hume, "Critique of Margaret Truman's singing performance at Constitution Hall," *Washington Post*, December 6, 1950. Excerpted by the Harry S. Truman Library and Museum, http://www.trumanlibrary.org/trivia/letter.htm.

13. Truman, *Off the Record*, 204.

14. Ibid.

15. Ibid.

16. Robert H. Ferrell, *Harry S. Truman: A Life* (Columbia: University of Missouri Press, 1994), 329.

17. McCullough, *Truman*, 989–91.

18. Brian Burnes, *Harry S. Truman: His Life and Times* (Kansas City: Kansas City Star Books, 2003), 15; Alan Schroeder, *Celebrity-in-Chief* (Boulder: Westview Press, 2004), 257.

19. Truman, *Off the Record*, 356.

20. Geoffrey Perret, *Eisenhower* (Avon: Adams Media, 1999), 586–87.

21. Eisenhower Presidential Library & Museum, "Ike and Mamie's Favorites: Ike's Favorite Music," http://www.eisenhower.archives.gov/all_about_ike/favorites.html. The list was prepared by White House personnel, January 23, 1954.

22. "The List: Music for the Presidents," *Washington Times*, October 9, 2010, http://www.washingtontimes.com/news/2010/oct/9/list-music-presidents/.

23. David Eisenhower and Julie Nixon Eisenhower, *Going Home to Glory: A Memoir of Life with Dwight D. Eisenhower, 1961–1969* (New York: Simon and Schuster, 2010), 85.

24. Schroeder, *Celebrity-in-Chief*, 122.

25. Gail Collins, *Scorpion Tongues: Gossip, Celebrity, and American Politics* (New York: William Morrow, 1998), 156.

26. Thomas A. Bogar, *American Presidents Attend the Theatre* (Jefferson, NC: McFarland, 2006), 300–2.

27. Ibid., 296.

28. Claire Suddath, "A Brief History of Campaign Songs Whether it's Stevie Wonder or Tippecanoe and Tyler, Too—You can't run for President without some catchy theme music," *Time*, http://www.time.com/time/specials/packages/article/0,28804,1840981_1840998_1840902,00.html #ixzz1yBQRMm8o, accessed June 18, 2012.

29. LBJ Library Staff, comp., "LBJ's Favorites: Music/Songs," http://www.lbjlib.utexas.edu/johnson/archives.hom/faqs/favorites/lbjtable.asp.

30. Arthur Schlesinger, "Memorandum to John F. Kennedy, February 6, 1961," John F. Kennedy Library, President's Office Files, Box 65A, "Schlesinger, Arthur M., 11/60-2/61"; Tevi Troy, *Intellectuals and the American Presidency: Philosophers, Jesters, or Technicians* (Lanham: Rowman and Littlefield, 2002), 34.

31. Letter, "President John F. Kennedy to Pablo Casals, May 24th, 1961"; Letter, "Pablo Casals to President John F. Kennedy, April 1st, 1961"; Memo, Letitia Baldridge to Evelyn Lincoln, October 10, 1961, John F. Kennedy Library, Papers of John F. Kennedy, Presidential Papers,

President's Office Files, Special Correspondence, Casals, Pablo, 1876–1973, Digital Identifier: JFKPOF-028-020, http://www.jfklibrary.org/Asset-Viewer/Archives/JFKPOF-028-020.aspx.

32. Clint Hill and Lisa McCubbin, *Mrs. Kennedy and Me: An Intimate Memoir* (New York: Gallery, 2012), 104.

33. Sally Bedell Smith, "Private Camelot," *Vanity Fair*, May 2004, http://www.vanityfair.com/society/features/2004/05/jackie-kennedy-200405. Excerpt from Sally Bedell Smith, *Grace and Power: The Private World of the Kennedy White House* (New York: Random House, 2004).

34. Paul Hume, "Brilliant Gathering at White House Entranced by Fabled Pablo Casals," *Washington Post*, November 14, 1961, A1.

35. Baldridge, "Hand-written directions to President John F. Kennedy, November 13th, 1961," John F. Kennedy Library, Papers of John F. Kennedy, Presidential Papers, President's Office Files, Special Correspondence, Casals, Pablo, 1876–1973, Digital Identifier: JFKPOF-028-020, http://www.jfklibrary.org/Asset-Viewer/Archives/JFKPOF-028-020.aspx.

36. Hume, "Brilliant Gathering at White House Entranced by Fabled Pablo Casals," A1, B7.

37. Dorothy McCardle, "Casals Triumph is Encore After Half Century," *Washington Post*, November 14, 1961, B7, B9.

38. Letter, "Pablo Casals to President John F. Kennedy, November 17th, 1961," John F. Kennedy Library, Papers of John F. Kennedy, Presidential Papers, President's Office Files, Special Correspondence, Casals, Pablo, 1876–1973, Digital Identifier: J FKPOF-028-020, http://www.jfklibrary.org/Asset-Viewer/Archives/JFKPOF-028-020.aspx.

39. Tevi Troy, *Intellectuals and the American Presidency.*

40. Donna M. Binkiewicz, *Federalizing the Muse: United States Arts Policy and the National Endowment for the Arts, 1965–1980* (Chapel Hill, University of North Carolina Press, 2004), 49.

41. C. Edward Spann and Michael E. Williams Sr., *Presidential Praise: Our Presidents and their Hymns* (Macon: Mercer University Press, 2008), 241.

42. Thomas C. Reeves, *A Question of Character: A Life of John F. Kennedy* (New York: Arrow, 1992), 316.

43. Bogar, *American Presidents Attend the Theatre*, 306.

44. Michael O'Brien, *John F. Kennedy: A Biography* (New York: Thomas Dunne/St. Martin's, 2005), xii.

45. Theodore H. White, "FOR PRESIDENT KENNEDY: An Epilogue," *Life* 6 (December 1963): 158–59.

46. O'Brien, *John F. Kennedy*, xii.

47. Robert D. McFadden, "Death of a First Lady; Jacqueline Kennedy Onassis Dies of Cancer at 64," *New York Times*, May 20, 1994, http://www.nytimes.com/learning/general/onthisday/bday/0728.html.

48. Bogar, *American Presidents Attend the Theatre*, 303.

49. Gore Vidal, *Palimpsest: A Memoir* (New York: Random House, 1995), 121, 181. In addition to the familial bond, Kennedy and Vidal also each had legendary libidos. As Vidal dished in his 1995 memoir, "I calculated, at 25, that I had had more than a thousand sexual encounters, not a world record (my near contemporaries Jack Kennedy, Marlon Brando, and Tennessee Williams were all keeping up), but not bad, considering that I never got a venereal disease like Jack … or suffered from jealousy like Tennessee."

50. O'Brien, *John F. Kennedy*, xiv.

51. Arthur Schlesinger, "Foreword to the 2002 edition," *A Thousand Days: John F. Kennedy in the White House* (New York: Houghton Mifflin, 2002), xi.

52. Bogar, *American Presidents Attend the Theatre*, 303.

53. Gil Troy, *Affairs of State: The Rise and Rejection of the Presidential Couple Since World War II* (New York: The Free Press, 1997), 119.

54. Tom DeFrank, "Remembering Gerald Ford," *Anderson Cooper 360 Degrees*, CNN, December 27, 2006, http://transcripts.cnn.com/TRANSCRIPTS/0612/27/acd.01.html.

55. Jim Newton, *Eisenhower: The White House Years* (New York: Doubleday, 2011), 296.

56. Richard Reeves, *President Nixon: Alone in the White House* (New York: Simon & Schuster, 2007), 42.

57. Arthur Schlesinger, *A Life in the Twentieth Century: Innocent Beginnings, 1917–1950* (New York: Houghton Mifflin, 2000), 138.

58. "A Medal for Duke and a Kiss for the Chief," *Life*, May 9, 1969, 97.

59. Craig Brown, "Memorable meetings," *Guardian*, September 30, 2011, http://www.guardian.co.uk/books/2011/sep/30/craig-brown-101-improbable-encounters.

60. Mark Feeney, *Nixon at the Movies: A Book About Belief* (Chicago: University of Chicago Press, 2004), 218.

61. "Interview Egil 'Bud' Krogh, Jr.," *Frontline*, PBS, 2000, http://www.pbs.org/wgbh/pages/frontline/shows/drugs/interviews/krogh.html.

62. Brown, "Memorable meetings," *Guardian*, September 30, 2011, http://www.guardian.co.uk/books/2011/sep/30/craig-brown-101-improbable-encounters.

63. "The Nixon-Presley Meeting," George Washington University National Security Archive, June 5, 2012, http://www.gwu.edu/~nsarchiv/nsa/elvis/elnix.html.

64. Feeney, *Nixon at the Movies*, 218.

65. Pat Moynihan, "Memo to H. R. Haldeman and John Ehrlichman, July 24, 1970," Nixon Archives, WHSF, Staff Member and Office Files, John D. Ehrlichman, Box 21, "Moynihan Report, July 24, 1970." Quoted in Troy, *Intellectuals and the American Presidency*.

66. Marc Myers, "She Went Chasing Rabbits," interview with Grace Slick, *Wall Street Journal*, April 29, 2011, http://online.wsj.com/article/SB10001424052748703778104576287303493094530.html#printMode.

67. David Greenberg, *Nixon's Shadow: The History of an Image* (New York: W. W. Norton, 2003), 193.

68. Lester J. Feder, "Song of the South: Country music, race, region, and the politics of culture, 1920–1974," Ph.D. dissertation (Los Angeles: University of California, 2006), 214.

69. Ibid.

70. Bruce J. Schulman, *The Seventies: The Great Shift in American Culture, Society, and Politics* (New York: Da Capo Press, 2002), 39.

71. Lester J. Feder, "Song of the South: Country music, race, region, and the politics of culture, 1920–1974," Ph.D. dissertation (Los Angeles: University of California, 2006), 193–94, 198.

72. Jefferson R. Cowie, *Stayin' Alive: The 1970s and the Last Days of the Working Class* (New York: New Press, 2010), 257.

73. Ibid., 210.

74. Ibid., 257. Cash was incredibly prolific and had plenty of blue-collar tunes. But when he performed other artists' works, they were all American folk tunes or Gospel. He didn't do covers until late in his career, most notably a celebrated retool of Nine Inch Nails' "Hurt."

75. John Berlau, "The Battle Over 'Okie From Muskogee,'" *Weekly Standard* 1, no. 47 (August 19, 1996).

76. Ibid.

77. Richard Goldstein, "My Country Music Problem—and Yours," *Mademoiselle*, June 1973, 114–15, 185.

78. Ibid., 114–15.

79. B. Jowett, *The Dialogues of Plato, Vol. 2* (New York: Scribner & Sons, 1907), 248.

80. Will Durant, *The Story of Philosophy* (New York: Simon & Schuster, 2006), 32.

81. Dave Zimmer, *Crosby, Stills, and Nash: The Biography* (New York: Da Capo Press, 1984), 198.

82. James Sullivan, "Willie Nelson Sparks an 'Austin Torpedo' on White House Roof—Twisted Tales," Spinner, March 21, 2011, http://www.spinner.com/2011/03/21/willie-nelson-jimmy-carter-pot/.

83. Jimmy Carter, *Jimmy Carter: White House Diary* (New York: Farrar, Straus, and Giroux, 2010), 125, 135.

84. Chris Willman, "Q&A with Willie Nelson and Jimmy Carter: The ex-President and country legend discuss their friendship and their CMT music special," *Entertainment Weekly*, December 3, 2004, http://www.ew.com/ew/article/0,,831928,00.html.

85. Gil Troy, *Morning in America: How Ronald Reagan Invented The 1980s* (Princeton: Princeton University Press, 2005), 163.

86. Todd Leopold, "Analysis: The Age of Reagan," CNN, June 16, 2004, http://articles.cnn.com/2004-06-16/entertainment/reagan.80s_1_cosby-show-pop-culture-family-ties?_s=PM:SHOWBIZ.

87. Jim Cullen, *Born in the USA: Bruce Springsteen and the American Tradition* (Middletown: Wesleyan University Press, 2005), 7.

88. Troy, *Morning in America*, 163.

89. Leopold, "Analysis: The Age of Reagan."

90. David Remnick, "We Are Alive: Bruce Springsteen at sixty-two," *New Yorker*, July 30, 2012, http://www.newyorker.com/reporting/2012/07/30/120730fa_fact_remnick.

91. Rob Kirkpatrick, *The Words And Music of Bruce Springsteen* (Westport: Praeger, 2007), 79.

92. Nick Lewis, "Campaign songs can be powerful–or perturbing–political tools," *National Post*, February 14, 2008, http://www.nationalpost.com/story.html?id=308907&s=Related+Topics&is=Will.I.Am&it=Person.

93. Caryn James, "Beyond Fleetwood Mac and the Sax," *New York Times*, June 3, 1997, http://www.nytimes.com/1997/06/03/arts/beyond-fleetwood-mac-and-the-sax.html.

94. Geoff Boucher, "Songs in the Key of Presidency," *Los Angeles Times*, October 11, 2000, http://edition.cnn.com/2000/ALLPOLITICS/stories/10/11/latimes.campaign.songs/.

95. Ken Tucker, "Bill Clinton: Rock & Roll President," *Entertainment Weekly*, June 6, 1997, http://www.ew.com/ew/article/0,,288235,00.html.

96. James, "Beyond Fleetwood Mac and the Sax."

97. Philip Terzian, "The Anachronistic Candidate: Mitt Romney, Throwback," *Weekly Standard*, September 10, 2012, 16.

98. James, "Beyond Fleetwood Mac and the Sax."

99. Boller, *Presidential Diversions*, 338.

100. Chris Kaltenbach, "Clinton Proves Himself a Rock and Roll President," *Baltimore Sun*, June 3, 1997, http://articles.baltimoresun.com/1997-06-03/features/1997154115_1_snipes-dateline-nbc-connery.

101. David Samuels, "The Rap on Rap: The 'black music' that isn't either," *New Republic*, November 11, 1991, 24–29.

102. "Rapper Ice-T Defends Song Against Spreading Boycott," *New York Times*, June 19, 1992, http://www.nytimes.com/1992/06/19/arts/rapper-ice t defends-song-against-spreading-boycott.html.

103. Anthony Lewis, "Abroad at Home: Black and White," *New York Times*, June 18 1992, http://www.nytimes.com/1992/06/18/opinion/abroad-at-home-black-and-white.html.

104. Clarence Page, "Bill Clinton's Debt To Sister Souljah," *Chicago Tribune*, October 28, 1992, http://articles.chicagotribune.com/1992-10-28/news/9204070622_1_sister-souljah-bill-clinton-reagan-democrats.

105. Andrew Rosenthal, "THE 1992 CAMPAIGN: White House; Bush Denounces Rap Recording and Gives D'Amato a Hand," *New York Times*, June 30, 1992, http://www.nytimes.com/1992/06/30/us/1992-campaign-white-house-bush-denounces-rap-recording-gives-d-amato-hand.html?src=pm.

106. "Tom Petty's War on Michele Bachmann," *Daily Beast*, June 29, 2011, http://www.thedailybeast.com/articles/2011/06/29/tom-petty-against-michele-bachmann-springsteen-against-ronald-reagan-musicians-vs-politicians.html; Matt Labash, "Sing a Song of Howard Dean: The revival, if you can call it that, of campaign songs," *Weekly Standard* 9, no. 18 (January 19, 2004), http://www.weeklystandard.com/print/Content/Public/Articles/000/000/003/581okxhu.asp.

107. Cary Darling, "Politicians need more spin control when it comes to campaign tunes," *Fort Worth Star-Telegram*, August 30, 2012, http://www.kansascity.com/2012/08/29/3786204/politicians-need-more-spin-control.html.

108. Robin Abcarian, "Tuning in to the Bushes: Country music, foreign film, art and other first couple fascinations," *Los Angeles Times*, February 13, 2005, http://articles.latimes.com/2005/feb/13/entertainment/ca-bushculture13.

109. Tom Brokaw, "Interview with President George W. Bush," *New York Times*, April 25, 2003, http://www.nytimes.com/2003/04/25/international/worldspecial/25BUSH-TEXT.html?pagewanted=all.

110. Kanye West, remarks at "A Concert for Hurricane Relief," NBC, 2005.

111. Ken Tucker, "George Bush really does not 'appreciate' Kanye West's Katrina criticism: 'The worst moment of my presidency,'" *Entertainment Weekly*, November 2, 2010, http://watching-tv.ew.com/2010/11/02/george-bush-kanye-west-lauer-today/.

Chapter 8

1. David Nasaw, "Learning To Go To The Movies," *American Heritage* 44, no. 7 (November 1993), http://www.americanheritage.com/content/learning-go-movies?page=show.

2. Ibid.

3. Ibid.

4. Peter Bowen, "Presidential Projections," *Film in Focus*, September 19, 2008, http://www.filminfocus.com/article/presidential_projections.

5. Walter Prichard Eaton, "Class-Consciousness and the 'Movies,'" *Atlantic Monthly*, January 1915, http://www.theatlantic.com/issues/15jan/eaton.htm.

6. Giuliana Muscio, *Hollywood's New Deal* (Philadelphia: Temple University Press, 1997), 40.

7. Greg Mitchell, *The Campaign of the Century: Upton Sinclair's Race for Governor of California and the Birth of Media Politics* (Sausalito: PoliPoint Press, 2010).

8. Richard Sheridan Ames, "The Screen Enters Politics," *Harper's Monthly Magazine*, March 1935, 473–82.

9. Michael S. Shull, "Franklin and Eleanor Roosevelt," 184–90; Peter C. Rollins, ed., *The Columbia Companion to American History on Film: How the Movies Have Portrayed the American Past* (New York: Columbia University Press, 2003), 184.

10. Nathan Ward, "Following Fala," *American Heritage* 44, no. 2 (April 1993), http://www.americanheritage.com/content/1943-fifty-years-ago-0.

11. Shull, "Franklin and Eleanor Roosevelt," 184.

12. Bowen, "Presidential Projections."

13. Nisid Hajari, "All the President's Movies," *Entertainment Weekly*, April 30, 1993, http://www.ew.com/ew/article/0,,306429,00.html.

14. Kenneth T. Walsh, *From Mount Vernon to Crawford: A History of the Presidents and their Retreats* (New York: Hyperion, 2005), 117.

15. Bowen, "Presidential Projections."

16. Alan Schroeder, *Celebrity-in-Chief* (Boulder: Westview Press, 2004), 185.

17. Nancy Gibbs and Michael Duffy, *The Presidents Club: Inside the World's Most Exclusive Fraternity* (New York: Simon & Schuster, 2012), 251.

18. Bowen, "Presidential Projections"; Thomas A. Bogar, *American Presidents Attend the Theatre* (Jefferson, NC: McFarland, 2006), 300.

19. Scott Butki, "Interview: David Eisenhower, Author of Going Home To Glory: A Memoir of Life with Dwight D. Eisenhower, 1961–1969," *Seattle Post Intelligencer*, April 26, 2011, http://www.seattlepi.com/lifestyle/blogcritics/article/Interview-David-Eisenhower-Author-of-Going-841345.php#ixzz20ANQkcJQ.

20. Schroeder, *Celebrity-in-Chief*, 185.

21. W. Dale Nelson, *The President Is at Camp David* (Syracuse: Syracuse University Press, 2000), 44.

22. Jim Newton, *Eisenhower: The White House Years* (New York: Doubleday, 2011), 290.

23. Kim Phillips-Fein, *Invisible Hands: The Making of the Conservative Movement from the New Deal to Reagan* (New York: W. W. Norton, 2009), 56.

24. J. Hoberman, "How the Western Was Lost," *Village Voice*, August 27, 1991, http://puffin.creighton.edu/fapa/Bruce/0New%20Film%20as%20Art%20webfiles/HowtheWestern%20was%20lost/How_the_western_was_lost.htm.

25. Marth Joynt Kumar, "All the Presidents' Movies," *Political Communication* 24, no. 1 (January 2007).

26. Michael Medved, *Hollywood vs. America* (New York: Harper Collins, 1992), 278.

27. Schroeder, *Celebrity-in-Chief*, 188.

28. Note: this list, while perhaps exhausting, is—incredibly—not exhaustive. It is also not definitive. See for example Alex Michelini, "Jackie's Sex Revenge She Had Fling With Actor To Get Back At Cheatin' Jack, Book Sez," *New York Daily News*, June 18, 1996, http://articles.nydailynews.com/1996-06-18/news/18008863_1_christopher-andersen-audrey-hepburn-jack-and-jackie.

29. Gibbs and Duffy, *The Presidents Club*, 116.

30. Mimi Alford, *Once Upon a Secret* (New York: Random House, 2012), 87.

31. Arthur Schlesinger, *A Thousand Days: John F. Kennedy in the White House* (New York: Houghton Mifflin, 2002), 666.

32. Julian Borger, "The Best Perk in the White House," *Guardian*, June 3, 2004, http://www.guardian.co.uk/film/2004/jun/04/1.

33. Alford, *Once Upon a Secret*, 95.

34. Bogar, *American Presidents Attend the Theatre*, 306.

35. Borger, "The Best Perk in the White House."

36. Gibbs and Duffy, *The Presidents Club*, 186.

37. Robert Cara, *Master of the Senate: The Years of Lyndon Johnson*, vol. 3 (New York: Vintage, 2003), 343.

38. Walsh, *From Mount Vernon to Crawford*, 161.

39. Michael Freedland, *Gregory Peck: A Biography* (New York: W. Morrow, 1980), 197.

40. Kumar, "All the Presidents' Movies."

41. Lynn Haney, *Gregory Peck: A Charmed Life* (New York: Carrol and Graf, 2003), 345.

42. Elisabeth Bumiller, "White House Letter: Even Bush, No Movie Buff, Enjoys Getting Big Picture," *New York Times*, March 7, 2005, http://www.nytimes.com/2005/03/07/politics/07letter.html.

43. Kumar, "All the Presidents' Movies."

44. Mark Feeney, *Nixon at the Movies: A Book about Belief* (University of Chicago, 2004), 11–13.

45. Ibid.

46. Kumar, "All the Presidents' Movies," *Political Communication* 24, no. 1 (January 2007).

47. For those of you dying of curiosity, the last movie shown in the Nixon White House was *Around the World in 80 Days*.

48. David Greenberg, *Nixon's Shadow: The History Of An Image* (New York: W. W. Norton, 2003), 252; Elizabeth Drew, "Richard M. Nixon," *New York Times*, 2007, 33.

49. Greenberg, *Nixon's Shadow*, 252.

50. Kumar, "All the Presidents' Movies." One area in which movie watching did have an impact in the Nixon White House was in the area of flag pins. After seeing the Robert Redford movie *The Candidate*, Nixon Chief of Staff H. R. Haldeman suggested that the Nixon White House follow the example of the Redford character and start wearing American flag pins on their lapels, a suggestion Nixon eagerly adopted.

51. Hank DeZutter, "First Profile: What Makes Obama Run?," *Chicago Reader*, December 8, 1995, http://www1.chicagoreader.com/obama_reader/what_makes_obama_run/.

52. Feeney, *Nixon at the Movies*, 85, 275.

53. "High Noon: The Presidents' Choice," *Guardian*, August 5, 2003, http://www.guardian.co.uk/film/2003/aug/05/usa.world.

54. Feeney, *Nixon at the Movies*, 11–13.

55. Schroeder, *Celebrity-in-Chief*, 184–85.

56. Ronald Brownstein, *The Power and the Glitter: The Hollywood-Washington Connection* (New York: Pantheon, 1990), 121.

57. Jimmy Carter, "A Vision of the Outside World," *Journal of the University Film Association* 30, no. 1 (Winter 1978): 3–4.

58. Kumar, "All the Presidents' Movies."

59. Ibid.

60. Robert Brent Toplin, *History by Hollywood: The Use and Abuse of the American Past* (Champaign: University of Illinois Press, 1996), 197–98.

61. Kevin Mattson, *"What the Heck Are You Up To, Mr. President?"*: *Jimmy Carter, America's "Malaise," and the Speech That Should Have Changed the Country* (New York: Bloomsbury, 2009), 26.

62. Borger, "The Best Perk in the White House."

63. Tevi Troy, "What's Playing at the White House Movie Theater?," *Washingtonian*, February 2011, http://www.tevitroy.org/8840/white-house-movie-theater.

64. Jimmy Carter, *White House Diary* (New York: Farrar, Straus, and Giroux, 2010), 103.

65. Mattson, *"What the Heck Are You up To, Mr. President?,"* 68.

66. Kumar, "All the Presidents' Movies."

67. Mattson, *"What the Heck Are You Up To, Mr. President?,"* 26–27.

68. Richard Grenier, "A New Patriotism?," *Commentary*, April 1979, http:\\www.commentary magazine.com/article/a-new-patriotism/#.

69. Mattson, *"What the Heck Are You Up To, Mr. President?,"* 26–27.

70. Kumar, "All the Presidents' Movies."

71. Schroeder, *Celebrity-in-Chief*, 187.

72. Walsh, *From Mount Vernon to Crawford*, 298.

73. Borger, "The Best Perk in the White House."

74. Gil Troy, *Morning in America: How Ronald Reagan Invented The 1980s* (Princeton, Princeton University Press), 11, 192

75. Lou Cannon, "The Reagan Presidency: Every Night at the Movies," *Los Angeles Times*, April 28, 1991, http://articles.latimes.com/1991-04-28/opinion/op-1295_1_ronald-reagan/2.

76. Richard Reeves, *President Reagan: The Triumph of Imagination* (New York: Simon & Schuster, 2005), 516.

77. Bogar, *American Presidents Attend the Theatre*, 360.

78. Bumiller, "White House Letter: Even Bush, No Movie Buff, Enjoys Getting Big Picture."

79. George W. Bush, *Decision Points* (New York: Crown, 2010), 230, 272–73.

80. Schroeder, *Celebrity-in-Chief*, 172.

81. Bill Clinton, *My Life* (New York: Knopf, 2004), 36.

82. Boller, *Presidential Diversions: Presidents at Play from George Washington to George W. Bush* (New York: Houghton Mifflin, 2007), 345–47.

83. Schroeder, *Celebrity-in-Chief*, 173.

84. Peter Baker, *The Breach: Inside the Impeachment and Trial and William Jefferson Clinton* (New York: Scribner, 2000), 103–4. The comment could have referred to whether the President should resign—or to whether the guest in question would also have been willing to bestow her favors on the president in a similar fashion.

85.   Schroeder, *Celebrity-in-Chief*, 172.

86.   Stephanie Zacharek, "Everyone's a critic—even Bill Clinton," *Salon Magazine* (February 8, 2000), http://www.salon.com/2000/02/08/clinton_ebert/.

87.   Kumar, "All the Presidents' Movies."

Chapter 9

1.   Daniel Boorstin, *The Image: A Guide to Psuedo-Events* (New York: Vintage, 1987), 229.

2.   Roger Butterfield, "The Camera Comes To The White House," *American Heritage* 15, no. 5 (August 1964), http://www.americanheritage.com/content/camera-comes-white-house?page=show.

3.   Boorstin, *The Image*, 64.

4.   Kiron Skinner, Annelise Anderson, and Martin Anderson, *Reagan in His Own Hand* (New York: Free Press, 2001), xiv.

5.   Robert Morrison, "James Jackson Kilpatrick, 1920–2010," *The Blog of The Family Research Council*, August 17, 2010, http://www.frcblog.com/2010/08/james-jackson-kilpatrick-1920-2010/.

6.   Daniel J. Boorstin, *The Americans: The Democratic Experience* (New York: Random House, 1973), 397.

7.   Ibid.

8.   Robert Heinlein, *Stranger in a Strange Land* (New York: Ace Books, 1987), 89 ("babble machine"), 131 ("babble box"). Note: reprint edition. The original was published by G. P. Putnam Sons in 1961.

9.   Gary Edgerton, *The Columbia History of American Television* (New York: Columbia University Press, 2007), xi–31.

10.   Leo Bogart, *The Age of Television: A Study of Viewing Habits and Impact of Television on American Life* (New York: Frederick Ungar Publishing, 1956), 8.

11.   Edgerton, *The Columbia History of American Television*, xi–31.

12.   Bogart, *The Age of Television*, 8.

13.   Thomas K. McCraw, *American Business, 1920–2000: How It Worked* (Wheeling: Harlan Davidson, 2000), 129.

14.   Bogart, *The Age of Television*, 8–9.

15.   Carl Sferrazza Anthony, *America's First Families: An Inside View of 200 Years of Private Life in the White House* (New York: Touchstone, 2000), 51.

16.   Jonathan Eig, *Opening Day: The Story of Jackie Robinson's First Season* (New York: Simon & Schuster, 2007), 239.

17. Roger Simon, "Party agenda: Cheeseheads, But No Surprises," *Politico*, August 2, 2012, http://www.politico.com/news/stories/0712/79144.html.

18. Bogart, *The Age of Television*, 11.

19. Richard Alan Schwartz, *The 1950s* (New York: Facts on File, 2003), 438.

20. Thomas Patrick Doherty, *Cold War, Cool Medium: Television, McCarthyism, and American Culture* (New York: ColumbiaUniversity Press, 2003), 51.

21. Christopher Anderson, "I LOVE LUCY," Museum of Broadcast Communications, http://www.museum.tv/eotvsection.php?entrycode=ilovelucy.

22. Doherty, *Cold War, Cool Medium*, 51.

23. Jim Newton, *Eisenhower: The White House Years* (New York: Doubleday, 2011), 146.

24. Craig Allen, *Eisenhower and the Mass Media: Peace, Prosperity, & Prime-Time TV* (Chapel Hill: University of North Carolina Press, 1993), 31; Doherty, *Cold War, Cool Medium: Television, McCarthyism, and American Culture*, 57.

25. Ken Tucker, "Good Timing, Good Delivery," *Entertainment Weekly*, January 21, 1994, http://www.ew.com/ew/article/0,,300799,00.html.

26. Kenneth Walsh, *From Mount Vernon to Crawford: A History of the Presidents and Their Retreats* (New York: Hyperion, 2005), 128–29; Museum Management Program, "POP CULTURE: Gadgets & Gizmos," Nps.gov, Eisenhower National Historical Site Virtual Museum Exhibit, http://www.nps.gov/history/museum/exhibits/eise/gadgetsMore.html.

27. Allen, *Eisenhower and the Mass Media*, 31.

28. Herbert S. Parmet, *Eisenhower and the American Crusades* (New Brunswick: Transaction, 1999), 5.

29. Allen, *Eisenhower and the Mass Media*, 24.

30. Parmet, *Eisenhower and the American Crusades*, 57.

31. Allen, *Eisenhower and the Mass Media*, 24.

32. Parmet, *Eisenhower and the American Crusades*, 5.

33. Newton, *Eisenhower: The White House Years*, 67.

34. Dick Cavett, *Talk Show, Enhanced Edition: Confrontations, Pointed Commentary, and Off-Screen Secrets* (New York: Macmillan, 2011).

35. Parmet, *Eisenhower and the American Crusades*, 489.

36. Allan L. Damon, "Presidential Accessibility," *American Heritage* 25, no. 3 (April 1974), http://www.americanheritage.com/content/presidential-accessibility?page=show.

37. Heinlein, *Stranger in a Strange Land*.

38. Allen, *Eisenhower and the Mass Media*, 7.

39. Jennifer Epstein, "Obama tells kids to study, not watch 'Real Housewives,'" *Politico*, July 25, 2012, http://www.politico.com/politico44/2012/07/obama-tells-kids-to-study-not-watch-real-housewives-130139.html.

40. Allen, *Eisenhower and the Mass Media*, 8.

41. Damon, "Presidential Accessibility."

42. Allen, *Eisenhower and the Mass Media*, 7.

43. Alan Schroeder, *Presidential Debates: Fifty Years of High-Risk TV* (New York: Columbia University Press, 2008), 177.

44. Ibid., 5.

45. Robert A. Caro, *The Passage of Power* (New York: Alfred A. Knopf, 2012), 49.

46. Erik Barnouw, *Tube of Plenty: The Evolution of American Television* (New York: Oxford University Press, 1990), 271.

47. "Teddy" was, of course, Kennedy's younger brother Edward. With respect to Meader, he was the subject of a devastating joke from the comedian Lenny Bruce. Not long after Kennedy's tragic death, Bruce would shock audiences by shaking his head and saying either, "Man, poor Vaughn Meader" or "Vaughn Meader is screwed." The joke was prescient, as audiences lost all interest in Meader's act after Kennedy's assassination. Clips of Kennedy's humorous comments from his press conferences can be found online on Youtube at JFK63Conspiracy, "The JFK Show," Youtube, October 7, 2010, http://www.youtube.com/watch?v=mXDLLUOxmsY.

48. Schroeder, *Celebrity-in-Chief*, 276.

49. J. Fred MacDonald, "John F. Kennedy and Television," J. Fred MacDonald, http://www.jfredmacdonald.com/trm/ivjfk.htm.; "John F. Kennedy and the Press," John F. Kennedy Presidential Library and Museum, http://www.jfklibrary.org/JFK/JFK-in-History/John-F-Kennedy-and-the-Press.aspx.

50. John Barnes, *The Lesson and Legacy of a President: John F. Kennedy on Leadership* (New York: AMACOM, 2007), 71–72.

51. Boorstin, *The Image*, 17.

52. Stephen E. Kercher, *Revel with a Cause: Liberal Satire in Postwar America* (Chicago: University of Chicago, 2006), 357.

53. Peter C. Rollins and John E. O'Connor, *Hollywood's White House: The American Presidency in Film and History* (Lexington: University of Kentucky, 2005).

54. Caro, *The Passage of Power*, 341.

55. Ibid., 342.

56. O'Brien, *John F. Kennedy*, 817.

57. Newt Minow, "Reaction to Newt Minnow's Vast Wasteland Speech," interview on his 1961 "Vast Wasteland" speech to TV broadcasters, EMMYTVLEGENDS.ORG, http://www.youtube.com/watch?v=uZJJSb5Nu50&noredirect=1.

58. Paul Varner, *The A to Z of Westerns in Cinema* (Lanham, MD: Scarecrow, 2009), 207.

59. Paul Cantor, *Gilligan Unbound: Popular Culture in the Age of Globalization* (Lanham: Rowman & Littlefield, 2001), 68, 179.

60. Randall Bennett Woods, *LBJ: Architect of American Ambition* (New York: Free Press, 2006), 400.

61. Stephen Vaughn, "Review: The Presidency and the Press: LBJ and Vietnam," *Reviews in American History* 13, no. 4 (December 1985): 616-621, http://www.jstor.org/pss/2702599.

62. Caro, *The Passage of Power*, 205.

63. Vaughn, "Review: The Presidency and the Press: LBJ and Vietnam."

64. Schroeder, *Celebrity-in-Chief*, 278.

65. "Opinion: L.B.J.'s Musings about the Media," *Time*, February 14, 1969, http://www.time.com/time/magazine/article/0,9171,900647,00.html.

66. Ibid. Interestingly, Richard Nixon had the three TV devices removed from the Oval Office.

67. Walsh, *From Mount Vernon to Crawford*, 163.

68. Ibid.

69. Robert Dallek, *Flawed Giant: Lyndon Johnson and His Times, 1961–1973* (New York: Oxford University Press, 1999), 286. Safer, in addition to being Canadian, was also Jewish, which may have added to Johnson's suspicions. During the 1967 Six Day War, Johnson called Jewish White House aides Ben Wattenberg and Larry Levinson "Zionist dupes." Joseph A. Califano Jr., *The Triumph & Tragedy of Lyndon Johnson* (New York: Simon & Schuster, 1991), 205.

70. Jack Valenti, "Lyndon Johnson: An Awesome Engine of a Man," edited by Thomas W. Cowger and Sherwin Markman, *Lyndon Johnson Remembered: An Intimate Portrait of a Presidency* (Lanham, MD: Rowman& Littlefield, 2003), 37.

71. Dallek, *Flawed Giant*, 452.

72. Ibid., 368.

73. As he did with the lead in *High Noon*, perennial presidential favorite John Wayne also is reported to have turned down the Dillon role as well.

74. Lyndon B. Johnson and Michael R. Beschloss, *Taking Charge: The Johnson White House Tapes, 1963–1964* (New York: Simon & Schuster, 1997), 236.

75. Carl Sferrazza Anthony, *America's First Families: An Inside View of 200 Years of Private Life in the White House* (New York: Touchstone, 2000), 248. In today's Hollywood, a Democratic first lady would have relatively little reason to worry about the presence of a Republican cast member—and if a modern day Kitty were a member of the GOP, she'd likely be in the closet.

76. James Arness and James E. Wise, *James Arness: An Autobiography* (Jefferson, NC: McFarland, 2001), 287.

77. For a detailed discussion of the Festival of the Arts and its disastrous outcome, see Tevi Troy, *Intellectuals and the American Presidency: Philosophers, Jesters, or Technicians?* (Lanham: Rowman & Littlefield, 2002), 60–68.

78. Dallek, *Flawed Giant*, 281.

79. Robert Dallek, "Three New Revelations About LBJ," *Atlantic*, April 1998, http://www.theatlantic.com/past/docs/issues/98apr/lbj.htm.

80. Michael Baruch Grossman and Martha Joynt Kumar, "The White House and the News Media: The Phases of Their Relationship," *Political Science Quarterly* 94, no. 1 (Spring, 1979): 37–53, http://www.jstor.org/stable/pdfplus/2150155.pdf.

81. Vaughn, "Review: The Presidency and the Press: LBJ and Vietnam."

82. Daniel C. Hallin, "Vietnam on Television," The Museum of Broadcast Communications, http://www.museum.tv/eotvsection.php?entrycode=vietnamonte.

83. Theodore White, *The Making of the President, 1968* (New York: Harper Perennial, 1969), 460.

84. Jonathan Aitken, *Charles W. Colson: A Life Redeemed* (Colorado Springs: WaterBrook Press, 2005), 160.

85. George Allen, *What Washington Can Learn From the World of Sports* (Washington, D.C.: Regnery, 2010), 3.

86. Paul F. Boller Jr., *Presidential Diversions: Presidents at Play from George Washington to George W. Bush* (New York: Houghton Mifflin, 2007), 289–90.

87. Michael Barone, "Conventional Wisdom," *Wall Street Journal*, August 24, 2012, http://online.wsj.com/article/SB10000872396390444358404577609230859623286.html.

88. Walsh, *From Mount Vernon to Crawford*, 179.

89. Charles Colson, *Born Again* (Grand Rapids: Chosen Books, 2008), 113.

90. Walsh, *From Mount Vernon to Crawford*, 184.

91. Jordy Yager, "Journalist recalls the honor of being on Nixon's Enemies List," The Hill, January 6, 2009, http://thehill.com/capital-living/20243-journalist-recalls-the-honor-of-being-on-nixons-enemies-list.

92. Ben Shapiro, *Primetime Propaganda: The True Hollywood Story of How the Left Took over Your TV* (New York: Broadside, 2011), 287–88.

93. Ibid., 288.

94. Ibid., 159.

95. Schroeder, *Celebrity-in-Chief*, 184.

96. Richard M. Nixon, John D. Ehrlichman, and H. R. Haldeman, Oval Office Conversation, May 13, 1971, between 10:30am and 12:30pm—498–505, http://www.csdp.org; http://www.csdp.org/research/nixonpot.txt.

97. Jay Sharbutt, "Ron Nessen: Ford's Funny Front Man," *Free Lance-Star* (Fredericksburg), April 19, 1976.

98. Richard Nixon, "Checkers Speech," September 23, 1952.

99. Garry Wills, *Nixon Agonistes: The Crisis of the Self-Made Man* (New York: Mariner Books, 2002), 92; Newton, *Eisenhower: The White House Years*.

100. "Ailes: The Selling of Toughness," *Time*, February 8, 1988, http://www.time.com/time/magazine/article/0,9171,966619,00.html#ixzz22JCTFK4g.

101. Nancy Gibbs and Michael Duffy, *The Presidents Club: Inside the World's Most Exclusive Fraternity* (New York: Simon & Schuster, 2012), 232.

102. Donald Rumsfeld, *Known and Unknown: A Memoir* (New York: Sentinel, 2011), 625.

103. Schroeder, *Celebrity-in-Chief*, 280.

104. Rollins and O'Connor, *Hollywood's White House*, 340.

105. "President Gerald Ford dies at 93," ESPN, December 28, 2006, http://sports.espn.go.com/espn/news/story?id=2709062.

106. Mark Leibovich, "Chevy Chase as the Klutz in Chief, and a President Who Was in on the Joke," *New York Times*, December 29, 2006, http://www.nytimes.com/2006/12/29/washington/29chevy.html.

107. Walsh, *From Mount Vernon to Crawford*, 192.

108. "President Gerald Ford dies at 93," ESPN.

109. Rollins and O'Connor. *Hollywood's White House*, 337.

110. Leibovich, "Chevy Chase as the Klutz in Chief, and a President Who Was in on the Joke."

111. Rumsfeld, *Known and Unknown*, 188.

112. Laura Bush, *Spoken from the Heart* (New York: Scribner, 2010), 326.

113. Schroeder, *Celebrity-in-Chief*, 267.

114. Sharbutt, "Ron Nessen: Ford's Funny Front Man," *Free Lance-Star* (Fredricksburg), April 19, 1976, 19.

115. Rollins and O'Connor, *Hollywood's White House*, 337.

116. Leibovich, "Chevy Chase as the Klutz in Chief, and a President Who Was in on the Joke," *New York Times*, December 29, 2006, http://www.nytimes.com/2006/12/29/washington/29chevy.html.

117. Tina Fey, *Bossypants* (New York: Little Stranger, 2011).

118. Grossman and Kumar, "The White House and the News Media: The Phases of Their Relationship."

119. Beverly Gherman, *Jimmy Carter* (Minneapolis: Lerner, 2004), 35.

120. Rollins and O'Connor, *Hollywood's White House*, 339.

121. Robert Locander, "Carter and the Press: The First Two Years," *Presidential Studies Quarterly* 10, no. 1 (Winter, 1980): 106–20, http://www.jstor.org/stable/pdfplus/27547539.pdf?acceptTC=true.

122. Roger Mudd, *The Place to Be: Washington, CBS, and the Glory Days of Television News* (Philadelphia: Perseus, 2008), 355.

123. Jonathan Martin, "Roger Mudd: Ted Kennedy recollection a 'fantasy,'" *Politico*, September 20, 2009, http://dyn.politico.com/printstory.cfm?uuid=CDEADAB8-18FE-70B2-A8244AE4ED54AB46.

124. Shapiro, *Primetime Propaganda*, 46.

125. Horace Newcomb, *Encyclopedia of Television*, 2nd ed. (New York: Fitzrey Dearborn, 2004), 852.

126. Nikki Finke, "Does Mr. Middle-of-the-Road Lean Left?," *LA Weekly*, September 16, 2004, http://www.laweekly.com/2004-09-16/news/does-mr-middle-of-the-road-lean-left/.

127. "The Iranian Hostage Crisis," PBS American Experience, http://www.pbs.org/wgbh/americanexperience/features/general-article/carter-hostage-crisis/.

128. Francis Fitzgerald, *Way Out There in the Blue* (New York: Simon & Schuster, 2000), 54. They were married in 1952.

129. James Sutherland, *Ronald Reagan* (New York: Penguin Group, 2008), 102.

130. Fitzgerald, *Way Out There in the Blue*, 216.

131. Steven F. Hayward, *The Age of Reagan: The Fall of the Old Liberal Order: 1964–1980* (Roseville: Prima Publishing, 2001), 399.

132. Don Steinberg, "This Election is No Laughing Matter," *Wall Street Journal*, August 31, 2012, D1, D6.

133. Richard Aldous, *Reagan and Thatcher: The Difficult Relationship* (New York: W. W. Norton, 2012), 51.

134. Gibbs and Duffy, *The Presidents Club*, 209.

135. Steven V. Roberts, "Former Aide Questions Signing of Reagan's Initials," *New York Times*, September 16, 1988, http://www.nytimes.com/1988/09/16/us/former-aide-questions-signing-of-reagan-s-initials.html.

136. Peter Hannaford and Charles D. Hobbs, *Remembering Reagan* (Washington: Regnery Publishing, 1994), 34.

137. Ronald Reagan, "Speech on the Challenger Disaster," January 28, 1986.

138. Walsh, *From Mount Vernon to Crawford*, 298.

139. Aldous, *Reagan and Thatcher*, 256.

140. Mark Hertsgaard, *On Bended Knee: The Press and the Reagan Presidency* (New York: Farrar, Straus, and Giroux, 1988), 46.

141. Aldous, *Reagan and Thatcher*, 32.

142. Hertsgaard, *On Bended Knee*, 51.

143. Gil Troy, *Morning in America: How Ronald Reagan Invented The 1980s* (Princeton, Princeton University Press), 11.

144. Hertsgaard, *On Bended Knee*, 3. It is a curious and insufficiently noted phenomenon that former Democratic staffers such as Burke seem to be able to get jobs as news professionals at the three major networks, but that this rarely happens to Republicans. Tim Russert and George Stephanopoulos are also exemplars of this phenomenon. With the sole exception of Diane Sawyer, who worked in the Nixon White House, Republican staffers only appear on the big three networks in commentary slots specifically reserved for providing the Republican point of view. Ex-Democrats, in contrast, get to report the news.

145. Rollins and O'Connor, *Hollywood's White House*, 340.

146. Hertsgaard, *On Bended Knee*, 3.

147. Glenn Elert, "Television and the Presidency: How the News Affects Our Perceptions," hypertextbook.com, March 24, 1992, http://hypertextbook.com/eworld/president.shtml.

148. Stephen Weisman, "The President and the Press: The Art of Controlled Access," *New York Times Magazine*, October 14, 1984.

149. Hertsgaard, *On Bended Knee*, 3.

150. Richard Stengel, David Beckwith, and Mary Cronin, "Bushwhacked!," *Time*, February 8, 1988.

151. Cantor, *Gilligan Unbound*, 68.

152. Ibid.

153. George Bush, *All the Best, George Bush: My Life In Letters and Other Writings* (New York: Scribner, 1999), 621.

154. George C. Edwards, Martin P. Wattenberg, and Robert L. Lineberry, *Government in America: People, Politics, and Policy, Brief Edition*, 11th ed. (London: Longman, 2011), 162.

155. Newcomb, *Encyclopedia of Television*, 388.

156. Tucker, "Good Timing, Good Delivery."

157. Schroeder, *Celebrity-in-Chief*, 185; Walsh, *From Mount Vernon to Crawford*, 128–29; Museum Management Program, "POP CULTURE: Gadgets & Gizmos," Nps.gov, Eisenhower National Historical Site Virtual Museum Exhibit, http://www.nps.gov/history/museum/exhibits/eise/gadgetsMore.html.

158. Michael Wines, "Views on Single Motherhood Are Multiple at White House," *New York Times*, May 21, 1992, http://www.nytimes.com/1992/05/21/us/views-on-single-motherhood-are-multiple-at-white-house.html?pagewanted=all&src=pm.

159. Jonathan Gray, *Watching with The Simpsons: Television, Parody, and Intertextuality* (New York: Routledge, 2006), 7.

160. "A Brief History of *The Simpsons*," *The Simpsons* Archive, http://www.snpp.com/other/articles/briefhistory.html.

161. Shapiro, *Primetime Propaganda*, 174.

162. Mark I. Pinsky, *The Gospel According to the Simpsons: Bigger and Possibly Even Better* (Louisville: WestminsterJohn Knox Press, 2007), 6.

163. Cantor, *Gilligan Unbound*, 68.

164. Gibbs and Duffy, *The Presidents Club*, 421.

165. "Martin Sheen Shares Worldview on Charlie Rose: An Excerpt from the Interview," MartinSheen.net, October 14, 2002, http://martinsheen.net/id110.html.

166. Terry McAuliffe, *What A Party! My Life Among Democrats: Presidents, Candidates, Donors, Activists, Alligators, and Other Wild Animals* (New York: St. Martin's, 2007), 173.

167. Aaron Sorkin, "A News Hour with Jim Lehrer Transcript: Aaron Sorkin," interview by Terence Smith, PBS, September 27, 2000, http://www.pbs.org/newshour/media/west_wing/sorkin.html.

168. Chris Lehmann, "The Feel Good Presidency," *Atlantic*, March 2001, http://www.theatlantic.com/magazine/archive/2001/03/the-feel-good-presidency/2138/.

169. Robert E. Denton, *Images, Scandal, and Communication Strategies of the Clinton Presidency* (Westport, CT: Praeger Publishers, 2003), 10.

170. John Gartner, *In Search of Bill Clinton: A Psychological Biography* (New York: St. Martin's, 2008), 135.

171. Denton, *Images, Scandal, and Communication Strategies of the Clinton Presidency*, 10.

172. Fred Greenstein, "The Presidential Leadership Style of Bill Clinton: An Early Appraisal," *Political Science Quarterly* 108, no. 4 (Winter 1993–94): 589–601, http://www.jstor.org/discover/10.2307/2152401?uid=2&uid=4&sid=21102073918397.

173. Denton, *Images, Scandal, and Communication Strategies of the Clinton Presidency*, 10.

174. John F. Harris, *The Survivor: Bill Clinton in the White House* (United States: Random House, 2005), 147.

175. McAuliffe, *What A Party!*, 173.

176. Paul J. Gough, "Bill Clinton a fan of '24' and 'I Love Lucy,'" Reuters, March 26, 2007, http://www.reuters.com/article/idUSN2531004820070326.

177. Bob Woodward, *Obama's Wars* (New York: Simon and Schuster, 2010), 74.

178. Joan Ryan, "Bush Pursues 'Next Endeavor,'" *San Francisco Chronicle*, February 25, 2000, http://www.sfgate.com/politics/article/Bush-Pursues-Next-Endeavor-Personable-3240428.php.

179. Edwin Chen, "Bush Joins Debate on TV Standards," *Los Angeles Times*, January 29, 2005, http://articles.latimes.com/2005/jan/29/nation/na-bush29.

180. Paul Kengor, *God and George W. Bush* (New York: HarperCollins, 2004), 76.

181. Walsh, *From Mount Vernon to Crawford*, 256.

182. Douglas Kellner, *Grand Theft 2000: Media Spectacle and a Stolen Election* (Lanham: Rowman & Littlefield, 2001), 101.

183. Amy Chozick, "Obama Is an Avid Reader, and Critic, of the News," *New York Times*, August 7, 2012, http://www.nytimes.com/2012/08/08/us/politics/obama-is-an-avid-reader-and-critic-of-news-media-coverage.html?_r=1&pagewanted=all&pagewanted=print.

184. Fred I. Greenstein, "George W. Bush and the Politics of Agenda Control," *The Presidential Difference: Leadership Style from FDR to George W. Bush* (Princeton: Princeton University Press, 2004), https://pup.princeton.edu/chapters/s7804.html.

185. Nielsen, "State of the Media: Trends in TV viewing,—2011 TV Upfronts," blog, http://blog.nielsen.com/nielsenwire/wp-content/uploads/2011/04/State-of-the-Media-2011-TV-Upfronts.pdf.

Chapter 10

1. Amie Parnes, "Move Over Oprah? Obama Sells Books," *Politico*, May 30, 2009, http://dyn.politico.com/printstory.cfm?uuid=8FA074B3-18FE-70B2-A8CCC68D3A33C43D.

2. Kenneth T. Walsh, *From Mount Vernon to Crawford: A History of the Presidents and Their Retreats* (New York: Hyperion, 2005), 107.

3. David McCullough, *Truman* (New York: Simon & Schuster, 1992), 253.

4. Walsh, *From Mount Vernon to Crawford*, 107.

5. McCullough, *Truman*, 33–34.

6. Michael Beschloss, *Presidential Courage: Brave Leaders and How They Changed America, 1789–1989* (New York: Simon & Schuster, 2007), 211.

7. Jon Meacham, "How to Read Like a President," *New York Times Book Review*, November 2, 2008, http://www.nytimes.com/2008/11/02/books/review/Meacham-t.html.

8. McCullough, *Truman*, 77.

9. Paul F. Boller Jr., *Presidential Diversions: Presidents at Play from George Washington to George W. Bush* (Orlando: Harcourt Books, 2007), 244.

10. Robert H. Ferrell, *Harry S. Truman: A Life* (Columbia: University of Missouri Press, 1994), 108.

11. Walsh, *From Mount Vernon to Crawford*, 113.

12. Boller, *Presidential Diversions*, 244.

13. Beschloss, *Presidential Courage*, 211.

14. Michael Benson, *Harry S. Truman and the Founding of Israel* (Westport: Praeger, 1997), 189.

15. John Lewis Gaddis, "Ending Tyranny," *American Interest*, (September/October, 2008), http://www.the-american-interest.com/article.cfm?piece=459.

16. Allan L. Damon, "Presidential Accessibility" *American Heritage* 25, no. 3 (April 1974), http://www.americanheritage.com/content/presidential-accessibility?page=show.

17. Boller, *Presidential Diversions*, 261.

18. David Eisenhower, interview with Scott Butki, "Interview: David Eisenhower, Author of *Going Home To Glory: A Memoir of Life with Dwight D. Eisenhower, 1961–1969*," *Seattle Post Intelligencer*, April 26, 2011, http://www.seattlepi.com/lifestyle/blogcritics/article/Interview-David-Eisenhower-Author-of-Going-841345.php#ixzz20ANQkcJQ.

19. Jim Newton, *Eisenhower: The White House Years* (New York: Doubleday, 2011), 31.

20. Dwight D. Eisenhower. "Remarks at the Dartmouth College Commencement Exercises," Hanover, New Hampshire, June 14, 1953.

21. Walsh, *From Mount Vernon to Crawford*, 130.

22. Damon Linker, "Against Common Sense," blog, *New Republic*, November 30, 2009, http://www.tnr.com/blog/damon-linker/against-common-sense.

23. Newton, *Eisenhower: The White House Years*, 211.

24. Nancy Gibbs and Michael Duffy, *The Presidents Club: Inside the World's Most Exclusive Fraternity* (New York: Simon & Schuster, 2012), 115.

25. Arthur Schlesinger, "Memorandum to John F. Kennedy, February 6, 1961," John F. Kennedy Library, President's Office Files, Box 65A, "Schlesinger, Arthur M., 11/60-2/61"; Tevi Troy, *Intellectuals and the American Presidency: Philosophers, Jesters, or Technicians* (Lanham: Rowman & Littlefield, 2002), 34.

26. Troy, *Intellectuals and the American Presidency*, 9.

27. Franklin Foer, "The Browbeater," review of Dwight MacDonald, *The Browbeater: Masscult and Midcult: Essays Against the American Grain* 242, no. 4914, *New Republic*, edited by John Summers, December 15, 2011, http://www.tnr.com/article/books-and-arts/magazine/97782/dwight-macdonald-midcult-masscult?page=0,1.

28. Michael Medved, "Obama's Revealing Book Bag," *Daily Beast*, August 23, 2011, http://www.thedailybeast.com/articles/2011/08/23/obama-s-fictional-world-a-peek-at-his-vacation-reading-list.print.html.

29. Michael O'Brien, *John F. Kennedy: A Biography* (New York: Thomas Dunne/St. Martin's, 2005), 793–94.

30. Arthur Schlesinger, *A Thousand Days: John F. Kennedy in the White House* (New York: Houghton Mifflin, 2002), 105.

31. Norman Podhoretz, *Making It* (New York: Harper & Row, 1967), 313.

32. Schlesinger, *A Thousand Days*, 105.

33. O'Brien, *John F. Kennedy: A Biography*, xii.

34. Bruce Jay Friedman, *Lucky Bruce: A Literary Memoir* (New York: Biblioasis, 2011), 223.

35. Ken Gormley, *Archibald Cox: Conscience of a Nation* (Reading, MA: Addison-Wesley, 1997), 102.

36. Walsh, *From Mount Vernon to Crawford*, 146–47.

37. Garry Wills, *The Kennedy Imprisonment* (New York: Pocket Books, 1983), 138.

38. Herb Parmet, *Jack: The Struggles of John F. Kennedy* (New York, Doubleday 1983), 320–23.

39. Wills, *The Kennedy Imprisonment*, 134.

40. Ibid., 139.

41. O'Brien, *John F. Kennedy: A Biography*, 338.

42. James Piereson, *Camelot and the Cultural Revolution: How the Assassination of John F. Kennedy Shattered American Liberalism* (New York: Encounter Books, 2007), 325, fn. 23.

43. Wills, *The Kennedy Imprisonment*, 136.

44. Michiko Kakutani, "Critic's Notebook; How Books Have Shaped U.S. Policy," *New York Times*, April 5, 2003, http://www.nytimes.com/2003/04/05/books/critic-s-notebook-how-books-have-shaped-us-policy.html?pagewanted=all&src=pm.

45. Nicholas Lemann, "The Unfinished War," *Atlantic*, December 1988, http://www.the atlantic.com/past/politics/poverty/lemunf1.htm.

46. Ibid.

47. "The Best-Read Presidents," *Daily Beast*, February 14, 2010, http://www.thedailybeast. com/galleries/2010/02/14/the-best-read-presidents.html#slide6.

48. Nicholas D. Kristof, "Obama and the War on Brains," *New York Times*, November 9, 2008, http://www.nytimes.com/2008/11/09/opinion/09kristof.html.

49. Stephen E. Ambrose, *Nixon*, vol. 1, *The Education of a Politician, 1913–1962* (New York: Touchstone, 1987), 26–27, 56, 236.

50. Theodore White, "Making of the President 1968," *Life*, July 11, 1969, 48B.

51. Ambrose, *Nixon,* 1:542.

52. Richard Nixon, *RN: The Memoirs of Richard Nixon*, vol. 2 (New York: Warner Books, 1979), 108.

53. Richard Reeves, *President Nixon: Alone in the White House* (New York: Simon & Schuster, 2001), 542.

54. Robert D. Novak, *The Prince of Darkness: 50 Years Reporting in Washington* (New York: Crown Forum, 2007), 254–55.

55. Emma Brown, "Robert A. Goldwin, 87; political scientist, White House adviser," obituary for Robert A. Goldwin, *Washington Post*, January 22, 2010, http://www.washingtonpost. com/wp-dyn/content/article/2010/01/21/AR2010012104481.html. For more on Goldwin's intellectual outreach efforts, see Troy, *Intellectuals and the American Presidency*, 113–28.

56. Kenneth T. Walsh, *Air Force One: A History of the Presidents and their Planes* (New York: Hyperion, 2003), 114.

57. Andrew J. Glass, "Catholic Church Missal, Not Bible, used by Johnson for Oath at Dallas," *Washington Post*, February 26, 1967.

58. Peter Bergen, *Manhunt: The Ten-Year Search for Bin Laden—from 9/11 to Abbottabad* (New York: Crown, 2012) 17.

59. Jimmy Carter, *An Hour before Daylight: Memories of a Rural Boyhood* (New York: Simon & Schuster, 2001), 31–32.

60. Ibid., 212.

61. Jimmy Carter, *Christmas in Plains: Memories* (New York: Simon & Schuster, 2001), 59.

62. Jimmy Carter, *Sharing Good Times* (New York: Simon & Schuster, 2005), 55.

63. Caroline Kennedy, *Jacqueline Kennedy: Historic Conversations On Life With John F. Kennedy*, foreword by Caroline Kennedy, interviews by Arthur M. Schlesinger, introduction and annotations by Michael Beschloss (New York: Hyperion, 2011), second conversation, 44, footnote 10.

64. Jimmy Carter, *White House Diaries* (New York: Picador USA, 2011), 126. *Time* called Herzog one of the best novels in the English language since the beginning of *Time*.

65. Ibid., 126, 172.

66. Christopher Lasch, *The Culture of Narcissism: American Life in an Age of Diminishing Expectations* (New York: Norton, 1979).

67. Kevin Mattson, *What the Heck Are You Up To, Mr. President?* (New York: Bloomsbury, 2009), 43–44.

68. Ibid., 43–44.

69. Ibid., 55.

70. Troy, *Intellectuals and the American Presidency*, 136–39.

71. Ibid.

72. Jon Meacham, "How to Read Like a President," *New York Times Book Review*, November 2, 2008, http://www.nytimes.com/2008/11/02/books/review/Meacham-t.html.

73. Richard Aldous, *Reagan and Thatcher: The Difficult Relationship* (New York: W. W. Norton, 2012), 28.

74. Douglas Brinkley, ed., *The Reagan Diaries* (New York: HarperCollins, 2007), x.

75. Aldous, *Reagan and Thatcher*, 16.

76. Steven F. Hayward, *The Age of Reagan: The Fall of the Old Liberal Order, 1964–1980* (Roseville: Prima Publishing, 2001), 399.

77. Walsh, *From Mount Vernon to Crawford*, 216.

78. Fred Barnes, "The Real Reagan, In His Own Words," *Weekly Standard* 25 (June 2012): 25.

79. Robert Lekachman, "Virtuous Men And Perfect Weapons," review of *Red Storm Rising*, by Tom Clancy. *New York Times Book Review*, July 27, 1986, http://www.nytimes.com/1986/07/27/books/virtuous-men-and-perfect-weapons.html?&pagewanted=all.

80. Charles Kolb, *White House Daze: The Unmaking of Domestic Policy in the Bush Years* (New York: Free Press, 1994), 347.

81. Peter Robinson, *How Ronald Reagan Changed My Life* (New York: ReganBooks, 2003), 119; Larissa MacFarquhar, "The Gilder Effect," *New Yorker*, May 29, 2000, http://www.newyorker.com/archive/2000/05/29/2000_05_29_102_TNY_LIBRY_000020935#ixzz236IK62Lh.

82. Michael Duffy and Dan Goodgame, *Marching in Place: The Status Quo Presidency of George Bush* (New York: Simon and Schuster, 1992), 33.

83. William Safire, "ON LANGUAGE: Growing Down Grows Up," *New York Times Magazine*, November 15, 1992, http://www.nytimes.com/1992/11/15/magazine/on-language-growing-down-grows-up.html?pagewanted=all&src=pm.

84. Interview with Garry Wills, "Amish Romance, Israeli Identity, more," NPR, October 25, 2010, http://www.nytimes.com/keyword/economy.

85. George H. W. Bush, interview in Williamsburg, Virginia, June 2, 1995, http://www.achievement.org/autodoc/page/bus0int-1.

86. Duffy and Goodgame, *Marching in Place*, 42.

87. Ronald Kessler, *Inside the Secret Service: Behind the Scenes with Agents in the Line of Fire and the Presidents They Protect* (New York: Crown, 2009), 134.

88. George Bush, *All the Best, George Bush: My Life in Letters and Other Writings* (New York: Scribner, 1999), 42.

89. Ibid., 219.

90. Ibid., 564.

91. Bruce Jay Friedman, *Lucky Bruce: A Literary Memoir* (New York: Biblioasis, 2011), 223. Friedman also reports that he solved the mystery of Plimpton's indescribable accent. When asked directly where exactly that accent came from, Plimpton acknowledged that it was "an affectation."

92. Troy, *Intellectuals and the American Presidency*, 157.

93. Bill Clinton, *My Life* (New York: Knopf, 2004), prologue, 3.

94. Ibid., 10.

95. Ibid., 100, 148, 167, 186, 235, 414, 788.

96. Samuel Jacobs, "Obama's Book List Gaffe," *Daily Beast*, August 24, 2009, http://www.thedailybeast.com/articles/2009/08/24/the-obama-book-club.html?cid=hp:blogunit1.

97. Margaret Carlson, James Carney, and Michael Duffy, "I Didn't Get Hired to Fix Everything: BILL CLINTON," *Time*, September 27, 1993, http://www.time.com/time/magazine/article/0,9171,979265,00.html#ixzz23SbYWPI3.

98. Walsh, *From Mount Vernon to Crawford*, 242.

99. Victoria Will, "Bill Clinton's World," interview with Bill Clinton by Peter Baker and Susan Glasser, *Foreign Policy*, December 2009, http://www.foreignpolicy.com/articles/2009/11/19/bill_clintons_world?page=full.

100. Laura Rozen, "Robert Kaplan: The controversial *Balkan Ghosts* put him on the map. His opinionated, darkly seductive reports of an unraveling world have kept him there," *Salon*, April 17, 2001, http://dir.salon.com/people/bc/2001/04/17/kaplan/index.html?pn=4.

101. Parnes, "Move Over Oprah? Obama Sells Books."

102. Bill Clinton, interviewed by Brian Lamb, Booknotes, C-SPAN, December 15, 1996, http://www.booknotes.org/Watch/77223-1/President+Bill+Clinton.aspx.

103. Elizabeth Renzetti, "Celebrity, summer and little white lies about beach reading (yes, Fabio; no, Proust)," *Globe and Mail*, August 5, 2011, http://www.theglobeandmail.com/news/

arts/elizabeth-renzetti/celebrity-summer-and-little-white-lies-about-beach-reading-yes-fabio-no-proust/article2121550/.

104. "The Gifts," *Washington Post*, September 22, 1998, A30, http://www.washingtonpost.com/wp-srv/politics/special/clinton/stories/evigifts092298.htm.

105. Thomas A. Bogar, *American Presidents Attend the Theatre: The Playgoing Experiences of Each Chief Executive* (Jefferson, NC: McFarland, 2006), 358.

106. Daniel Gross, *Bull Run: Wall Street, the Democrats, and the New Politics of Personal Finance* (New York: Public Affairs, 2000), 189.

107. Steve Chapman, "Don't Hate Bush Because He's Dumb: Dimwits often make good presidents," *Slate*, October 12, 2000, http://www.dev.slate.com/articles/news_and_politics/high_concept/2000/10/dont_hate_bush_because_hes_dumb.html.

108. Karl Rove, "Bush Is a Book Lover," *Wall Street Journal*, December 26, 2008, http://online.wsj.com/article/SB123025595706634689.html.

109. "Peter Robinson Interview with Guest George W. Bush," Uncommon Knowledge with Peter Robinson, Hoover Institution, July 18, 2012, http://www.hoover.org/multimedia/uncommon-knowledge/122646.

110. Rove, "Bush Is a Book Lover."

111. George W. Bush, Decision Points (New York: Crown, 2010), 14.

112. Walt Harrington, "Dubya and Me," *American Scholar* (Autumn 2011), http://theamericanscholar.org/dubya-and-me/.

113. Alan Fram, "One in Four Read No Books Last Year," *Washington Post*, August 21, 2007, http://www.washingtonpost.com/wp-dyn/content/article/2007/08/21/AR2007082101045.html.

114. Rove, "Bush Is a Book Lover."

115. Harrington, "Dubya and Me."

116. Ibid.

117. Rove, "Bush Is a Book Lover."

118. Warren Vieth, "Bush Salts His Summer With Eclectic Reading List," *Los Angeles Times*, August 16, 2005, http://articles.latimes.com/2005/aug/16/nation/na-bushread16.

119. Harrington, "Dubya and Me."

120. Bush, *Decision Points*, 106.

121. Ibid., 159.

122. "Bill Clinton's 21 Favorite Books," Associated Press, February 11, 2009, http://www.cbsnews.com/stories/2003/11/21/politics/main585068.shtml.

123. Harrington, "Dubya and Me."

124. Peter Baker, "As Democracy Push Falters, Bush Feels Like a 'Dissident,'" *Washington Post*, August 20, 2007, http://www.washingtonpost.com/wp-dyn/content/article/2007/08/19/AR2007081901720.html.

125. Gaddis, "Ending Tyranny."

126. Michael Medved, "Obama's Revealing Book Bag," *Daily Beast*, August 23, 2011, http://www.thedailybeast.com/articles/2011/08/23/obama-s-fictional-world-a-peek-at-his-vacation-reading-list.print.html.

127. Michiko Kakutani, "From Books, New President Found Voice," *New York Times*, January 18, 2009, http://www.nytimes.com/2009/01/19/books/19read.html?pagewanted=all.

128. Richard Cohen, "Reading Into Bush's Book List," *Washington Post*, December 30, 2008.

129. Kristof, "Obama and the War on Brains," *New York Times*, November 9, 2008, http://www.nytimes.com/2008/11/09/opinion/09kristof.html.

130. While I am not a fan of anonymous sources and have said so publicly (see Troy, "Condi's Mystery Men," *Washingtonian*, December 2011, http://www.tevitroy.org/10801/condi-mystery-men), the former aide who told me this story specifically asked that I keep his name private.

131. Walter Isaacson, "Republican Convention: George Bush: My Heritage Is Part of Who I Am," *Time*, August 7, 2000.

132. Rove, "Bush Is a Book Lover."

133. "Peter Robinson Interview with Guest George W. Bush," *Uncommon Knowledge with Peter Robinson*.

134. Gore Vidal, "Geopolitical Thoughts: Requiem for the American Empire," *Nation*, January 11, 1986.

135. Emily Parker, "To Be Read by All Parties," *New York Times*, February 19, 2012, http://mobile.nytimes.com/2012/02/19/books/review/the-impact-of-books-on-washington-policy.xml.

Chapter 11

1. Barack Obama, *Dreams from My Father: A Story of Race and Inheritance* (New York: Crown, 2007), 62.

2. David Maraniss, *Barack Obama: The Story* (New York: Simon & Schuster, 2012), 68.

3. Ibid., 243.

4. Ibid., 159.

5. Obama, *Dreams from My Father*, 67–68.

6. Ibid., 46, 52.

7. Caitlin McDevitt, "Lt. Uhura Tweets Photo with Obama," *Politico*, April 4, 2012, http://www.politico.com/blogs/click/2012/04/star-trek-star-obama-had-a-crush-on-me-119594.html.

8. Emily Heil, "Obama's 'Jedi mind meld' mixes sci-fi worlds," *Washington Post*, March 1, 2013, http://www.washingtonpost.com/blogs/in-the-loop/post/obamas-jedi-mind-meld-mixes-sci-fi-worlds/2013/03/01/749ca984-8291-11e2-a350-49866afab584_blog.html.

9. Obama, *Dreams from My Father*, 78.

10. David Remnick, *The Bridge: The Life and Rise of Barack Obama* (New York: Alfred A. Knopf, 2010), 100.

11. Maraniss, *Barack Obama: The Story*, 346.

12. Obama, *Dreams from My Father*, 10, 123.

13. Glenn Thrush, *Politico Playbook 2012: Obama's Last Stand* (New York: Random House, 2012).

14. Peter Baker, "Onset of Woes Casts Pall Over Obama's Policy Aspirations," *New York Times*, May 16, 2013, A1, http://www.nytimes.com/2013/05/16/us/politics/new-controversies-may-undermine-obama.html?pagewanted=all&_r=0.

15. Michael Lewis, "Obama's Way," *Vanity Fair*, October 2012.

16. Mark Hemmingway, "Was Obama Too Busy Watching Television to Respond to Benghazi Attack?," *Weekly Standard*, November 5, 2012, http://www.weeklystandard.com/blogs/was-obama-too-busy-watching-television-respond-bengahzi-attack_660358.html.

17. Amie Parnes, "Obama's TV: Sports, surprises," *Politico*, April 8, 2009, http://dyn.politico.com/printstory.cfm?uuid=832DC694-18FE-70B2-A8E8869255D98AA3.

18. Thrush, *Politico Playbook 2012*.

19. Maraniss, *Barack Obama: The Story*, 281, 286, 289. For those not up to date on their 1970s NBA stars, "Iceman" was George Gervin of the San Antonio Spurs, and "Earl the Pearl" was the New York Knicks' Earl Monroe.

20. Joel Meares, "Q & A: *New York Times* Reporter Michael Powell," *Columbia Journalism Review*, http://www.cjr.org/behind_the_news/q_a_new_york_times_reporter_mi.php?page=all.

21. Parnes, "Obama's TV: Sports, surprises."

22. Jodi Kantor, *The Obamas* (New York: Little Brown, 2012), 55.

23. Bob Woodward, *The Price of Politics* (New York: Simon & Schuster, 2012), 47.

24. Parnes, "Obama's TV: Sports, surprises."

25. Bill Simmons, "B.S. Report Transcript: Barack Obama," THE B.S. REPORT, March 1, 2012, http://www.grantland.com/blog/the-triangle/post/_/id/18690/b-s-report-transcript-barack-obama.

26. Maraniss, *Barack Obama: The Story*, 288.

27. Parnes, "Obama's TV: Sports, surprises."

28. "President Barack Obama a fan of 'Homeland', says drama series star Damian Lewis," Daily News, February 10, 2012, http://www.nydailynews.com/entertainment/television/president-barack-obama-a-fan-homeland-drama-series-star-damian-lewis-article-1.1020669.

29. David Jackson, "Stars come out for Obama," *USA Today*, September 27, 2011, http://content.usatoday.com/communities/theoval/post/2011/09/the-stars-come-out-for-obama/1#.UDZgU6DOO8o.

30. Warren Littlefield with T. R. Pearson, *Top of the Rock: Inside the Rise and Fall of Must See TV* (New York: Doubleday, 2012), 320.

31. Caitlin McDevitt, "Show creator zings Ann Romney for watching 'Modern Family,'" *Politico*, August 28, 2012, http://www.politico.com/blogs/click/2012/08/show-creator-zings-ann-romney-for-watching-modern-133552.html.

32. In 1976, Betty Ford appeared on the Mary Tyler Moore show. After the first lady introduced herself to Mary Richards over the phone, Richards responded with a classic line: "Hi, Betty. This is Mary . . . Queen of Scots." The Reliable Source, "Michelle Obama's 'iCarly' appearance and other first ladies on sitcoms," *Washington Post*, January 13, 2012, http://www.washingtonpost.com/blogs/reliable-source/post/michelle-obamas-icarly-appearance-and-other-first-ladies-on-sitcoms/2012/01/12/gIQAg4gYuP_blog.html.

33. Jordan Zakarin, "'Homeland' Producers on Being Obama's Favorite Show, Shooting Season 2 in Israel," *Hollywood Reporter*, May 21, 2012, http://www.hollywoodreporter.com/live-feed/homeland-producers-obamas-favorite-show-327282.

34. Bill Carter, "The Terrorist Plot Even Obama Loves," *New York Times*, September 16, 2012, AR1, AR16.

35. Ken Tucker, "President Obama and his TV faves: 'Entourage' and Omar on 'The Wire,'" *Entertainment Weekly*, April 8, 2009, http://watching-tv.ew.com/2009/04/08/.

36. Parnes, "Obama's TV: Sports, surprises."

37. Valerie Richardson, "They really, really like Obama, but not sure they'll back him," *Washington Times*, September 3, 2012, A1, A9.

38. Parnes, "Obama's TV: Sports, surprises."

39. Sunlen Miller, "The 'Wild Things' Were at the White House this Weekend," ABC News, October 19, 2009, http://abcnews.go.com/blogs/politics/2009/10/the-wild-things-were-at-the-white-house-this-weekend/.

40. Scott Wilson, "Obama Breaks Out of the Inside-the-Beltway Bubble," *Washington Post*, September 2, 2012, A25.

41. Reid J. Epstein, "Obama: RNC fare for 'black-and-white TV,'" *Politico*, September 1, 2012, http://www.politico.com/politico44/2012/09/obama-rnc-fare-for-blackandwhite-tv-134057.html.

42. Jordan Zakarin, "President Obama Guests on 'Jimmy Fallon,' Slow-Jams the News and Talks Student Loans," Hollywood Reporter, April 24, 2012, http://www.hollywoodreporter.com/live-feed/president-obama-guests-jimmy-fallon-slow-jam-the-news-315696.

43. Patricia McDonough, "TV Viewing Among Kids at an Eight-Year High," blog, Nielsen Wire, October 26, 2009, http://blog.nielsen.com/nielsenwire/media_entertainment/tv-viewing-among-kids-at-an-eight-year-high/print/.

44. Jennifer Epstein, "Obama tells kids to study, not watch 'Real Housewives,'" *Politico*, July 25, 2012, http://www.politico.com/politico44/2012/07/obama-tells-kids-to-study-not-watch-real-housewives-130139.html.

45. Maraniss, *Barack Obama: The Story*, 316.

46. Obama, *Dreams from My Father*, 103.

47. David Mendell, *Obama: From Promise to Power* (New York: HarperCollins, 2007), 59.

48. Maraniss, *Barack Obama: The Story*, 376.

49. Ibid., 492.

50. Stanley Kurtz, *Radical-in-Chief: Barack Obama and the Untold Story of American Socialism* (New York: Threshold, 2010), 44.

51. Maraniss, *Barack Obama: The Story*, 552.

52. Remnick, *The Bridge*, 425–26.

53. Robert Wright, "Bibi Netanyahu's Bible Story," *Atlantic* Online, March 6, 2012, http://www.theatlantic.com/international/archive/2012/03/bibi-netanyahus-bible-story/254044/.

54. Daniel Halper, "Kind of newish, not so Jewish 'New American Haggadah' updates Passover story," *Washington Times*, April 4, 2012, http://www.washingtontimes.com/news/2012/apr/4/new-american-haggadah-fashionably-updates-the-old-/print/.

55. Jason Zengerle, "The Israeli Desert," *New York Magazine*, June 3, 2012, http://nymag.com/news/features/peter-beinart-2012-6/.

56. Todd S. Purdum, "Team of Mascots," *Vanity Fair*, July 2012, http://www.vanityfair.com/politics/2012/07/obama-cabinet-team-rivals-lincoln; Stanley Fish, "The Obama Show," *New York Times*, September 21, 2009, http://opinionator.blogs.nytimes.com/2009/09/21/the-obama-show/.

57. Michiko Kakutani, "From Books, New President Found Voice," *New York Times*, January 18, 2009, http://www.nytimes.com/2009/01/19/books/19read.html?pagewanted=all.

58. Amie Parnes, "Move Over Oprah? Obama Sells Books," *Politico*, May 30, 2009, http://dyn. politico.com/printstory.cfm?uuid=8FA074B3-18FE-70B2-A8CCC68D3A33C43D.

59. Purdum, "Team of Mascots."

60. David Jackson, "Obama, reading up on Roosevelt (Theodore)," *USA Today*, March 9, 2010, http://content.usatoday.com/communities/theoval/post/2010/03/obama-reading-up-on-roosevelt-theodore/1.

61. John Wilwol, "Interview with Barbara Meade," *Washingtonian*, April 2013, 44.

62. Tevi Troy, "Freedom Frenzy: A Look at Presidential Reading Lists," National Review Online, September 11, 2010, http://www.nationalreview.com/articles/246248/i-freedom-i-frenzy-look-presidential-reading-lists-tevi-troy.

63. Caitlin McDevitt, "Franzen to Obama: Put Down the Novels," blog, *Politico*, January 30, 2012, http://www.politico.com/blogs/click/2012/01/franzen-to-obama-put-down-the-novels-112790.html.

64. Parnes, "Move Over Oprah?"

65. "Jonathan Franzen Uncorrected," interview with Jonathan Franzen, October 4, 2001, PowellsBooks.Blog, October 10, 2006, http://www.powells.com/blog/interviews/jonathan-franzen-uncorrected-by-dave/.

66. Melissa Bell, "President Obama's book bump slump," blog, *Washington Post*, August 23, 2011, http://www.washingtonpost.com/blogs/blogpost/post/president-obamas-book-bump-slump/2011/08/23/gIQAKKrtYJ_blog.html.

67. Peter Baker, "Education of a President," *New York Times Magazine*, October 12, 2010, http://www.nytimes.com/2010/10/17/magazine/17obama-t.html?pagewanted=all.

68. Perry Bacon Jr., "President Begins Vacation With a Smile," *Washington Post*, December 25, 2010, http://www.washingtonpost.com/wp-dyn/content/article/2010/12/24/AR2010122402852.html.

69. "Scandal over Obama's Martha's Vineyard reading list," *Baltimore Sun*, August 25, 2009, http://weblogs.baltimoresun.com/entertainment/books/blog/2009/08/scandal_over_obamas_marthas_vi.html.

70. Gabriel Sherman, "The New Republic: Obama's Bromance," NPR, August 31, 2009, http://www.npr.org/templates/story/story.php?storyId=112399581.

71. Jonathan Martin, "Silence of the lamb chops," *Politico*, January 14, 2009, http://www.politico.com/news/stories/0109/17441.html.

72. Kristof, "Obama and the War on Brains."

73. Rebecca Mead, "What Do You Call It?," *New Yorker*, January 4, 2010, http://www.newyorker.com/talk/comment/2010/01/04/100104taco_talk_mead#ixzz259X6bonA.

74. Walter Kirn, "Clash of the Archetypes: The most compelling election in years," *New Republic*, September 13, 2012, 5–6.

75. James T. Kloppenberg, *Reading Obama: Dreams, Hopes, and the American Political Tradition* (Princeton: Princeton University Press, 2011), 172.

76. Patricia Cohen, "In Writings of Obama, a Philosophy Is Unearthed," *New York Times*, October 27, 2010, http://www.nytimes.com/2010/10/28/books/28klopp.html.

77. Parnes, "Obama's TV: Sports, surprises."

78. Carol E. Lee and Monica Langley, "A More Worried Obama Battles to Win Second Term," *Wall Street Journal*, September 1–2, 2012, A1, A4. (Quote is on A4.)

79. Julie Mason, "Obama laments his lost 'cool,'" *Politico*, June 26, 2011, http://dyn.politico.com/printstory.cfm?uuid=733137A7-1570-42D8-9A11-EC44A12A42B6.

80. Hillary Busis, "Presidential PopWatch round-up on Barack Obama: Kardashian hater, SpongeBob lover, and stealth Cool Dad," *Entertainment Weekly*, August 16, 2012, http://popwatch.ew.com/2012/08/16/barack-obama-pop-culture/.

81. Howard Fineman, "Obama, Our Celebrity President, Faces Real World Test," *Huffington Post*, February 25, 2013, http://www.huffingtonpost.com/howard-fineman/obama-celebrity-president_b_2760776.html.

82. Mason, "Obama laments his lost 'cool.'"

83. Emily Miller, "Hollywood's president: Obama uses movie stars to raise money, but not campaign," *Washington Times*, May 2, 2012, http://www.washingtontimes.com/news/2012/may/1/hollywoods-president/.

84. David Nakamura, "Obama Rallies Hollywood Supporters On Fundraising Trip," *Washington Post*, February 15, 2012, http://www.washingtonpost.com/politics/obama-eager-to-soothe-hollywood-supporters-on-fundraising-trip/2012/02/14/gIQAwL3NFR_story.html.

85. Chris Richards, "Worshiping the Tao of Bruce," *Washington Post*, September 15, 2012, C1.

86. Dave Itzkoff, "Message to Your Grandma: Vote Obama," *New York Times*, October 6, 2008, http://www.nytimes.com/2008/10/07/arts/television/07sara.html.

87. Ken Thomas, "Obama Campaign to Release Documentary," Associated Press, March 7, 2012, http://www.tulsaworld.com/scene/article.aspx?subjectid=371&articleid=20120307_371_0_WSIGOr203916.

88. Craig Ferguson, "The Late Late Show with Craig Ferguson," CBS, September 4, 2012.

89. Don Steinberg, "This Election is No Laughing Matter," *Wall Street Journal*, August 31, 2012, D1, D6.

90. Miller, "Hollywood's president: Obama uses movie stars to raise money, but not campaign."

91. Edward Klein, *The Amateur: Barack Obama in the White House* (Washington: Regnery, 2012), 190.

92. Kantor, *The Obamas*, 134.

93. Keith Koffler, "Mr. President: Get Common Out of the East Room," White House Dossier, May 11, 2011, http://www.whitehousedossier.com/2011/05/11/president-common-east-room/.

94. Dylan Byers, "Gay marriage: Why Robin Roberts got the exclusive," *Politico*, May 9, 2012, http://www.politico.com/news/stories/0512/76139.html#ixzz265saOwz3.

95. Simmons, "B.S. Report Transcript: Barack Obama."

96. Barack Obama, Presidential Press Conference, White House Office of the Press Secretary, April 27, 2011.

97. Joe Biden, interview on Meet the Press, May 6, 2012.

98. Thrush, *Politico Playbook 2012*.

99. Paul Farhi, "Obama's Gay Marriage Stance Revealed in Controversial Way," *Washington Post*, May 9, 2012, http://www.washingtonpost.com/lifestyle/style/obamas-gay-marriage-stance-revealed-in-conversational-way/2012/05/09/gIQAPej8DU_print.html.

100. Thrush, *Politico Playbook 2012*.

101. Paul Farhi, "Journalists complain the White House press office has become overly combative," *Washington Post*, December 22, 2011, http://www.washingtonpost.com/lifestyle/style/journalists-complain-the-white-house-press-office-has-become-overly-combative/2011/12/20/gIQAvRnTAP_story.html.

102. Kantor, *The Obamas*, 64.

103. "White House Escalates War of Words With Fox News," Fox News, October 12, 2009, http://www.foxnews.com/politics/2009/10/12/white-house-escalates-war-words-fox-news/.

104. Barack Obama, interview with Jann Wenner and Eric Bates, "Obama in Command: The Rolling Stone Interview," *Rolling Stone*, October 14, 2010, http://www.rollingstone.com/politics/news/obama-in-command-br-the-rolling-stone-interview-20100928.

105. Parnes, "Obama's TV: Sports, surprises."

106. Wilson, "Obama Breaks Out of the Inside-the-Beltway Bubble," A25.

107. Amy Chozick, "Obama Is an Avid Reader, and Critic, of the News," *New York Times*, August 7, 2012, http://www.nytimes.com/2012/08/08/us/politics/obama-is-an-avid-reader-and-critic-of-news-media-coverage.html?_r=1&pagewanted=all&pagewanted=print.

108. Ibid.

109. Simmons, "B.S. Report Transcript: Barack Obama."

110. John Kass, "Obama swings and misses at Sox lore," *Chicago Tribune*, April 7, 2010, http://articles.chicagotribune.com/2010-04-07/news/ct-met-kass-0407-20100407_1_sox-fan-sox-lore-famer-carlton-fisk.

111. "President Obama's interview with David Letterman," CBS News, September 18, 2012, 6:38 – 6:53, http://www.cbsnews.com/video/watch/?id=7422156n.

112. Zakarin, "President Obama Guests on 'Jimmy Fallon,' Slow-Jams the News and Talks Student Loans."

113. Byron Tau, "Obama weighs in on 'Call Me Maybe,'" *Politico*, August 17, 2012, http://www.politico.com/politico44/2012/08/obama-weighs-in-on-call-me-maybe-132396.html.

114. Lisa DeMoraes, "The road to the White House runs through … 'The View'?," *Washington Post*, September 21, 2012, C4.

115. Sam Stein, appearance on *Morning Joe*, MSNBC, September 18, 2012.

116. Benjy Sarlin, "Obama's Softball Interviews Irk White House Press, GOP," Talking Points Memo, August 17, 2012, http://2012.talkingpointsmemo.com/2012/08/obamas-softball-interviews-irk-white-house-press-gop.php.

117. Jonah Goldberg, "Interview with Jonah Goldberg," *Piers Morgan*, April 30, 2012, http://transcripts.cnn.com/TRANSCRIPTS/1204/30/pmt.01.html.

118. Aaron Blake, "Obama adviser says *People* magazine 'equally important' as political media," *Washington Post*, August 19, 2012, http://www.washingtonpost.com/blogs/the-fix/wp/2012/08/19/obama-adviser-says-people-magazine-equally-important-as-national-media/?print=1.

119. Ruth Marcus, "It's going to be a long slog," *Washington Post*, February 28, 2013, http://www.washingtonpost.com/opinions/ruth-marcus-its-going-to-be-a-long-slog/2013/02/28/576c32d0-81e7-11e2-b99e-6baf4ebe42df_story.html

120. Alan Greenblatt, "Does President Obama Know When To Say When?," NPR, March 2, 2013, http://www.npr.org/blogs/itsallpolitics/2013/03/02/173243509/does-president-obama-know-when-to-say-when.

121. Daniel Boorstin, *The Image: A Guide to Pseudo-Events* (New York: Vintage, 1987), 249.

Conclusion

1. Irving Kristol, "High, Low, and Modern: Some Thoughts on Popular Culture and Popular Government," *The Neoconservative Persuasion: Selected Essays, 1942–2009*, edited by

Gertrude Himmelfarb, foreword by William Kristol (New York: Basic Books, 2011), 105–106.

2.   Camille Paglia, *Vamps & Tramps: New Essays* (New York: Vintage, 1994), 346.

3.   Michael J. Hogan, *The Ambiguous Legacy: U.S. Foreign Relations in the "American Century,"* (Cambridge: Cambridge University Press, 1999), 8.

4.   Laura Ingraham, *Of Thee I Zing* (New York: Threshold, 2012), 3.

5.   Kristol, "High, Low, and Modern: Some Thoughts on Popular Culture and Popular Government," *The Neoconservative Persuasion*, 105–106.

INDEX